EMBODIED LIVES

Ancient Maya and Egyptian cultures present evidence of similar concerns with body and self: monumental art depicts complex costume and standards of beauty, and ornaments, cosmetics, and items of dress used by the living are recovered in tombs in which the bodies of the dead were arrayed. Despite the centrality of such practices, these two civilizations had very different ways of treating, understanding and experiencing the body.

Taking bodily materiality as a crucial starting point to the understanding and formation of self in any society, Lynn Meskell and Rosemary Joyce offer a new approach to both civilizations centred on understanding embodiment. They examine a wide range of archaeological data, using it to explore issues such as the sexual body, mind/body dualism, body modification, and magical practices.

Drawing on insights from feminist theory, art history, phenomenology, anthropology, and psychoanalysis, the book sheds new light on Ancient Egyptian and Maya cultures. Theorizing the body across two cultures, this book shows how a comparative project can open up new lines of inquiry by raising questions about accepted assumptions. Drawing attention to the long-term histories and specificities of embodiment, it makes the case for the importance of ancient materials for contemporary theorization of the body.

Lynn M. Meskell is Associate Professor in the Department of Anthropology, Columbia University. Her previous books include *Archaeology under Fire* (edited, Routledge 1998), *Archaeologies of Social Life* (1999), and *Private Life in New Kingdom Egypt* (2002).

Rosemary A. Joyce is Professor of Anthropology at the University of California, Berkeley. Her recent books include *The Languages of Archaeology* (2002), *Gender and Power in Prehispanic Mesoamerica* (2001), and *Beyond Kinship* (edited with Susan D. Gillespie, 2000).

D1559276

EMBODIED LIVES

Figuring Ancient Maya and Egyptian Experience

Lynn M. Meskell and Rosemary A. Joyce

Routledge
Taylor & Francis Group

LONDON AND NEW YORK

First published 2003
by Routledge
11 New Fetter Lane, London EC4P 4EE
Simultaneously published in the USA and Canada
by Routledge
29 West 35th Street, New York, NY 10001

Routledge is an imprint of the Taylor & Francis Group

Typeset in Galliard by
Bookcraft Ltd, Stroud, Gloucestershire
Printed and bound in Great Britain by
MPG Books Ltd, Bodmin

British Library Cataloguing in Publication Data
A catalogue record for this book is available from the British Library

Library of Congress Cataloging in Publication Data
Meskell, Lynn.
Embodied Lives : figuring ancient Maya and Egyptian experience/
Lynn M. Meskell and Rosemary A. Joyce.
p. cm.
Includes bibliographical references and index.
1. Mayas–Antiquities. 2. Mayas–Funeral customs and rites. 3. Human
remains (Archaeology)–Latin America. 4. Body, Human–Symbolic
aspects–Latin America. 5. Egyptians–Antiquities. 6. Egyptians–Funeral
customs and rites. 7. Human remains (Archaeology)–Egypt. 8. Body,
Human–Symbolic aspects–Egypt. 9. Latin America–Antiquities.
10. Egypt–Antiquities. I. Joyce, Rosemary A., 1956– II. Title.
F1435.M553 2003
306.9'097281'09021–dc21   2003045937

ISBN 0–415–25310–1 (hbk)
ISBN 0–415–25311–X (pbk)

FOR JOAN AND JACK
LMM

FOR CAROLYN AND MICHAEL
RAJ

CONTENTS

FIGURES

FIGURES

FOREWORD

The phenomenology of lived experience

The human body has become a topic of intensive study in the last two decades, and its development has challenged and changed the intellectual contours of anthropology and sociology. Scientific and technological advances in medicine and genetics, particularly the new reproductive technologies and cloning techniques, have given the human body a problematic legal and social status. In futuristic visions of health and illness, aging and death no longer appear to be irreducible facts about the human condition. The development of the body as a topic of research in the humanities and social sciences is a response to these technological changes, and to the social movements that are associated with them—such as the women's movement and green politics on the one side and religious fundamentalism and conservative politics on the other. In contemporary sociology the body has been studied in a variety of contexts: in advertising and popular consumerism; in medical and ethical debates about the self and cloning; in research on the social meaning of AIDS/HIV; in postmodern reflections on cybernetics, cyberbodies and cyberpunk; and in the analysis of the trade in body organs between North and South. The body has been a dominant theme in feminist research on the changing social roles of women, female identity and sexuality, but it has gained a new urgency with the development of reproduction outside the womb. The body has been a crucial issue in queer theory in understanding masculinity, trans-sexuality and men's health. The body has thus emerged as a central feature of the sociological imagination, because its vulnerability and plasticity have been exposed by new genetic technologies that have raised questions about the possibility of a posthuman future. The cultural dominance of the body in social and political debate is not difficult to document or to comprehend, but the very complexity of the issues has raised intractable problems about how to study the body. Indeed, our most pressing question is: what is the body?

It is puzzling that, while the study of the body has enjoyed such a rampant growth in anthropology, sociology and history, it has not had much discernible impact on archaeology as a discipline. *Embodied Lives* is thus a remarkable book, because it establishes a new field of inquiry and provides a conceptual map for re-organizing and redirecting the work of archaeologists. Lynn Meskell and Rosemary Joyce take a decisive stand on how this field should develop through a critical reflection on the legacy of Michel Foucault, and what they call "discourse determinism," namely the tendency to regard the body as merely a cultural effect of discursive formations. Their work is explicitly a contribution to the phenomenology of embodied lives in the immediate, practical, everyday world rather than a reflection on the abstract body as a text or a system of signs. Their book is not a contribution to the deconstruction of the body as a system of archaeological traces, but an inquiry into body matters (blood, semen and tears) and fundamental social processes (reproduction, death and transubstantiation). Their research uncovers the complexity and diversity of the social institutions through which the human body is conveyed and how it is reconstructed through mortuary arts and other funeral technologies. Their bold and imaginative creation of an embodied archaeology explores the everyday world of Ancient Mayan and Egyptian cultures from the perspective of the tasks of embodiment in production and reproduction. The arrival of the lived body is a palpable turning point in contemporary archaeological theory.

Although one can, in the social sciences, trace this debate about the body and society back to the early writings of Karl Marx in the notion of *praxis*, its contemporary inspiration has come from a diversity of sources: the philosophy of Martin Heidegger, the phenomenology of Maurice Merleau-Ponty, the cultural anthropology of Mary Douglas, the feminist philosophy of Simone de Beauvoir, and the history of systems of knowledge of Michel Foucault. In more specific terms, the cultural study of the body began to surface in the late 1970s. For example, the American Anthropological Association held a conference on the anthropology of the body to reconsider the conventional debate about nature and cultural practice. Modern anthropology has attempted to avoid treating the body as a given or natural fact, and has, following Marcel Mauss, emphasized the notion of "bodily practices" that human beings must acquire and develop if they are to cope successfully with their world. Eating and walking, sleeping and copulating are body practices that express our place in society and constitute our individuality. These notions have in recent anthropological scholarship been expressed by Pierre Bourdieu in terms of the concepts of *hexis* and *habitus* in which our dispositions and tastes are organized. For example, within the everyday habitus of social classes, the body is a site of endless practices by which we invest symbolic capital with the result that the body is a living testament to hierarchies of social power. The body is permanently shaped and represented by the different aesthetics of social classes.

In part, the recovery of the body for contemporary research has depended on philosophical anthropology. For example, the controversial work of Arnold Gehlen has been important for the research of Hans Joas, Alex Honneth and Wolf Lepenies in Germany, and in the United States for Peter

Berger and Thomas Luckmann. Gehlen argued that in order to cope with their "world openness," human beings have to create a cultural sphere to replace or to supplement their instinctual world. It is their ontological incompleteness that provides an anthropological explanation for the origins of social institutions. Berger and Luckmann adopted this position to argue that, since human beings are biologically underdeveloped, they have to construct a "sacred canopy" around themselves in order to complete or supplement their biology. Institutions are the social bridges between humans and their physical environment, and it is through these institutions that human life becomes coherent, meaningful and continuous. In filling the gap created by instinctual deprivation, institutions provide humans with relief from the tensions generated by undirected, unfocused and abundant instinctual drives. The mortuary and funeral rituals that traditionally surround death are examples of such institutions that provide routine methods to deal with dead bodies and their decay and decomposition.

Despite the richness of these intellectual foundations, the contemporary anthropology and sociology of the body would have remained underdeveloped without feminist theory. Simone de Beauvoir's study of the "second sex" in 1949 was a major contribution to the study of the body in society, and in particular to the patriarchal regulation of the female body. Her study was a contribution to the phenomenology of the gendered body, because she showed that women are not born but become women through social and psychological processes that construct them as eternally and essentially female. Her research on human aging also demonstrated the social invisibility and powerlessness of women in old age. Her work inaugurated a tradition of research on the socially constructed character of sexuality, but the paradox of this legacy has often been that the emphasis on the socially constructed quality of women's bodies in cultural studies has led to the disappearance of the lived body and embodiment as themes in feminist research. It is important to recapture the intellectual importance of the phenomenology of human embodiment in order to avoid the reduction of bodies to cultural texts. *Embodied Lives* thus has a double significance: it seeks to explore the phenomenology of the body in archaeology with an acute sensitivity to how gender was a dominant principle of the organization of the life-world of Mayan and Egyptian civilization.

There are many strands to the anthropological and sociological analysis of the body, but one unifying theme has been a profound distrust of the legacy of Cartesian dualism. In philosophical terms, the discovery of the importance of the body is connected with an implicit, and occasionally explicit, rejection of the Cartesian division between mind and body, in which the human body was merely a mechanical extension of the mind. Descartes' *cogito ergo sum* had the effect of exorcising the body from the rational apprehension of the world. The body was interpreted as merely a contingent vehicle for the consciousness of the mind, and the imperial subject, inconveniently equipped with its mechanical supports, surveyed and appropriated everything before him. The masculine subject is important here, because the mind was conceptualized as a sort of cognitive Odysseus whose journey through life was a triumph over physical adversity; it was a triumph over nature that prepared the way for the Enlightenment. This Olympian view of the subject has come under attack from a number of angles.

Merleau-Ponty's phenomenology of perception criticized the Cartesian division of (active) mind and (passive) body by arguing that the world is neither given to us neutrally to examine at our leisure nor is it wholly constructed in a social vacuum by the knowing isolated subject. In this "philosophy of ambiguity," he argued that consciousness can never be understood correctly without paying attention to the embodied existence of conscious individuals. For Merleau-Ponty, all consciousness is perceptual, but philosophers have ignored the phenomenon of perceptual activity, that is the experiences of perception in the life-world are the experiences of an embodied subject, whose perception of their world is always from the point of view of the body. This archaeology of perception of the life-world was rooted in the body in the everyday world, and hence all perceptions of reality are inherently contingent. Merleau-Ponty's view of the contingencies that confront our being in the world gave his work an immediate appeal to French existentialism.

This phenomenological orientation to embodiment contrasts sharply with the legacy of Foucault, whose work owes a great deal to the "anti-humanism" of Heidegger. Heidegger's philosophy of time had displaced the conscious subject of traditional Kantian philosophy by developing the concept of *Dasein* ("there-being") to argue that there is no pre-given human essence. Foucault, employing Heidegger against French existentialism, created an archaeological study of systems of knowledge ("discursive formations") that exist and develop independently of human intentions and beliefs, and as a result he rejected the centrality of the subject in the study of changes in knowledge. In his archaeological inquiries into the origins of homosexuality in classical Greece, he was not concerned to understand the phenomenology of sexual experiences, but rather to understand the "truth" of sex in relation to ideologies of masculinity and political power. These were studies, not of the facticity of everyday sexual activity, but rather inquiries into the abstract discursive systems that created the possibility of sex. Although Foucault's archaeology of knowledge was enormously important and creative, his legacy has often resulted in work that is dogmatic, narrow and imitative. Post-structuralist thought has become an orthodoxy in which the study of embodiment in the life-world of men and women is rigidly and blindly rejected in favour of research on systems of knowledge that slavishly imitate Foucault. As a result, Foucault's ethical project to show how the contingency of knowledge falsely pretends to certainty and thus limits our scope for action has often been neglected.

We might say, therefore, that there are two separate traditions in the anthropology and sociological study of the body. There is either the cultural decoding of the *body* as a system of meaning that has a definite structure existing separately from the intentions and conceptions of individuals, or there is the phenomenological study of *embodiment* that attempts to understand human practices that are organized around the life course (of birth, maturation, reproduction and death). *Embodied Lives* is an intellectual project, as the title indicates, that attempts to understand and recreate the lived experiences of human beings through archaeological investigation of the cultural artefacts of ancient Mayan and Egyptian civilizations. The authors uncover an astonishing world of embodiment where the complexity of bodies, hybrid creatures, sexual identities, and persons presents a constant challenge to our own post-industrial world, and in particular to our taken-for-granted notions about the individual and the body.

Their perspective on embodiment is also feminist. *Embodied Lives* is an account of phallic cultures in which there is a fluid economy of human and divine secretions that reproduce the world. The tears, sweat and semen of the gods become self-sustaining substances that have dramatic reproductive capacities. Material worlds are conjured up through the masturbatory exuberance of gods, and castration was the ultimate sign of power over the bodies of enemies. Because ancient Egypt was patriarchal, the penis and the act of penetration defined a chain of cultural value and significance in terms of having and not having, of being and not being. Puns on the semantic ambiguities of the phallus and poison created a network of meanings associated with violence, sex and male dominance, and phallic worship was central to Egyptian religion. Rituals and theology both played on the parallel notions of the erect penis and life, and hence the erect phallus defies death and points to life beyond death and the possibility of resurrection. The story of the conflict between Seth and Horus involved violence in which masculinity was threatened and gave rise to a parallel set of symbols: tears and semen; eyes and testicles. Because sexuality is defined by the presence of the penis, women are classified by its lack. These patriarchal assumptions shaped the social world of both Mayan and Egyptian civilizations. Representations of sexual power in Egypt contrasted the clothed male body with the naked and revealed female body. In Mayan society, there was a powerful homoerotic culture that was represented through images of athletic young men, and ball game playing, dancing and military activities dominated courtly art. In Classic Mayan art, there is a parallel drawn between the male penis and the tongue, and in bloodletting rituals the perforation of the male penis had a counterpart in the perforation of the female tongue, expressing a further connection between spittle and semen. Mayan patriarchal representations of sexual subordination often show the woman's tongue in submission to the male penis.

The anthropology of the body has often provided compelling support for cultural relativism that is associated with the ethnographic tradition of fieldwork research. The ethnographic imagination has in particular uncovered a bewildering diversity of cultural practices associated with the body. There appears to be no particular coherence to human cultures; on the contrary, everywhere there is diversity and difference. *Embodied Lives* can also be read as a phenomenological inquiry into the mind-boggling diversity of body-practices and representations. In Mayan and Egyptian worlds, bodies could exist beyond the boundary of the skin; there were fantastic hybrid bodies constructed through animals and humans; gods created worlds through scattering their sperm; men had gigantic genitalia; and their penises enjoyed erection in death. There is ample evidence here that human beings were embodied differently in the phenomenal world, and yet there is at least one major ontological issue that underpins this complex world, which is, I would suggest, the vulnerability of embodiment. The phallic culture of the ancient world of patriarchal power was constantly threatened by castration, but more importantly life and the living body were permanently threatened by death. In this sense, mummification was, as Meskell and Joyce so cleverly show, equivalent to the preservation of the body through its violation. The human body was never considered to be divine, and it required considerable modification and reconstruction to achieve perfection after death. The Egyptian mummy aimed to achieve a perfectly preserved image of the dead person, thereby transmuting the body into a simulacrum of itself. Mummification transformed the former living, sensual body into a new object. In addition to the fabrication of the body, there were elaborate precautions to safeguard and protect the dangerous borders and orifices of the body. The nostrils, ears and anus were often covered with resin to protect the individual from external, supernatural threats. However cunning the art of the embalmer, threats to the safety of the individual were ever present, and mummification could never quite solve the tensions between a desire for divinity and the rigidity and intractability of the dead body. The stiffness of the corpse contradicted the flexibility of living tissue, and the embalmer's arts were always compromised by the stubborn process of decay. The spells of the Book of the Dead point to this unresolved contradiction between the quest for divinity and the inescapable fact of putrefaction.

Classic Mayan culture exhibits a different set of attitudes and practices towards death and the dead body. Mayan people made no attempt to preserve the body or to counter the inevitable decay of the flesh. The hot climate of Egypt and the wet and humid conditions of central America may have contributed significantly to different mortuary practices. While the Mayan dead were left to decay, there was a clear sense that the personhood of the dead continued to have a place among the living. The disappearance of the flesh was not a cause for horror, and death did not preclude continuing membership of a social group, because the ancestors were buried in house compounds that were integral to social life. Dead bodies were not treated in any way to stop the process of physical decay, but they were provided with elaborate costumes and masks that ensured that the face and identity of the dead were sustained. These masks were often attached to the flesh of the dead person and at other times actually replaced the head of the deceased where decapitation had taken place. While bodily integrity does not appear to have been an issue for Mayan people, the point was to connect the dead with the future, and this projection was sometimes achieved through the use of the bones of the dead by the living, for example as ornaments.

I do not disagree with the argument in *Embodied Lives* that we cannot treat Egyptian mummification or Mayan mortuary rites as evidence that human attitudes towards death are universal. Meskell and Joyce present compelling evidence to the contrary; Mayan and Egyptian societies had very different approaches to sexuality, death and the human body. There is evidence however that embodiment means that human beings are vulnerable and that they share a common ontological insecurity. This is what phenomenology tells us. Merleau-Ponty's phenomenology of perceptual experience impresses us with the uncertainty and instability of our modes of apprehending and comprehending the world, and hence it must drive home an inescapable sense of the contingencies of the life-world. Although Mayan and Egyptian mortuarial and funeral practices were very different, they have one thing in common: they express a perplexity about the world in which death turns the living body into a putrefied mess and eventually into a not-body. Egyptian and Mayan visions of hell were different, but they both addressed the problem of human death and the conundrum of non-existence. Although Mayans may have contemplated the not-body with less existential horror than Egyptians, who went to extraordinary lengths to bring about mummification, death in both cultures exposed the vulnerability of our being-in-the-world and the precariousness of human institutions. In western Christianity, the body also played a major part in understanding evil and holiness. Theologians solved the paradox of Christ's perfect humanity and his divinity by developing the doctrine of his immaculate birth by a virgin whose womb was not penetrated; we might say that Mary was not wounded by the Annunciation. The problem of death and decay was resolved through the resurrection stories of Lazarus and Jesus in the New Testament, in which the wounding and death of Christ on the Cross was merely a prelude to his resurrection and entry into Paradise. Our embodiment in the world is characterized by its precariousness, and we can argue plausibly that religions are cultural modes that seek to address our vulnerability by mythology and by bodily practices that attempt for example to disguise our death by giving our face a mask or through the mummification of the corpse. Doctrines of resurrection and practices of mummification are both cultural institutions that address our experiences of the incompleteness of embodied lives in the everyday world.

These facts about the social world may be grasped by phenomenology, but they are less easily and effectively understood by the textual strategies of structuralism, that is by "discourse determinism." Vulnerability literally means that human beings have the capacity to be wounded, or opened up. According to Diodorus, embalmers who were responsible for the visceral incision on a corpse often ran away to avoid being stoned and abused. While this process was necessary for embalming, it was regarded as an abhorrent act. It was an act against bodily integrity; it was a wounding. *Embodied Lives* is an inspirational contribution not simply to an archaeology of the body but to any humanistic inquiry into the phenomenology of life and death.

Professor Bryan S. Turner
Faculty of Social and Political Sciences
University of Cambridge

ACKNOWLEDGMENTS

Victoria Peters, former editor of Archaeology at Routledge, originally commissioned this book and we want to thank her for suggesting to us such a stimulating and challenging project. Julene Barnes and Richard Stoneman have subsequently seen the project to fruition and we thank them too for their patience and support. To Bryan Turner, we are immensely indebted for not only reading the book but for his gracious endorsement of our overall endeavor.

Special thanks go to Richard Parkinson, Stephen Quirke, and Terry Wilfong who each read various Egyptian sections of the book and to John Baines, Gay Robins, Hubertus Muench, Liz Frood, and John Taylor for numerous helpful suggestions and ideas. Lynn Meskell is also indebted to Chris Gosden for many stimulating conversations and for his ongoing support and friendship. Another pleasant summer in Oxford allowed her to complete her research and she is grateful to the Warden and Fellows of New College Oxford for making that possible. A Columbia University Arts and Sciences Summer Fellowship funded her work in Oxford, and the book was finished during her sabbatical at the School of American Research in Santa Fe. She would like to acknowledge Richard Leventhal, her colleagues at SAR, and the National Endowment for the Humanities for their support.

Rosemary Joyce would like to acknowledge the indispensable inspiration of many conversations with Mary Weismantel, Susan Gillespie, and Julia Hendon, whose effects are patent throughout, even more than citation can make clear. Key invitations from Jeffrey Quilter, Cecelia Klein, Rob Schmidt and Barb Voss, Amelia Trevelyan and Lowell Gustafson, and Ruth Van Dyke and Susan Alcock provided opportunities to develop work that might otherwise not have flourished to form part of the present book. This work was partially prepared while Rosemary Joyce was a Fellow at the Center for Advanced Study in the Behavioral Sciences. She is grateful for the financial support provided by Grant 2000–5633 and the "Hewlett Fellow" Grant 98–2124 from the William and Flora Hewlett Foundation. She is even more grateful for the generous intellectual community at CASBS, particularly Judy Walkowitz, Dorothy Hodgson, and the other participants in the Gender and Feminist Studies reading group.

ACKNOWLEDGMENTS

For their help with illustrations, Lynn Meskell would like to thank Rosemarie Drenkhahn at the Kestner Museum in Hannover; Tanya Watkins and Richard Parkinson at the British Museum in London; Helen Whitehouse at the Ashmolean Museum in Oxford; Bob Wilkins at the Institute for Archaeology, Oxford; Nathan Pendlebury at the National Museum and Galleries on Merseyside; and Jaromir Málek at the Griffith Institute in Oxford. James Conlon also provided the map of Egypt and helped with illustrations. Rosemary Joyce would like to thank Victoria Canney, Viva Fisher and Donna Dickerson of the Peabody Museum; David Stuart and Ian Graham of the Corpus of Maya Hieroglyphic Inscriptions at the Peabody Museum, Harvard University; Norman Hammond of Boston University; John S. Henderson of Cornell University; and Justin and Barbara Kerr for their assistance with and permission for use of illustrations. Rus Sheptak deserves a particular acknowledgment for facilitating Rosemary Joyce's final art work, including giving permission for use of his original photographic images.

Lynn Meskell would like to thank her students, Marisa Lazzari, Carrie Nakamura, Aziz Meshiea, Anna Boozer and Matt Palus, who were extremely helpful with resources and readings. Rosemary Joyce would similarly like to thank Jeanne Lopiparo, Scott Hutson, Kira Blaisdell-Sloan, and Holly Bachand for their willingness to debate concepts that have found their way into this work, and the stimulation to thought that they have consistently provided.

We are both grateful to our students for their willingness to discuss ideas and for challenging the ways in which we can write archaeology.

Lynn M. Meskell and Rosemary A. Joyce

1

INTRODUCTION

This book is an experiment in comparative analysis. We begin with the assumption that it can be productive to ask the same questions about two very different places and times. This is not because we expect to discover any simple explanatory framework that transcends history. Rather, we believe that it is through a constant tacking between historical specificities that unexamined postulates are exposed; this is one reason why archaeology matters as something more than antiquarian or aesthetic particularism.

Each of us has previously published extensive arguments concerning social identities in our areas of specialization: the study of ancient Egypt and precolumbian Mesoamerica (Meskell 1999a, 2002; Joyce 2001a). We realized that our arguments, while distinct in many ways, converged on an appreciation of the significance of embodied experience in ancient lives. Rather than seeing this as an utterly inaccessible aspect of individual existence, we further agreed that archaeologists were well positioned to explore embodied lives, because the materiality of those lives is still with us today. Perhaps surprisingly, archaeological scholarship has had minimal impact upon the outpouring of recent research into the discursive constructions of personhood, gender, sexuality and embodiment. Ethnographic writing has had a wider sphere of influence in terms of presenting lived experience within the context of cultural difference. We suggest that archaeology is well placed to make similar cultural comparisons with the added interpolation of long time depth to add another dimension of complexity in terms of social difference and possibility. This book is the materialization of such a venture.

We do not begin here with an overview of previous research on either the Classic Maya or New Kingdom Egyptians; given the depth of scholarship in both fields, we would never emerge from such an introduction. Instead, we introduce significant research on which we depend and to which we respond throughout the chapters that follow. We offer here only a critical assessment of the materials from which we draw out the constructions and experiences of self and embodiment in our respective cultural domains. Nor do we attempt to provide in this introduction an overview of theory of embodiment and experience; our debts there too will be obvious as our arguments proceed.

1

A number of important works have been central to our understandings of embodiment starting with Turner's early path-breaking work (1984), the phenomenology of Merleau-Ponty (1962), the psychoanalytic perspectives of Lacan (2001, 1996), ethnographic readings (Csordas 1994; Jackson 1989; Munn 1986; Taussig 1993) and the radical refiguring of the body through the writing of a wide circle of feminists (Butler 1990, 1993; Gatens 1996; Grosz 1994, 1995). Our perspectives are broadly phenomenological and feminist, but to say that is to reveal little, since both phenomenology and feminist thought cover such wide ground. Both kinds of orientation share an emphasis on collapsing the distinction between action and theory, and existential thought and embodied practice. It is on that ground that we begin here with a simple orientation to the places and times that concern us in the remainder of this book.

New Kingdom Egypt

As a chronological period, the New Kingdom is thought to begin in 1539 BC, with the accession of Ahmose, and to finish in 1075 BC with the end of Ramesses XI's reign (Figure 1.1). Iconographic evidence suggests that the Egyptians themselves looked back upon the New Kingdom as a distinct period of time. The military turmoil and struggles for power during Ramesses XI's reign (reg. 1104 BC to 1075 BC) were seen as discrete historical markers. During the last decade of his reign a new system of era dating was introduced which apparently acknowledged the end of one cycle and the beginning of another one. In view of the evidence, it is justifiable to think about Bronze Age Egypt between 1539 BC and 1075 BC as a specific historical era (Meskell 2002: 19).

The New Kingdom is a particularly rich period from which to unpack complex cultural notions of lived experience and the embodied self, both in living and otherworldly contexts. Archaeologists have at their disposal a wealth of textual, iconographic and archaeological materials that offer a window into ancient life. However, all have their specific caveats. First, Egyptian history was written from an elite perspective, using the sources generated by pharaohs and their officials. This ensures that their legacy is inflected with the biases of class and gender since literacy was almost entirely restricted to the male, scribal class, which may have formed up to 5 percent of the total population (Baines 1991: 132).

The experience of the elite was very different from that of the vast majority of the Egyptian populace. By virtue of their wealth and station, the elite constructed monuments that have survived to a greater degree than those of the middle or lower strata. Their aspirations and connections reached levels of society unattainable, perhaps almost unimaginable, for the rest. The majority of society lived in relative poverty and simplicity. Agricultural laborers formed the backbone of Egyptian society, yet we know little of their lives other than

Figure 1.1   Map of Egypt. Courtesy of James Conlon.

that they struggled through a life of poverty and hardship. There were other groups of workers we might classify as artisans, including higher status foremen and supervisors, lower ranking craftsmen and laborers, like those from Deir el Medina. Many of these individuals left substantial written and material remains, which have enabled scholars to examine other dimensions to Egyptian social life (Meskell 1998a, 2000a). The New Kingdom has yielded the greatest number of personal documents and inscriptions of any period before the Graeco-Roman, many from the settlement site of Deir el Medina. These offer unprecedented insights into historical events, village happenings and personal histories. These daily, sometimes intimate, narratives give their interpreters the impression of being able to "know" the people of the New Kingdom, since many of their sentiments, aspirations and concerns resonate with our own. But the act of translation presents a hermeneutic dilemma in itself, although it provides an evocative connective bridge between ancients and moderns.

Iconography is another major source for New Kingdom life, and it lies at the nexus of textual and archaeological evidence. Word and image were deeply intertwined in Egypt. Both were efficacious and could be functionally powerful in this world and the next. As with documentary evidence, the weight of material stems from the elite, and throughout this book numerous royal examples are employed. Visual representation is similarly inscribed by cultural politics. Elite images should be seen within a discourse of perfection where all failings were erased. They cannot be taken as face value renderings of ordinary life or its historical specificities. Much tomb representation is unsurprisingly directed toward concerns for attaining the afterlife. Such images were largely constructed by and for male subjects.

Archaeology offers a counter to the documentary and iconographic record produced by an all-male elite, in that it can shed light on the silent masses—women, children, foreigners, the non-elite and individuals of servile status. We have material evidence for household activities and domestic life that were not the subjects of written texts. Moreover, archaeological evidence can hint at more subversive trends that explicitly defy the hegemony of the textual record. While much of our discussion is directed toward lived experience, the weight of archaeological analysis in Egypt has been biased towards mortuary studies and must be balanced with studies of village and urban life. Throughout we aim for a dialogic relationship between our evidential sources.

Given the depth of information for Egypt, we can offer specific accounts of concepts of time, crucial in any understanding of embodied being and its corollary extension into the next world. The Egyptians did not have a general word that can be glossed as time. One construction of time, *nḥḥ*, was associated with cyclical time, like the repeated dawning of the new day which parallels the conceptual cycle of rebirth, in which time is a spiral of patterned repetitions and a coil of countless rebirths. Creation was not a single past

4

event, but a series of "first times" of sacred regenerative moments recurring regularly within the sacred space of temples through the media of rituals and architecture (Shafer 1997). Operating in tandem was the concept of _dt_, which we might translate as linear time. It occurs in references to the night and to the ruler of death, Osiris. Together these concepts determine and embody the spatial structure of the created world and constitute its temporal shape (Hornung 1992).

Time was primarily divided into human or divine time, what might be called "here-time" and "there-time." Earthly life could be broken into increments of years, _rnpwt_, months, _3bdw_, days, _hrw_, hours, _wnwt_, and moments, _3wt_ (Bochi 1994: 56). Two calendars were operative in Egypt: the lunar calendar was religious in function whereas the civil calendar was used in daily life. The civil calendar consisted of twelve months of 30 days and 5 additional days, making a total of 365 days. This was a cycle that simply repeated itself. Given the cyclical nature of the Nile itself, this probably played an important role in the creation of the civil calendar: the first season refers to the inundation (Depuydt 1997). Days were divided into twenty-four hours, twelve for day and twelve for night, whilst hours were not divided.

The ancient Egyptians also had a concept of the lifetime, called _ꜥḥꜥw_ (Hornung 1992: 58). The ideal life span was 100 years plus an extra decade or two to attain ultimate wisdom: the corporeal realities of life were very different. Egyptian ideology may have stressed the wonders of the next life, yet the sentiments expressed in didactic texts amongst others are inflected with fear and dread at the realization of bodily death. The identity of each individual was accumulated through life and was used to determine the deceased's fate at the pivotal day of judgment. One's earthly identity and character were somatic entities or aspects of the individual that persisted after corporeal death and, as such, were subject to a cyclical process of development.

The Classic Maya world

The counterpoint to New Kingdom Egypt is provided by research on the Classic Maya societies of Central America (Figure 1.2). The remains of ancient Maya settlements extend throughout eastern Mexico, Guatemala, Belize, and western Honduras and El Salvador (Henderson 1997). Archaeologists identify sites in these regions as constructions of predecessors of the indigenous people who occupied the same territory when the first Europeans entered the region in the early sixteenth century. Millions of descendants of these people, who were subjected to colonization by Europeans, still live in the region today, having survived five centuries of economic and political exploitation, including a series of bloody wars in the late twentieth century.

When used to refer to the living indigenous people who occupy the region today, whose ancestors met the first European invasions with military

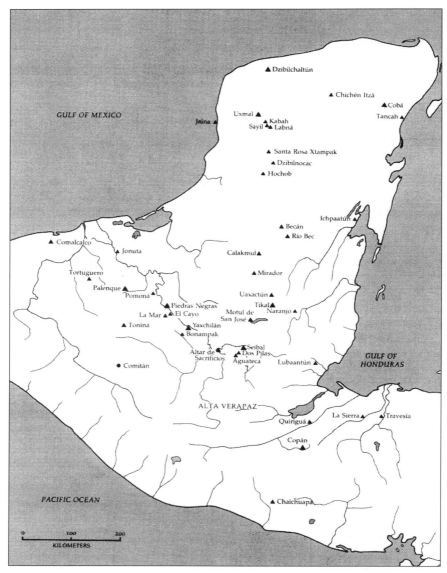

Figure 1.2 Map of the Classic Maya world. Courtesy of John S. Henderson (Henderson 1997).

resistance, and who are presumed to be descendants of the inhabitants of archaeological sites in the region, "Maya" denotes a historical tradition, an ethnic group, and a set of related languages. It is an artificial lumping together of different groups of people who were never integrated into a single polity, and who quite possibly never thought of themselves as a single people. Usually taken for granted, the use of the term "Classic Maya" deserves some explicit defense, especially in a book that is concerned with exploring experiences of individual people in the past.

The full Classic period is generally assigned dates of AD 250 to AD 830 (Culbert 1973, 1991). These dates bracket a period during which a single calendar was employed across the region in inscriptions on public monuments (Milbrath 1999). The calendar itself predates the Classic, and was used by non-Maya people (Aveni 1980). A version was still in use among Maya people when the first Spanish reports of their culture were written in the sixteenth century, although not for public monumental inscriptions and in slightly different form (Paxton 2001). The AD 250 beginning date of the archaeological Classic period actually post-dates the earliest Maya use of the calendar, and the earliest Maya monuments now known (Coe 1976; Justeson 1986). The conventional end date for the Classic period at c. AD 830, coinciding with the end of a major period of about 400 years in the Maya calendar, actually marks the beginning of a time of transition in the use of writing, monuments, and calendars throughout the region. Over a span of about 200 years following AD 830, the use of inscriptions on public monuments became uncommon, and dating systems shifted toward practices described in the sixteenth century AD. While the beginning and ending dates of the Classic period cannot, in consequence, be treated as sharp points of demarcation of a cultural tradition (as was implied by the older concept of the "collapse" of the Classic Maya), between these dates the use of writing, the calendar, and public monuments was pervasive across the Maya lowlands. Significantly, the use of a common calendar that allowed historical records to be pinpointed in a single temporal scheme at a scale of thousands of years suggests that at least literate inhabitants of Classic Maya cities did consider themselves to be participants in a common historical epoch, comparable to the apparent status of New Kingdom Egypt in the Egyptian historical tradition.

Unlike the situation in Egypt, where the documentary record provides abundant evidence of real social complexity, the Classic Maya inscriptional record has been greatly depleted by poor conditions for preservation of perishable materials. Classic Maya paintings depict scribes at work in noble courts, writing in fanfold books (Coe 1977). Scholars assume these books were like the very few codices preserved from later Maya societies, made of bark paper coated with lime plaster to provide an even surface for the brush. But no paper manuscripts have survived in legible form from Classic sites, even where abundant scribal paint pots and brush handles have been recovered (Inomata 2001b). For the Classic Maya, unlike ancient Egypt, we are dependent on small numbers of inscriptions carved or painted on imperishable pottery, bone, and stone objects and a much larger body of monumental inscriptions in stone and plaster stucco. The preserved textual record for the Classic Maya is thus limited; what would we have if only public monuments and inscriptions on personal objects were available for the ancient Egyptians? Our knowledge of the Classic Maya is biased toward the public record of dynastic history.

Progress in transcribing Classic Maya inscriptions has been based on the assumption that they represent ancient languages related to specific Maya languages recorded following European contact, with descendant languages spoken today, particularly Yucatec and members of the Cholan branch of Maya languages (Houston *et al.* 2000; Houston 2000). In this sense, the identification of the Classic sites as "Maya" clearly reflects an important degree of relationship of the living Maya people and the ancient builders of the sites. Nevertheless, it should be noted that Classic Cholan and Yucatec had long histories of independent development as languages as distinct as German and English. The amount of time elapsed between even the last Classic Maya inscriptions and the first European records of Maya languages is as great as the time between the composition of Chaucer's *Canterbury Tales* and the works of Shakespeare, and modern Maya speakers are as distant from the time of creation of the first European records as modern English speakers are from the author of *Hamlet*. Students of Classic Maya inscriptions face the challenge of working through written compositions from a span of time longer than the English tradition that begins with *Beowulf*. While researchers emphasize common threads, a reader should keep in mind that reality was no doubt characterized by greater historical, social, and cultural diversity than can today be documented.

The historical events recorded in dated Classic Maya inscriptions demonstrate that the independent Maya city-states were bound together in military and political alliances, cemented by social ties between noble families (Culbert 1991). As a network of closely linked ruling families presiding over allied and competing polities, Classic Maya nobles patronized the production of material goods, including artworks, that were stylistically similar. They presided over ceremonies, some clearly rooted in widely shared ideas about relations between humans and the supernatural world, that have left behind significant material traces. It is these signs of a "high culture" (Baines and Yoffee 1998) that archaeologists have taken as the basis for defining the Classic Maya as a coherent object of study (Joyce 2000c). As numerous specialists have argued, acceptance of this coherence needs to be balanced with attention to local differences, particularly in the degree and nature of economic integration, political hierarchy, social inequality, and religious conformity (Chase 1992; Hammond 1991; Hendon 1991, 1992; Sabloff and Henderson 1993). The comparative methodology that is an inescapable tool used to tease information out of the less abundant Classic Maya textual and visual records inevitably leads to an emphasis on what is shared, and a consequent de-emphasis of difference both within and between Classic Maya city states. The ideological impetus for the creation of much of the received documentary and visual record further tends to obscure viewpoints other than those of the ruling families (Marcus 1992). Fortunately, other lines of archaeological evidence have been developed that reinstate a sense of variability and dynamics among Classic Maya city states.

Settlement pattern studies and household archaeology, widely practiced in the Maya area, have demonstrated that Maya polities vary greatly in absolute size, and in the degree of economic differentiation among households that made up the monumental centers. Estimates of polity populations range from the thousands to the tens of thousands (Culbert and Rice 1990), with a tier of very large sites likely reaching more than 100,000 but less than 200,000 people. The stability of individual sites varies from city states that apparently lasted only two or three generations, to long-lived cities whose final dynasties claimed to have been in existence for nine or more generations. Households within sites also varied in size and longevity, some expanding to comprise multiple groups as large as other single households, with founders' houses remodeled over multiple generations until they resembled small palaces and temples (Hendon 1991; Tourtellot 1983). Some of the largest non-ruling households were a source of potential competition for ruling houses, encompassing enough labor to underwrite lavish ceremonies and even support the creation of artworks and monuments like those of the ruling families. In the absence of large domesticated animals, human labor was the critical resource for the agrarian economy of the Classic Maya city-states, many of which developed elaborate systems of water control and agricultural intensification directed at coping with sharp seasonal differences in rainfall. Labor concentrated in house compounds also provided the basis for most craft production, with specialization in pottery, shell and bone tool production, chipped stone and ground stone tool production, textile production and lapidary work all well represented archaeologically (Hendon 1997; Inomata 2001b).

Trying to write about the embodied lives of individuals in Classic Maya city-states requires attention to the probable effects on living experience of all of these differences among contexts. Monumental inscriptions and public artworks, with their stereotyped presentation of idealized lives, dominate much of what we think about the Classic Maya. As in Egypt, orderly and ideologically charged mortuary contexts give a richer glimpse of the experience of death that has dominated the way we think about Classic Maya experiences of embodiment and personhood.

Toward an embodied archaeology

In order to try to overcome the tendency of the most abundant sources, which in both cases stem from the lives and interests of a small segment of society, to dominate our understanding, in the chapters that follow we begin with lived experience and move toward the experience of death, eternity, and the extension of the self into a time after bodily integrity ceases. We do not attempt to present an idealization of a life cycle, but rather take as our starting point the experience of embodiment, as it can be picked out from the materials available

INTRODUCTION

to us. Archaeology, like many other disciplines, has been seduced by the body
as a site of inscription and a vehicle for representation (Meskell 1996). We aim
to move beyond a surface approach or a simple reading of the body to
consider the culturally embedded experience of embodiment. We find that in
both Egypt and the Classic Maya world, texts reiterate certain words related to
bodily experience, a terminology of embodiment. The body concepts singled
out discursively in text are also in play, both discursively and experientially, in
material culture and visual representations. Gaps and silences in the words and
practices we can describe begin to point to the sites where embodied experience may have been most charged.

Because embodiment is in no way a given, but instead is always in process, it
is a critical site of both social and personal investment. We explore the rich
material traces of the social and individual work of embodiment, work that in
fact is responsible for the existence of a large part of the material culture, art,
and objects of "high culture" that archaeologists have recovered in both
regions. Unlike scholars who focus entirely on elite materials, we are equally
concerned with a wider spectrum of potential experience, and that necessarily
encompasses those who are often hidden from history: women, children,
foreigners, the poor and those of servile status. In giving voice to ancient lives
the material record is especially important since it offers a much needed coun-
terbalance to the textual and inscriptional evidence that renders silent those
outside elite circles. The objects under investigation should be seen not simply
as representations of persons, but as constitutive of them. Their post-mortem
persistence ensures that a part of the personhood of past people endures to the
present. Objects associated with embodiment are more than mere costume or
props; they are extensions of the materiality of the embodied person.

This leads us to a consideration of the play of desire implied by the material-
ities of embodiment that have survived as resources for archaeological study.
In both locales, sexuality has been under-examined. The representation of
male sexuality, although quite distinct in nature, occupies a central place in
both traditions, signified literally by the objectification of the penis as a subject
for textual and visual discourse. We explore implications of the phallic culture
evident among the Classic Maya and New Kingdom Egyptians. These images
and texts inevitably raise questions about the fluid economies of ancient Maya
and Egyptian bodies, and of the demarcation of bodily boundaries and
boundaries of embodiment. Hybrids crossing human, animal, and botanical
species lead us to a consideration of boundaries and distinctions as experienced in these ancient civilizations. Our taxonomies must incorporate various
recombinant identities based upon human, animal and plant taxa. Tensions
between categories that we find familiar have very different expressions in
these other cultures, and raise the question of how this might reflect different
forms of corporeal alterity.

In both cases, the transformation of bodies from subjects to objects in death
plays across boundaries that might be assumed to demarcate the materiality of

the individual person. In different ways, Maya and Egyptian visions of the possible persistence of selfhood depend on the physical persistence of the body, and on the memory of the self that carries on through the actions of other people who come after the death of the individual embodied person. The possible future of the disembodied person was, in consequence, a subject of concern, the topic of hellish visions.

As archaeologists who take the material traces of these ancient people as beginning points for construing something about their experiences, we play a role in the continuing memory of these persons at least partly envisaged by the makers of the things that have lasted over centuries to become our points of departure. By asking different questions about these materials, we hope we have been able to conjure up something of the personhood of these very different times and places.

2

TERMINOLOGIES

Worldly bodies

The human body served as a metaphor for the world, for which the Egyptians had no word. The body was thus an important metaphor for conceptualizing the cosmos, and its cyclicity provided the template for the workings of the universe. Physical elements like earth, sky, moisture, air, and sun were all embodied, personified and divinized. These were imaginative geographies that had real time implications on earth and were equally important in the realm of death and the hereafter. Paralleling the bodies of the gods, the person of the king was depicted as a body comprising various members symbolizing his subjects (Frandsen 1997: 82), so that world order itself was expressed in corporeal terms, as it was among the Classic Maya as well (Gillespie 2000). Many aspects of human experience and the use of abstract categories—thought, emotion, time, social practice, and unbounded bodily phenomena—are often represented through the tropes of metaphor, metonymy and mental imagery (Frandsen 1997: 81; Lakoff and Johnson 1980: 177). In an early form of genesis (Allen 1988: 36), the creator god claims:

> *It was through my effectiveness that I brought about my body.*
> *I am the one who made me.*
> *It was as I wished, according to my heart, that I built myself*

The motif of bodily self-creation was central to Egyptian theology and the origin myths pertaining to divinities and mortals alike. In another account, the god Khnum fashioned the bodies of mortals and gods on the potters' wheel (Meeks and Favard-Meeks 1997: 54). There are many separate but overlapping myths of becoming and being. In one account, the creator god fabricated the other gods from his divine sweat, which is another phrase for the fragrance emanating from his body, and then created humanity from his own tears. There is a word play on the verbal association between "tear" and "human being" (Hornung 1982: 150). The gods' blindness and weeping are the backdrop for humanity's creation, ensuring that they can never partake in the clear and perfect sight of the gods. As such they are inevitably forced to live in partial vision and affliction. In the myth of the god Atum, he comes into being and creates himself out of air and moisture, earth and sky (Piankoff 1964: 19). In the Memphite Theology (Lichtheim 1980: 54) we read:

> *There took shape in the heart, there took shape on the tongue the form of Atum. For the very great one is Ptah, who gave [life] to all the gods and their kas through his heart and through his tongue, in which Horus has taken shape as Ptah, in which Thoth has taken shape as Ptah.*

Becoming and birthing oneself into being is an inherently corporeal act that always centers on the male divine body, at the expense of the complimentarity and agency of the female body and its fertile potentials. Godly bodies were specifically sexed, and theoretically they could not switch genders. Very few could be said to be gendered ambiguously. It is also recorded in the Heliopolitan Theology that the origin of the world was phallic (Figure 2.1). Ra-Atum, the original father, brought the world into being (Lichtheim 1980: 54):

> *he took his phallus in his fist and made sweet ejaculation from it, and the twins, Shu and Tefnut, were born. Ptah's Ennead is before him as teeth and lips. They are the semen and the hands of Atum. For the Ennead of Atum came into being through his semen and his fingers. But the Ennead is the teeth and lips in this mouth which pronounced the name of every thing, from which Shu and Tefnut came forth, and which gave birth to the Ennead.*

Other texts erase this primeval act of masturbation, instead suggesting that Atum sneezed or spat his offspring into being. The self-creation of Amun (NK Papyrus Leiden I 350) (Allen 1988: 49) is also an embodied coming into the world that was a literal and metaphorical self fashioning:

> *The one who crafted himself, whose appearance is unknown.*
> *Perfect aspect, which developed in a sacred emanation.*
> *Who built his processional images and created himself by himself.*
> *Perfect icon, whom his heart made perfect.*
> *Who knit his fluid together with his body to bring about his egg in isolation.*
> *Development of a development, model of birth.*

Egyptian thought was tacitly embodied and the structures employed developed out of bodily experience, grounded in perception and phenomenological experience. Human imaginative capacities are similarly embodied, since

Figure 2.1 Image of creation featuring Geb and Nut. Courtesy of the British Museum, EA 10018.

metaphor, metonymy, and images are also based on corporeal experience (Lakoff 1987: xiv). Being, destruction and becoming are the stages that humanity experiences in parallel to the cycles of the Egyptian gods (Piankoff 1964: 49). If every individual came out of the body of the god then they may too return to a godly state. The clearest potential for this return occurs through the inescapability of death and bodily annihilation. Paradoxically, it was only through one form of bodily death that a divine embodiment might be achieved. Books of the Netherworld such as the Amduat, the Book of Gates and Book of Caverns all tell of Ra's passage through the night of the netherworld and his battle with dark forces. His is also a journey of transformation from the dead, fleshed anthropomorphic body to the otherworldly body of the scarab, Khepri, which symbolizes eternal resurrection and becomings. All the beings he encounters in the netherworld are similarly the bodies, forms and images of the god himself. But how malleable and susceptible were divine bodies, in contrast to the inherent fragilities of the human experience?

Divine bodies had their own implicit materiality and could be hurt, and even die, yet generally the pain a divine body suffered did not affect its entire being. Identity of visible form was clearly important to the god's identity and yet they retained the capacity for transformation, albeit within the same gendered regime. Godly bodies could be mutilated and could bleed since they were made of flesh, a flesh that was often likened to gold. Most deities were described as having golden skin, hair that was black with blue hues like lapis, and those that differed signified special powers. Black or green skin, for example in the case of Osiris or Ptah, would indicate regenerative powers. The properties of non-biological taxonomies, specifically those of a precious nature, could be integrated as metaphorical layerings upon the divine. Eye color was also indicative: Seth's eyes were black linking him with darkness, whereas those of Horus were blue like the sky, Atum's were green since he was originally a serpent and so on (Meeks and Favard-Meeks 1997: 57). Each aspect of the divine's embodiment had a symbolic coding related to their own narrative of being.

Gods could also become ill and suffer pain, the eyes being the most vulnerable elements of their bodies (Meeks and Favard-Meeks 1997: 57). Injuries like the attack on the eye of Horus, or worms lodged in the eye of Atum, became famous tropes within Egyptian culture. The eye served as a metaphor for the moon, and one interpretation posits that the notion of worms may have stemmed from an impression of the moon's uneven surface as observed from earth. Perhaps connected was the fact that eye ailments were common to Egyptian mortals as well. Stories about the misadventures of the gods often paralleled humanity's difficulties and afflictions on earth. Yet for the most part the gods did not age, with the exception of the sun god Ra, harking back to his status as a primeval god. In sum, it was believed that divine bodies were essentially indestructible, and that even the gods could not destroy themselves: Seth is a good case in point. Osiris was the only embodied deity to die in the manner of an earthly death and be resigned to the world of the dead, rather than living. He had been killed once before-hand and had returned, but his second death was indeed fatal. This second death involved the gradual assembling and revivification of his numerous body parts by his wife Isis, although even this reconstitution did not restore him to life in a traditional manner (Meeks and Favard-Meeks 1997: 80). His divine being was given another sort of existence in the afterlife—a commanding vision of the underworld and power over all those who inevitably traversed it.

But for the most part, despite this malleability, the impenetrable nature of the godly body ensured that its profound essence remained inviolable (Meeks and Favard-Meeks 1997: 74). Following this principle, the substances of the divine also rendered them impervious to destruction, if not to assault. For example, the severed hands of Horus had their own life force. Separated from the body they continued to live an entirely other existence of their own, as told in spell 113 from the Book of the Dead. In some textual accounts the eyes of Horus were treated similarly, taking on a life and identity of their own. This re-centers the importance of member divinization, where the separability of the body and its members reflects the divinity and discursive power characteristic of the gods. Mortals could only aspire to such a literal transformation.

Through language, member divinization undoes the body and returns it to a fetish (Barthes 1974: 112).

> *My face is a falcon*
> *The top of my head is Re.*
> *My eyes are the Two Women, the Two Sisters,*
> *My nose is the Horus of the Netherworld,*
> *My mouth is the Sovereign of the West,*
> *My throat is Nun.*
> *My two arms are the Embracing One,*
> *My fingers are the Graspers.*
> *My breast is Khepri,*
> *My heart is the Horus-Sunen ...*
> *My anus is the great flood.*
> *My phallus is Tatenen,*
> *My glans is the Protected One in Old Cairo.*
> *My testicles are the Two Hidden Ones,*
> *My thighs are the two Goddesses ...*
> *The gods have transformed themselves into my body*
> (Hornung 1992; Piankoff 1964: 173–4)

Other divine bodies incorporated non-corporeal elements and became truly universal deities. In another form of hybridity the gods assimilated cosmic entities into their own somatic forms. Nut, the sky goddess, sprinkled her body with stars (see Figure 2.1), and Hathor was similarly depicted as a starry female body. In this schema, both goddesses were depicted nude, inherently sexualized, and could be represented as pregnant, about to birth the sun, thus bringing forth the new day. Nut was well known for her abilities to swallow the sun and stars through her mouth and to birth them anew from her vagina on a daily basis. The cycle of daily life was inherently sexualized in this manner, though its specifically female nature was never completely explored. What might it mean to have the sun progress through the body of a goddess, to have her swallow and birth it as the night passes to day? The myth suggests that the most mundane element of life was intensely corporeal and feminized. While creation itself must be perceived as entirely male, sexual and monadic, its ongoing aspects were embodied as female and fertile. The sun was said to appear in the morning *between the thighs of Nut*, and there is a clear sexual referent when the sun enters her body; it is likened to impregnation by the god, Re. The passage of the sun between these essentially male and female poles echoes the fact that the concepts of day and night similarly interact as male and female principles. In the description of Nut, her right arm is on the northwestern side, her left on the southeastern side. The western horizon is her mouth, and her vagina is the eastern horizon. So despite the enormous emphasis placed upon creation as a singularly male, phallic event to be celebrated and retold in numerous myths, the creation and maintenance of the world is iterated through the swallowing and birthing of the sun, the sexual functionality of the female body. This reminds us quite literally of the central tenet of phenomenological theory—that we are in the world through our body and we perceive that world within our body. When we remake that contact with the body and with the world, we concurrently rediscover ourselves, since the body is a natural embodiment of the self and the subject of perception (Merleau-Ponty 1962: 206).

Body language and personification

The materials from Egyptian and Mayan societies, existing before and separate from the tradition that runs from Platonic to Cartesian thought, give us a potential window on other ways of framing embodiment, distinct from concepts of duality, hierarchy and rational privilege. In developing this position further, we follow a number of "anti-Cartesian" traditions in which the body and associated problems of dualism have been centrally addressed in theorization ranging from phenomenology to psychoanalysis, and from critical social theory to feminist scholarship (Turner 1984, 1996). Phenomenological methods, as elaborated by Maurice Merleau-Ponty, enable us to apprehend the active forces of corporeality in new ways, as a sentient body embedded within environments, encountering paths, obstacles, and horizons of reality. A phenomenological language is needed to describe the postures, gestures, and operations that constitute the body's perceptual and practical competence (Lingis 1994). Inspired by scholars like Csordas (1994), through our consideration of these ancient materials we offer a critique of the passive, representationalist approach, typified by Foucauldian "discourse determinism," that has become pervasive in contemporary social theory (Meskell 1996, 1999a). Throughout this volume we espouse a more experientially grounded view of human embodiment as the existential basis of the individual's being-in-the-world. Meaning inheres in bodily behaviors, gestures and culturally contextual understandings of the self, rather than being the product of some prior disembodied *cogito*. Culture becomes a projection of the contextual body into the world (Williams and Bendelow 1998: 8). *Homo duplex*, the construct embedded within anthropology's own history, plays on the dualisms of self and other, sacred and profane, body and soul. The ancient Egyptian and Maya materials challenge and inspire us to reconfigure those old pervasive binaries and ultimately deprivilege the Western tradition.

In Egypt the living person was embedded in a number of foundational matrices, not unlike Strathern's (1988: 13) notion of the *dividual*:

> Far from being regarded as unique entities, Melanesian persons are as dividually as they are individually conceived. They contain a generalized sociality within. Indeed, persons are frequently constructed as

the plural and composite site of the relationships that produced them. The singular person can be imagined as a social microcosm.

In New Kingdom Egypt, there was the connectedness of the kin group, with those sharing the same title and rank, and the person's general position in the divine, royal, and human order of things, glossed as *Maat*. On a broad societal level the concept of the person and their role in the worldly schema was an important existential issue. At the same time, there was a strongly contoured sense of the *individual* as well, with particular emphasis on the narrative biography of the self. "The positive value of a person can tend toward unique achievements that changed someone's world, or toward their full and harmonious embodiment of the ideals and aspirations of their social group" (Baines 1999: 24). For elite men, this biographizing took the form of tomb biographies, stelae and statuary, foregrounding the name, titles and achievements. For others, such as women and lower status individuals, it might take the form of pictorial representation in meager form. In this sense, both dividual and individual constructions of self were embraced and co-existent.

Ripples of association linked the physical experience of the material body and its spiritual resonances and potentials. It is likely that the Egyptians perceived the human body as constructed and operating not as a single organism but more as a corporation, a loose association, of separate anatomical entities (Walker 1996: 283). The word *ḥ* commonly rendered as "body" can also refer to existential concepts of "self," "person" and "own," but also to the skin or body surface. Such a linguistic construction might underscore the Egyptian's preference for a skin-bound construction of the person or self. However, the construct of a bounded being in a material sense does not necessarily imply a rigid boundary in the incorporeal sense. But *ḥ* is more than just the physical matter or substance of the body; it is the physical aspect of a person or one of their "states of being." Other terms to denote the whole body were *ẖȝt* (refers to the dead body), *ẖt* (the torso), and *ḏt* (spiritual concept of the body). *Ḏt* is the eternal personal form that transcends the living physical body that could be depicted in a serpent-like or mummiform shape (Walker 1996: 17). *Ḥt*, written with a sign representing an animal belly, has a wider meaning as the locus of inner life, the location of thoughts, feelings and memories (te Velde 1990: 89). It referred to the whole abdomen and its organs and could extend to the chest and its organs, but should not be read inclusively as encompassing the entire body. The word was also used to denote a tree trunk or stem of a plant, so one can see similarities with the English terminology of trunk or torso. Medical texts similarly reveal the concept of joint, an extension of the word for part called *ʿty*. For the Egyptians, the ligaments, cartilages and potential spaces between the bones were more important than the bones themselves. Joints were the places where the body divided into its many separate entities, whereas we see the joints as points where the body is held together as a cohesive, singular entity. *Wpt*, a term meaning a dividing line, was used to delineate the body. There was a duality in the concept of how the body was structured such as the parting of the torso, the cranium, and the perineum (Walker 1996: 57). A conceptual importance was placed upon "setting apart," as an agent at the boundary of two things, simultaneously constituting a tangible link. Linking embodiment with cultural conceptions of the landscape, *wpwty* is the name given for a messenger who travels between two lands. As will become clear, the Egyptians were fond of the related structured notions of doubling and duality, evidenced in both corporeal constructions and worldviews.

Outlining the porous nature of the phenomenal body in Egyptian culture, constituents of the body known as *mtw* incorporated both corporeal and esoteric elements. In the Papyrus Ebers the *mtw* include blood vessels, ducts, tendons, muscles and perhaps nerves (Nunn 1996: 44). It may be best to translate *mtw* as conduits rather than vessels. A number of substances can be transported by the *mtw* such as blood, urine, air, semen, disease carrying entities, as well as benevolent or malevolent spirits. Semen and poison were often linked—as detailed in the mythological accounts of Seth impregnating Horus with poisonous semen—and were similar in written and phonetic form. In one text there was a total of twenty-two *mtw*, and it states that *all come to his heart. They distribute to his nose and all unite at the anus.* This accords with Egyptian concepts of the circulation of noxious substances and with the fundamental fluidity of embodied life. They believed that the breath of life entered through the right ear, whereas the breath of death entered through the left. Illness was often considered to be the work of demons penetrating the borders of the body, threatening its integrity. The Egyptians feared the accessibility and vulnerability of the body's orifices, reminiscent of contemporary concerns with the leaky borders of the body (Grosz 1994), especially pertinent to the cultural and biological specificities of the female body.

Flesh was called *iwf.* A linguistic determinative designated whether it referred to the flesh of the living as opposed to the dead. The same term could refer to skin, as in the foreskin, thus underscoring the indeterminacy of terminology. The term is often used in gynecological texts that refer to contraception, pregnancy or vaginal complaints. Thus the vagina was seen as flesh, as were internal organs such as the liver, spleen, lungs, intestines, heart, and kidneys. *R3-ib* has traditionally been considered the name given to the stomach, literally the mouth of the heart. This may signify that the stomach was the place where the inner self/psyche resides, or at least a portal to its location (Walker 1996: 128). Because they use the word *ib*, the Egyptians intentionally link the stomach to the metaphysical heart rather than the physical organ, known as *h3ty.* It is most likely the chest cavity that was considered the domain of the heart, metaphorically and literally a shrine for the *ib.* Scholars have pointed out, however, that there are slightly different contextual cadences for these terms depending on whether one is reading religious or medical texts. *Ib* refers to a non-anatomical entity, and can refer to the self

19

or person as an entirety. The *ib* was part of a person's manifestations and was non-corporeal, likening it to the other non-corporeal constituents of the self such as the *ka* or *ba*. It was one of the states of being that possessed significant amount of existential flexibility and permeability. The individual and the *ib* were written in an interchangeable way: *my heart was happy* is a well known example. Other embodied expressions were *wide of heart* (to be happy); *enduring of heart* (to be patient); *place the heart before* (to be anxious); *to place the heart before* (to pay attention to); *stout of heart* (to be brave) (Teeter 2000: 157). To *give one's heart* was a potent metaphor for sexual activity. This body language reflects the emotional nature that was assigned the body and its constituents. Rather than residing in the mental sphere, the Egyptian emotional world was rooted in the very matter of the individual body.

Specific bodily parts were likened to actions and states of being in meta-phorical and embodied ways. The image of the head in profile, *tp*, was used for the word "head," but also to be "the head" or "chief." What we translate as the word "on" is written with hieroglyphic determinative of the frontal face, while the word "top" is written with the image of the human head. The nose, *fnd*, was similarly a determinative used in words that signify the actions sniff, smell, rebuff, kiss, and to take pleasure. More phenomenologically, incense was depicted as the sweat of the gods, and inhaling it was a means of appre-hending them, of communing with them and being nourished by them. Light, sound, air, and fragrance were all strongly associated and redolent of divinity for the Egyptians. One of the most iconic symbols of the Egyptian repertoire was the *ankh* sign, still popular as a motif in contemporary jewelry, symbolizing the breath of life.

The words for eye, *irt*, were linked to concepts such as "to see" and "to make," *iri*, and were visually and phonetically the same. The symbol of the eye was also used as a determinative for words like look, blind, and wakeful. Tongues were given a special sort of agency, as seen in the Hymns to Senwosret III: *the tongue of his person restrains Nubia,* or the Teachings of Merikare where *the strong arm of the king is his tongue* (Parkinson 2000: 28). Ears unsurprisingly signified hearing and were often made material for ritual purposes, as votives paralleling the ear hieroglyph. Archaeologically we have uncovered numerous wooden votive ears that were offered at Deir el Bahri at Hathor's shrine. Hathor was the goddess *who listens*. This was crucial for a non-literate populace desperate for divine intervention. Limestone stelae covered with inscribed ears were popular in the Ramesside Period. They were set up in popular shrines within state temples or found in household contexts (Parkinson 1999: 67). The image conveys the meaning, and the message, without a text.

Body parts were multivalent images and the very process of writing and picturing them held potency. One evocative example is that of the penis, used as a linguistic determinative in the words "man," "male," "bull," "donkey." The penis with fluid issuing is used in words such as "semen," "poison,"

"urinate," "husband." Some have argued that the organ had no negative association, and that all such words are redolent of masculinity. But some clearly
also are inflected with danger and power.

Perhaps the most complex construction of a body part was reserved for the
heart, the center for the gravitational self. There were many spells in the Book
of the Dead for retaining the heart in death, for willing it to be loyal and for
generally protecting the heart (Faulkner 1985). The heart was essentialized,
almost prior to its existence as an entity. One could be *of hearts*, or a *unifier of
hearts*, and having one's heart with them was likened to being *in the body of
Geb and Nut*, the primordial gods of creation. Spell 30B was intended to stop
the heart from testifying against the deceased: *O my heart which I had from my
mother, O my heart of my different ages! Do not stand up as a witness against me.
Do not be opposed to me in the tribunal.* Suggestive here is the notion that the
heart was linked to the female line and that it mirrored the trajectory of the
lifecycle. It was the same heart that stayed with the individual, perhaps
compiling its own narrative biography. In written and verbal spells and in
material objects, there was a concern to ritually control the freedom and
potential waywardness of the heart. Heart scarabs were designed to protect
the heart at the crucial moment of judgment when the heart could be
thrown to the monstrous Ammit, the devourer. The scarab was placed
upon the dead body, directly over the heart, and was inscribed with spell
30B from the Book of the Dead. Sometimes they bore a human face, an
anthropomorphizing tactic that renders an isomorphic connection between
the individual and their heart. Heart scarabs were usually manufactured from
schist or green stone, called *nmhf,* which literally means *it does not float*, a
symbolic implication of keeping the balance pan used in the judgment process
sufficiently weighted down. And more aggressively, prior to the New
Kingdom, heart scarabs could be ritually killed, their mouths and eyes defaced
and damaged, presumably to inhibit their seeing or speaking any evil against
the deceased petitioner (Andrews 1994: 57).

Embodied being

At the individual embodied level the terminology of the self was complex and
multifaceted. While we have explored the corporeal constituents of the
person, there existed an immaterial substrate that the Egyptians regarded as
potentially even more crucial to the notion of being. As explored below, the
Cartesian split of mind and body was not operative in Egyptian culture (see
Chapter 4). Rather, the ancient Egyptians apprehended their inter-subjective
domain as the realm of thoughts, intentions, sensations, personal reflections
and individual characteristics (Assmann 1982, 1999). This private experience
of the self lay at the intersection of the vectors of sociality, consciousness, self-
experience and the material body. Multiply constituted, the self had several
components necessary for being, an inchoate group of entities based on

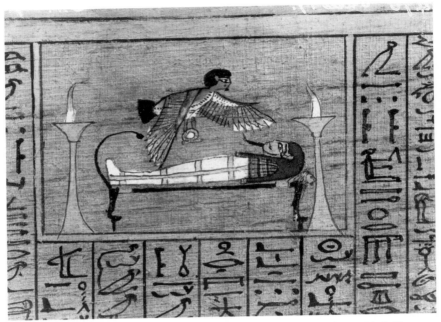

Figure 2.2 Detail from the Papyrus of Ani, showing Ani and his *ba* as a bird. Courtesy of the British Museum, EA 10470/7.

mirroring or doubling. We are still uncertain whether these operated primarily in death or were ever present during life.

The *ka*, glossed as twin self or vital force, and *ba*, character or individual identity, probably were considered present through life and persisted after death (Figure 2.2). The individual went to great lengths to ensure that these entities remained loyal and connected through the perils of the hereafter, since they were each an additional safeguard and guarantor of eternal life. Another important efficacious element of the self throughout life was the personal name or *rn* that was bestowed at birth and had personal and religious significance. The name had ritual potency, acting in a doubling capacity for the self, and further serving as a receptacle of individuality. It too could operate as a doppelganger if the physical body was compromised after death. Next was the heart, *ib*, the seat of intelligence for the Egyptians as opposed to the brain or mind, as well as the fount of knowledge, memory, and understanding. The Egyptians did not make the distinction between our taxonomies of "emotion" and "rational intelligence," since self-knowledge was grounded in a combined understanding.

A final component of the self was *heka* or personal magic, which was more connected to one's trajectory after death. Through ritual activity on the part of the kin group this personal magic was activated. For the deceased, the body and personality were preserved, whilst they were transformed in order to attain the next level of being, what was known as an *effective spirit*. This interior community was most at risk of dissolution at the point of death and the myriad spells recounted in the Books of the Netherworld were attempts to reintegrate and unify the various aspects of the embodied self (see Chapter 4).

Terms of embodiment

The ancient Maya world is not available for us to participate in and learn to understand as an ethnographer interested in lived experience can participate in contemporary Maya life (e.g. Hanks 1990). But the material world that ancient Maya persons experienced has not entirely vanished, either. We have available for our task a rich variety of material objects that furnished the homes, public spaces, and tombs of ancient Maya persons. The material context of ancient Maya experience shaped Maya personhood both subtly and overtly. An astonishing proportion of the material culture extant today was employed in practices of shaping the body. This includes not only the obvious examples of body ornaments, durable pieces of costume, and the tools used to produce them, but also the material settings for action, the rooms, benches, terraces, patios and walkways which Maya people traversed every day, which channeled their lived experiences and bodily practices in similar ways (Joyce 2001b; Joyce and Hendon 2000). It even includes the material artefacts employed to store, produce, process, and serve foods that literally nourished the body and metaphorically joined people to each other and the land around them (Hendon 1996, 1997, 1999, 2000, 2002; Joyce 1993, 2001b).

To the impressive array of material objects from the ancient Maya world that have survived to provide us with material for reflection, we can add an abundance of representations, both pictorial and textual (Miller 1999; Coe 1997), covering the surfaces of everything from costume ornaments (Joyce 2000b) to serving vessels (Reents-Budet 1994), and as monuments forming everything from the roofs of tombs to the demarcation of edges of the open living spaces we today call plazas (Tate 1992; Newsome 2001) and the secluded interior spaces of buildings (M. Miller 1986) and caves (Stone 1995). Representations provide a powerful and ambiguous source of evidence for understanding ancient Maya embodiment and personhood. Representations present stereotypes of ancient Maya experience, images of a universe populated primarily by young, male subjects (Joyce 1993, 2000d, 2001b). They thus systematically bias our vision of ancient Maya experience, if we make the mistake of taking the represented world as typical. But by the same token, ancient Maya representations provide us with insight into what aspects of ancient Maya personhood were most highly charged, the subjects of greatest interest and, potentially, of most contestation. By interpreting representations not as simple reflections of lived experience, but as paradigms that served as tacit and explicit models of idealized behavior, representations become a powerful entry point into foregrounded aspects of bodily experience.

The results of epigraphic studies of Maya inscriptions can be used to provide a beginning point for understanding embodiment from this perspective (e.g. Houston and Stuart 1989, 1996, 1998; Houston and Taube 2000; Stuart 1996). Such studies literally establish the terms of embodiment that lead us to understand embodied personhood in subtly and radically different ways from the taken-for-granted approaches of contemporary western philosophies. As has repeatedly been noted, the contemporary west has inherited a dualistic view of personhood in which the physical body is a gross vessel for a more refined spirit or mind (Turner 1984: 36–38). In this mind/body dualism, the mind or spirit is what dignifies personhood. In religious philosophies, the spirit is that which endures after the death and decay of the body. Non-religious dualism also posits an immaterial mind that endures beyond the fleshly self, in the form of recorded and communicated thought. These western views fundamentally separate a tangible physical body from an intangible metaphysical self.

Classic Maya texts and pictorial representations suggest a far different conception of embodiment—one that should not be assimilated to a simple mind/body dualism. The materially embodied Maya person was made up of blood and bone—substances that linked persons to relatives through their transmission from mothers and fathers (Gillespie and Joyce 1997; Gillespie 2001). The term once believed to literally represent blood (*k'ik'*) as a liquid animating fluid (Schele and Miller 1986) is now interpreted as a nonmaterial vital energy (*ch'ulel, k'ulel*) present in the blood, released through shedding blood in acts of personal sacrifice (Houston and Stuart 1996; Stuart 1988). Bone (*b'ak*) features prominently in texts as a reference to war captives claimed as trophies by their captors (Stuart 1985). The embodied person could be conceived of as a container or skin (Joyce 1993, 1998) enclosing these (and likely other) material substances and a variety of more immaterial, but by no means intangible, substances.

First among the recognized immaterial parts of the body was the *way* (Houston and Stuart 1989; Grube and Nahm 1994; compare Monaghan 1998: 141–144; Gossen 1996). These are depicted in animal form, and Gary Gossen (1996: 81–82) notes that in later Maya societies such spirits "originate or reside outside the body of their human counterpart, often in the bodies of animals" and "figure prominently in native theories of evil, well-being, fate, and destiny" (Figure 2.3). Described as a "spirit companion" or "co-essence," the *way* is named in Classic texts as a vision evoked in ritual (Figure 2.4). The word *way* literally refers to the dreaming state, during which the physical body might be immobile, but the *way* active. The relation between the embodied person and the co-essence, it has been suggested, was reciprocal, so that experiences of one affected the other. The relationship between a person and a *way* was not necessarily exclusive, opening up the possibility that the embodied person might have had connections to multiple *wayeb*, and that a particular

24

Figure 2.3 Animal/human hybrids representing *way* depicted on Classic Maya polychrome vase. Photograph K3040 © Justin Kerr. Used by permission.

Figure 2.4 *Way* invoked by a Classic Maya noble woman on Yaxchilan lintel 15, *c.* AD 755. The glyph for *way* is found in column F, row 1; the name of the *way*, including the term for serpent, comes immediately before this, at B2 and E1. This *way* is the co-essence of a supernatural being named at G1. Courtesy of Corpus of Maya Hieroglyphic Inscriptions, Peabody Museum, Harvard University.

Figure 2.5 Classic Maya polychrome vase showing immaterial substances emanating from the body. Photograph K2794 © Justin Kerr. Used by permission.

way might have been related to multiple people, through time or space. Monaghan (1998: 144), writing about the entire field of relations among persons and co-essences in native societies of the region, emphasizes that "as humans are uniquely defined by the particular webs of social relations they maintain, so too are coessential animals."

While the Classic Maya *way* is often represented as a kind of double, acting entirely outside the physical body, other immaterial parts of the person were represented as emanations from the body (Figure 2.5). In pictorial representation, sinuous scrolls marked with floral motifs appear to emerge from the anus and mouth, or are depicted reaching the nose and ears from other beings (Houston and Taube 2000). The immaterial but tangible substances—stench, scent, breath, speech, song, and noise—represented by such pictorial images are integral parts of the self and, to the extent that they reference phenomena that originate in the body, provide the embodied person with an inter-subjective materiality (compare Munn 1986). The substance of this class most widely recorded in Classic Maya texts is breath (*ik'*), recorded as one of the names of days in the divinatory calendar. A common expression for death contains this sign, and it was suggested quite early that it was based on a metaphor referring to the cessation of breath as part of death (Proskouriakoff 1963). More recently, epigraphers have read the sign linked with *ik'* in a coupled term for death as *tis*, "flatulence" (Houston and Taube 2000). Experientially, death marked the end of the inter-subjective transaction of immaterial bodily emanations.

Among the scroll-shaped emanations of the body, none have received more attention from epigraphers than vision scrolls (Houston and Stuart 1996; Houston and Taube 2000: 281–287). In texts, paired scrolls emerging from a detached eyeball—complete with a representation of an optic nerve—alternate with phonetic signs spelling the root for sight, *il* (Figure 2.6). As used most commonly in historical texts, this term records acts through which nobles witnessed important events in the lives of others. The pictorial image is one of a tangible visual field emerging from the eye of the watcher (*y-ichnal*)

26

Figure 2.6 Eyeball with optic nerve, part of a sculptural relief at Classic Maya Uxmal. Courtesy of Corpus of Maya Hieroglyphic Inscriptions, Peabody Museum, Harvard University.

understood by epigraphers as a "perceptual and interactional field" not entirely identical with the literal visual field (Houston and Taube 2000: 287–289). The eye is apparently to be understood as literally emanating a force, a metaphor for a sphere of command or control exercised through the sensory regard of a person.

Often accompanying references to vision in texts are references to an aspect of personhood recorded phonetically as *bah* (Houston and Stuart 1998). *Bah* can be used to signify a person's head, face, a mask, or a representation of the face, such as a carved stone monument (Stuart 1996: 158–165). The *bah* is linked intimately to selfhood, what Gillespie (2001: 83) notes Marcel Mauss (1985) called the *moi*, and distinguished from the *personne*. As Houston and Stuart (1998: 77) put it, "as the locus of identity, the face or head establishes individual difference and serves logically as the recipient of reflexive action" in Classic Maya inscriptions. The implication of deciphered Classic Maya texts is that in all of its senses, the *bah* is an enduring and identifiable part of a named person. As Matthew Looper (1995) has shown in an analysis of monuments at Quirigua, Guatemala, later nobles remained under the visual surveillance of deceased royal persons depicted in permanent form in stone monuments. The identity of the *personne* persisted over time in the medium of the visage, whether represented on a carved monument or in a substitute, such as a mask.

Monuments also carried another enduring aspect of the person—names. What are usually described as "names" in studies of Classic Maya inscriptions are a small set of highly stylized titles that circulate over generations, particulary noble families, and sometimes recur over broad areas (Montgomery 2002: 197–215). Examples of sequences of monumental inscriptions documenting events in the life of one person (e.g. Tate 1992: 130–132, 136–137) demonstrate that nominal references changed over the life span, with a child's name being replaced by one of the shared pool of adult names (Figure 2.7). Names, like co-essences, bone, and blood, and most likely the visage as well, were aspects of the embodied person that recurred in different individuals, linking them together as part of enduring personal identities multiply embodied over time (Gillespie 2001, 2002).

Figure 2.7 A lord named Chel-te in his youth, who later ruled as Shield Jaguar, in ritual performance with his adult predecessor, Bird Jaguar, on Yaxchilan lintel 2. The name of the youth is contained in column J, row 1. Courtesy of Corpus of Maya Hieroglyphic Inscriptions, Peabody Museum, Harvard University.

The persistence of names and visages facilitated the integration of a physical person with a history, a final aspect of Classic Maya personhood. We do not yet have an identified term for personal history or memory, but the overwhelming majority of the content of Classic Maya inscriptions can best be understood as precisely such accounts, making use of time statements that position the reader with respect to events in the near and distant past, and projected commemorative events in the future (Figure 2.8). Like names and visages, personal histories were linked in recurring patterns, facilitated by the use of cyclical calendars in which dates of the same name had divinatory import (Monaghan 1998). The terms for the date of birth of a person in the divinatory calendar could, in later Maya societies, function as an additional form of naming. Such calendar references embodied links to particular fates that might have formed an additional non-material, yet tangible, aspect of the person.

Blood and bone, face and eye, breath and sound, stench and scent, dreaming spirit and birth fate, name and history: it is unlikely that these exhaust the bodily terminology in use in everyday life among the Classic Maya. What the isolation of these bodily aspects in monumental texts and images does signal is the way that certain aspects of embodied existence were foregrounded as subjects of substantial importance to the patrons of historical

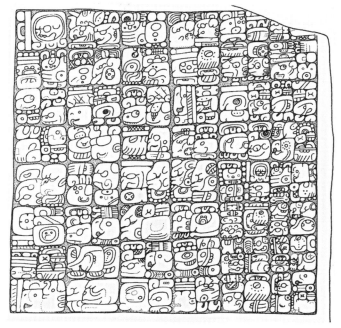

Figure 2.8 The personal history of a Maya lord. Yaxchilan lintel 10. Among the biographical information recorded is the lord's relationship to a woman named as his mother and the relationship of captor to captives metaphorized as his *b'ak*, prisoner/bone. Courtesy of Corpus of Maya Hieroglyphic Inscriptions, Peabody Museum, Harvard University.

monuments, and, as a result, as aspects of embodied experience subject to conscious reflection. Practices of the body, recorded in pictorial representations and also supported by material recovered archaeologically, reinforce and extend the Classic Maya inventory of focal body parts implied by texts. They allow us to begin to move away from the stereotypes presented in public records and begin to examine more concretely the lived experience of Classic Maya persons. To the extent that terms of embodiment and practices of the body coincide, they signal points of both tacit, experiential, and explicit, discursive construction of embodied personhood. Equally interesting are the tensions, silences, and gaps that the juxtaposition of practice and discourse reveals.

Practices of the body

The adult person normally represented in Classic Maya monumental images may be described as standing in emotionally serene and highly controlled poses (Houston 2001). She or he engages in a set of highly stylized gestures, which

29

Figure 2.9 Classic Maya dance posture, Xcalumkin jamb 7. Courtesy of Corpus of Maya Hieroglyphic Inscriptions, Peabody Museum, Harvard University.

have been likened to a form of sign language (Benson 1974; Schaffer 1991; compare Houston 2001: 209). Some of the most common stylized gestures are explicitly labeled in accompanying texts as "dance" (Grube 1992). To stand with knee bent and heel lifted (Figure 2.9), it appears, signifies dance steps (Schele 1988; Reents-Budet 1991). Like many Maya verbs, "dance" has as its root a noun, in this case "foot."

The equation of gesture (lifted foot) and highlighted action (dancing footwork) draws attention to other instances in which the pictorial icon used to record the word for an action takes the form of an image of a body part. Profile views of a hand supporting a variety of icons appear throughout Classic Maya inscriptions (Montgomery 2002: 163, 169–170, 179). The images they accompany routinely represent static human figures holding a range of regalia (Figure 2.10). The repetition of particular gestures by the human figures in the images parallels variation in the icon supported in the text by the hand that forms the root of these verbs (Schele and Miller 1986: 49, 53).

While to a contemporary western observer the figures are at rest, they clasp insignia of political and ritual roles, fingers folded around a handle in the position that would follow the gesture depicted as the verb. Despite the stillness of the body, conventions of texts and images combine to record the bodily actions of the person. These bodies, usually shown standing, are in action, not (as we might read them) at rest. But the actions in which they engage are tightly controlled, and do not ruffle the surface of the lavishly ornamented costumes the figures wear.

In fact, in most images, the body of the represented person is subordinated to the represented costume. This is especially true for figures identified in accompanying text as women (Figure 2.11). The only body parts that are visible when noble female persons are depicted in monumental art are the head, hands, and feet (Joyce 1996, 1999). These peripheral body parts are joined by representations of densely woven brocaded cloth, often overlaid with a diagonal network of beads, that normally covers the body (Proskouriakoff 1961; Bruhns 1988; Morris 1985a, 1985b). These cloth and beaded robes are never depicted as displaced around the flesh of the body (Joyce 1993, 1999). The linear designs of cloth robes and beaded over-robes flow without interruption across the chests of the noblewomen who wear them, with no sign of disarrangement

30

Figure 2.10 Classic Maya noble holding ritual object in a gesture recorded in the accompanying text. Yaxchilan lintel 1. The hand holding the mirror at column B, row 2 is associated with holding the personified hafted axe. Courtesy of Corpus of Maya Hieroglyphic Inscriptions, Peabody Museum, Harvard University.

from breasts below the cloth, clearly depicted in contemporary modeled figurines and painted polychrome vases (Figure 2.12). While the clothing of the male body often reveals more of the legs and arms (Joyce 2000d; see Chapter 6), the body of the highest ranking noble men also juxtaposes hands, feet and head to extremely elaborate costuming.

The Classic Maya body frames and thus acknowledges a head, hands, and feet as discursively relevant parts of the body. Details of these body parts are carefully rendered; the nails of fingers and toes, the sole of the foot, the articulation of the wrist with the arm, and the details of the face, all receive considerable attention. This form of depiction forcefully directs our attention to those bodily sites whose action is thematized in texts: the feet and hands. The isolation of the head, which appears in many images of women and men as if floating detached above a dense field of ornamentation, similarly reinforces the importance of the visage, *bah*, site of personal identification, and seat of the sensory effects of vision, speech, and hearing (Houston and Stuart 1998; Houston and Taube 2000). These corporeal parts were the focus of considerable bodily attention, attested to not only in pictorial images but through the

Figure 2.11 Portrait of Classic Maya noble man and woman, showing the exposure of the male body and contrast to the concealed female body. Yaxchilan lintel 24. Courtesy of Corpus of Maya Hieroglyphic Inscriptions, Peabody Museum, Harvard University.

Figure 2.12 Noble woman represented on Classic Maya pottery vase from Tayasal, showing the modeling of breasts in small scale art. Photograph K2707 © Justin Kerr. Used by permission.

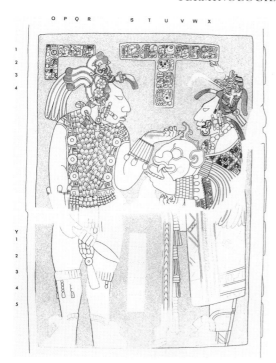

Figure 2.14
End of Classic Maya incised bone ornament from Copan. Photograph by Steve Burger. Museum object cat. no: 92–49–20/C202. N31825b. Courtesy of Peabody Museum, Harvard University, © President and Fellows of Harvard College.

Figure 2.13
Sloping head and bone hairpins in Classic Maya art, Yaxchilan lintel 26. Courtesy of Corpus of Maya Hieroglyphic Inscriptions, Peabody Museum, Harvard University.

recovery of material traces including body ornaments, especially those worn on the bodies of the buried dead.

Most obvious are bodily practices that emphasized various parts of the head. Images show Classic Maya figures with extremely exaggerated sloping foreheads, emphasized by shaving hair far above any likely natural hairline (Figure 2.13). A high proportion of crania recorded in Classic Maya burials actually had been artificially shaped into such backswept forms (Romero 1970: 65–67; Welsh 1988). While shaven hair does not persist in the conditions of the tropical forest, buried individuals at a number of sites were recovered with ornaments around the head like those shown in images. These include tubular beads, shown with locks of hair threaded through them, and long bone pins with elaborate terminals, sometimes carved with images and texts (Figure 2.14). The skull (Figure 2.15), it has been argued, was metaphorically understood as a seed (Schele and Friedel 1991). Perhaps specifically the elongated skull was equated with the maize cob (*ixim*), the head of the Classic

Figure 2.15 Classic Maya bead showing head enclosed in earth motif sprouting vegetation, recovered from the Cenote at Chichen Itza (Proskouriakoff 1974: Plate 43/10). © President and Fellows of Harvard College. Used by permission.

Figure 2.16 Classic Maya bead depicting the head of the maize god, with sloping forehead and tonsure suggesting vegetation, recovered from the Cenote at Chichen Itza (Proskouriakoff 1974: Plate 53b/6). © President and Fellows of Harvard College. Used by permission.

Maya maize god (Figure 2.16), who was depicted in Classic Maya art with a most exaggerated receding forehead (Taube 1985). At the same time, it is likely that the eye was understood, as it is in many descendant Maya languages, as the fruit or seed of the face (Campbell *et al.* 1986), re-emphasizing the identification between the person and the plant (see Chapter 5).

Shaped skulls, metaphorically identified with a removable, valued, plant part, were subject to "harvest" themselves (Figure 2.17), in practices employing "art-tools" (Graham 1992), axes elaborated on models of everyday utilitarian forms (Joyce 1998). The skulls of several royal burials at Tikal were removed in antiquity (A. Miller 1986). Images from contemporary monuments at the site, showing rulers holding decorated skulls (Figure 2.18), suggest that cranial bones were ornamented and preserved as items of regalia (A. Miller 1986: 46–51). Such practices are further suggested by other texts and images. The name of a prominent prisoner of a lord of Yaxchilan,

Figure 2.17 Decapitation scene from Classic Maya ballcourt. A decapitated figure kneels at the right of a rubber ball containing a skull, with plants sprouting from his severed throat. Facing him on the left stands a figure holding a leaf-shaped knife and the severed head. Great ballcourt, Chichen Itza. Photograph © Russell N. Sheptak. Used by permission.

Figure 2.18 Decorated skull held as regalia on Classic Maya Tikal stela 36. Photograph © Russell N. Sheptak. Used by permission.

Figure 2.19 Classic Maya bead depicting a human wearing a bird mask (Proskouriakoff 1974: Plate 59c/5). © President and Fellows of Harvard College. Used by permission.

"Jeweled Skull" (Proskouriakoff 1963), is one example. The shaping of the skull during life literally objectified it, making of it an independent object suitable for use after the death of the person, particularly to stand for the unique aspects of that person.

Skulls removed from burials at Tikal were replaced with jade masks (e.g. A. Miller 1986: Fig. 22). In other burials, masks covered the face of the deceased (compare Figure 2.19). An identification is suggested between the mask and the face, as a separable skin that covered the front of the head (Joyce 1998). In the central burial in the Temple of the Inscriptions at Palenque, this identification of face and mask was made literal by the painstaking gluing of a composite mosaic mask of jade and shell to the skin of the deceased (Gillespie 2001). Fragments of composite mosaic masks have been repeatedly reported in Classic Maya burials and tombs (e.g. Merwin and Vaillant 1932: Pl. 35a). The lack of any evidence of a substrate in even the most carefully excavated examples suggests that the adhesion of a permanent stony face to the decaying skin of the body may have been a more common practice than is currently recognized.

Solid one-piece stone masks are common items of Classic Maya costume, and masks of more flexible material are depicted in Classic Maya images, including a polychrome painted vase excavated at Tikal (Clancy *et al.* 1985: Fig. 8). Most often, Classic Maya masks depict anthropomorphic faces (Figure 2.20), emphasizing the identification of the fleshly countenance itself as a mask. In Classic Maya society, masking was a substitution of one constructed visage for another.

Other ornaments were routinely attached to the flesh of the head, both in life and in death (Figure 2.21). Some beads recovered archaeologically have been identified as lip ornaments (labrets), presumably inserted through a hole below the lower lip (Proskouriakoff 1974). Other beads may represent nose ornaments (Proskouriakoff 1974). Nose beads and labrets are poorly represented in pictorial images (Schele and Miller 1986: 69). But the sites on the

Figure 2.20 Classic Maya pendant showing a standing figure wearing three solid maskettes depicting anthropomorphic faces, as pendants and a fourth as a central belt ornament, recovered from the Cenote at Chichen Itza (Proskouriakoff 1974: Plate 67b/3). © President and Fellows of Harvard College. Used by permission.

head that they mark were clearly significant as interfaces from which emanated the immaterial aspects of the body represented as scrolls: speech, song, and breath (Houston and Taube 2000). In pictorial images, rather than representing the ornaments that are recovered archaeologically, artists often depicted beads hanging in the air in front of these bodily openings (Houston and Taube 2000: 265–267). Body ornaments not clearly represented in images may have been worn as a kind of materialization of the emergent presence of immaterial body essences (Figure 2.22).

Other forms of marking these passages are more obvious. While nasal piercings would not have survived the processes of post-mortem decay, like the cranium, teeth do remain intact. Researchers have recorded an astonishing range of dental modifications in Classic Maya burials (Romero 1970: 50–58; Welsh 1988). Circular jade and iron pyrite inlays were set in the teeth visible at the front of the mouth. Teeth might be notched or filed. Most intriguing, the central incisors could be filed to form a T-shape when viewed from the front. This made the person's mouth a replica of the linguistic sign *ik*, "breath." Paired with inlay of precious stones, this marking would permanently inscribe the precious emanation emerging from the mouth of the living person (Figure 2.23).

Most common, most elaborately depicted, and most varied, however, are ornaments depicted inserted through the earlobes of figures in Classic Maya images (Figure 2.24), and recovered in burials adjacent to the skull where they would have come to rest when the earlobes decayed (Figure 2.25). Classic Maya ear ornaments conform to a pattern with a long history in the region

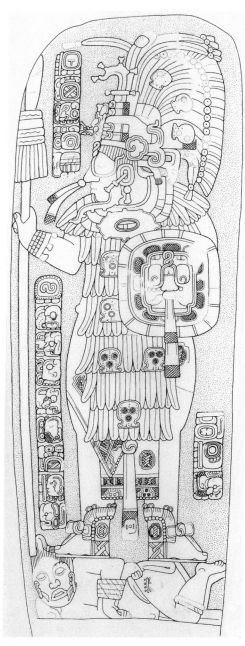

Figure 2.21 Classic Maya warrior showing nose bead and ear ornaments in use. Naranjo stela 21. Courtesy of Corpus of Maya Hieroglyphic Inscriptions, Peabody Museum, Harvard University.

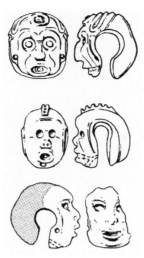

Figure 2.22 Classic Maya nose beads recovered from the Cenote at Chichen Itza
(Proskouriakoff 1974: Plate 47a). © President and Fellows of Harvard
College. Used by permission.

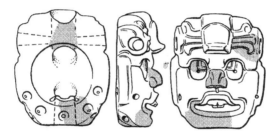

Figure 2.23 Classic Maya bead showing dental modification forming the *ik* sign,
recovered from the Cenote at Chichen Itza (Proskouriakoff 1974: Plate
59c/2). © President and Fellows of Harvard College. Used by
permission.

Figure 2.24 Detail showing Classic Maya ear ornament in use, with counterweight
beads below earlobe supporting projecting bead. Yaxchilan lintel 32.
Courtesy of Corpus of Maya Hieroglyphic Inscriptions, Peabody
Museum, Harvard University.

Figure 2.25 Pair of shell incised disks recovered from a Classic Maya burial at Holmul, depicting front flange of ear spools like those to which they originally were attached. Photograph N31839 by Hillel Burger. Museum object cat. nos: 11-6-20/C5619; and C5620. Courtesy of Peabody Museum, Harvard University, © President and Fellows of Harvard College.

(Joyce 2000c, 2001b; for the Maya, see Proskouriakoff 1974; Rands 1965: 563–565; and Woodbury 1965: 175–176). The simplest forms, represented in archaeological sites but rarely shown in monumental art, are so-called "napkin ring" ear spools, examples of which are found in fired clay and, more rarely, fine stone such as jade or obsidian (Figure 2.26). These simple tapered cylinders, with an average diameter of between 1.8 cm and 2.2 cm, would have been inserted through a hole in the earlobe achieved by initially piercing the ear for a narrow-diameter object and gradually widening the aperture with larger and larger spacers. Consequently, use of ear spools signifies a prior history of body modification, which in Mesoamerica began in childhood (Joyce 2000a). Describing these as part of "costume" misrepresents the degree to which their use was an extension of bodily materiality in media more durable than flesh. Like the mosaic masks directly applied to the skin, ear spools are better thought of as a cultural materialization of a preferred form of embodiment. In their most developed forms, Classic Maya ear spools substitute for the flesh of the living ear a culturally elaborated marker of the bodily site for reception of speech and song. The ornamentation of these most elaborate ear spools makes them resemble flowers, a visual metaphor for rhetorically elaborated sound (Houston and Taube 2000: 265, citing David Stuart).

To achieve this total substitution of durable constructed objects for perishable flesh, the Classic Maya employed a set of beads that fastened and provided counterweight to a spool with an asymmetric disk on one end (Figure 2.27). Napkin ring ear spools present only a narrow rim to a viewer standing in front of a person, and while this rim could be nicked, painted, or otherwise modified, the effect would have been extremely subtle. The narrow rim of some clay examples was slightly enlarged, folded out to form a narrow

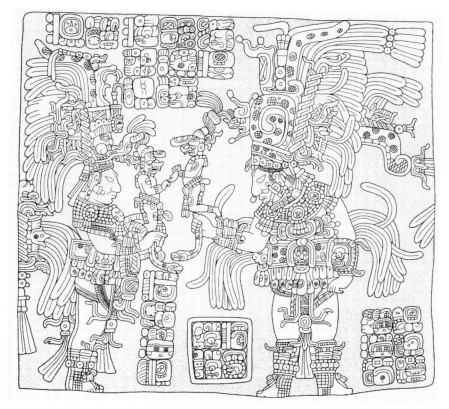

Fgiure 2.26 Classic Maya ear spools showing the contrast between plain ear spool with narrow edge (left) and ear spool with wide flange (right). Yaxchilan lintel 3. Courtesy of Corpus of Maya Hieroglyphic Inscriptions, Peabody Museum, Harvard University.

flange that was fluted, incised, or otherwise ornamented. This form was copied in other materials, including obsidian ear spools from a burial at Altun Ha, Belize. Much wider flanges were commonly created on jade earspools, and these are what most scholars have in mind when they talk about Classic Maya ear ornaments, whether in images or in texts, where earspools (*tup*) are recorded as parts of royal regalia (Macri 1997; Mathews 1979). The shaft of such ear ornaments is no wider than the average napkin ring ear spool. But the flange can extend much wider. The face of the flange was sculpted, and could even be incised with text (e.g. Justeson *et al.* 1988). In images, additional beads are shown suspended below the ear spool, and holes appropriate for attaching them are found on jade ear ornaments. Such beads served as a counterweight for the stone of the enlarged flange. A long central bead commonly protrudes from the neck of the spool, ending with a globular bead. Excavated

41

burials have all of the same elements, forming what is sometimes called an "earspool assemblage."

The effect of the ornamentation of the heads of Classic Maya nobles, as depicted in formal poses and as documented in their final burials, was to present a hybrid of flesh, bone, and culturally modified durable materials. The elaboration of this hybrid head made visible what were otherwise invisible aspects of the embodied person: sight, smell, speech, and hearing. The hybridity of these bodies extended the reach of these persons beyond their individual bodily boundaries, as ear ornaments must have represented not the flowery speech uttered by the person who wore them, but the appropriate and pleasing speech reaching their ears from other speakers.

While the head was, without question, much more intensely elaborated, other body parts isolated through representation also received their own hybrid extensions, prostheses that we can regard as not unlike the organic body parts which they supplement. "The body [is] the original prosthesis we all learn to manipulate, so that extending or replacing the body with other prostheses becomes a continuation of a process that began before we were born" (Hayles 1999: 3). Regalia grasped by figures, although open to removal (as are ear ornaments and the masks worn in life), also served as extensions of the hand, persisting as signs of the self like the prosthetic texts of the authors Hayles (1999: 125–127) explores.

The embodied, moving hand of Classic Maya subjects may have carried durable markers of otherwise invisible action, analogous to the nose and lip ornaments recovered by archaeologists. Items identified as rings have been recorded archaeologically (Merwin and Vaillant 1932: 88). By singling out certain fingers, rings would have referenced the complex gestural language depicted in Classic Maya art. Finger position is a major differentiating feature in Maya writing, where hands representing different verbs are distinguished primarily by the way fingers are depicted (Montgomery 2002: 161–196). Representations of hands commonly lack any indication of finger rings. Instead, the point of connection between hand and arm is usually marked by complex beaded ornaments (Figure 2.28). These underscore the motion of the hand and the relative immobility of the arm.

In images, both male and female figures wear elaborate sandals with high backs and complex ornaments above the instep (Figure 2.29). At least some of the ornamentation on sandals appears to represent feathers, which would have swayed as the person moved. As has been suggested for dance ornaments created by other Native American groups, the movement of the sandal ornaments may make visible the otherwise invisible motion of the feet, serving, like finger rings, labrets, and nose ornaments, to exteriorize aspects of the embodied self that might otherwise have been imperceptible.

Ultimately, the person represented in Classic Maya monumental art is a hybrid with a body composed culturally through the materialization of normally immaterial corporeal aspects, the extension of the fleshly body

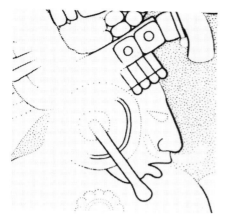

Figure 2.27
Detail showing wide flange of Classic Maya ear spool, with long bead protruding. Yaxchilan lintel 7. Courtesy of Corpus of Maya Hieroglyphic Inscriptions, Peabody Museum, Harvard University.

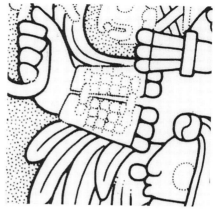

Figure 2.28
Detail of Classic Maya wrist ornament, with closure on inside of wrist shown. Yaxchilan lintel 32. Courtesy of Corpus of Maya Hieroglyphic Inscriptions, Peabody Museum, Harvard University.

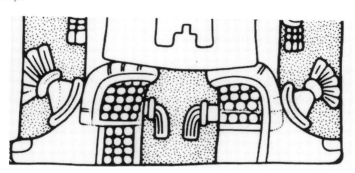

Fgiure 2.29 Detail of Classic Maya sandals with feathered ornaments. Yaxchilan lintel 32. Courtesy of Corpus of Maya Hieroglyphic Inscriptions, Peabody Museum, Harvard University.

through durable prosthetic devices, and the inculcation of the person in particular forms of bodily activity. The subjects of Classic Maya art, whether monuments or the figurines and painted pottery vessels created and consumed in noble households, cannot be taken as "typical" of Maya experience. Instead, they suggest the extreme stylization and aestheticization of embodied existence. But these subjects share with those who were not represented in images and texts a suite of experiences through which the adult, embodied person was produced. Based on archaeological traces, the embodiment of nobles was an exemplary, exaggerated form of practice used throughout society to materialize the Classic Maya *personne*.

3

MATERIALITIES

Materializing the body

As Gillespie (2001) argues, Classic Maya persons, while clearly having self-hood, were never the autonomous and disconnected individuals of contemporary methodological individualism. An account of the materialization of the embodied person, then, must be framed in terms of social interaction. Some of the practices of materializing the body have already been mentioned in passing above, notably the inheritance of ancestral names, calendrical fates, and co-essences (*way*), and the cultural modification of the skull, teeth, and ears. The practices that produced these effects formed part of a suite of performances that distinguished the adult, reproductive female gender position expressed in Classic Maya art (Joyce 2001b). The body was materialized as the product of the labor of adult women transforming matter in the physical environment into enculturated form (Joyce 1999). From this perspective, the embodied person was a relational self, the inalienable product of the labor of adults, exercised on the raw material of the infant (Joyce 2000a).

It is likely, although not certain, that the shaping of the embodied self was understood to begin before birth. Here, the loss to decay of all the paper documents produced by the Classic Maya has an inestimable effect on what we can say. Monuments routinely ignore the processes of reproduction; no monumental images show pregnant figures, birth, or even the suckling of newborns. Some monumental texts do present birth as a metaphoric relation between human nobles and deities (Schele 1979: 46–47; Houston 1996: 135–136). These references hint at a set of beliefs about the role of the living in creating the substance of the pre-born person, even if the subjects are, as in the case of Palenque, deities acting at the beginning of time, or historic rulers re-enacting those creation performances.

In some of these metaphoric texts, blood is cited as the substance linking the mother to her offspring. The provision of blood by the mother could be considered simply a naturalistic observation related to the physiology of reproduction, but this ignores considerable scholarship showing that different human societies interpret connections in substance between parents and offspring in

44

Figure 3.1 Classic Maya temple at Palenque identified as a symbolic sweatbath. Photograph © Russell Sheptak. Used by permission.

different ways (e.g. Héritier-Augé 1989). Although over-emphasized in some early scholarship, the significance of blood in Classic Maya society reflects a specific fluid economy discussed in more detail in Chapter 6. Bone, received from the father, may have been a counterpart to maternal blood, as Héritier-Augé (1989: 173) suggests for the Mesoamerican Otomí (compare Battaglia 1985). Blood, the fleeting substance of the body provided by the mother, and bone, the enduring material that persisted through the patriline, were clearly significant in Classic Maya concepts of personhood (Gillespie 2001: 90–91; Gillespie and Joyce 1997: 199). But just as the physical person was composed of far more than a duality of substances, so the materialization of the embodied person involved far more than the conjunction of female blood and male bone (Gillespie 2002).

One contribution to bodily substance that is less well understood was the steam produced by Classic Maya sweat baths (Figure 3.1). The Classic Maya rulers of Palenque constructed a set of temples recording the births of a trio of gods, with sanctuaries in the form of sweat baths (Houston 1996). Other durably constructed Classic Maya sweat baths may have had connections to similar metaphoric connections with birth in ritual practice. This suggests that for the Classic Maya sweat baths, including more perishable examples that formed part of rural settlements like the uniquely well preserved village at Joya del Ceren, El Salvador (Sweely 1999), were a site of pre-birth medical practices. The steam of sweat baths, depicted in the form of scrolls (Figure 3.2), may have been understood as a source of the invisible yet tangible substances

Figure 3.2   Scrolls as mist or steam on Ulua marble vase. Photograph © Russell N. Sheptak. Used by permission.

whose emission from the body during life was marked in Classic Maya art with breath, speech and stench scrolls. The source of this breath may have been not simply one of the parents, but the localized social group or the collective ancestors whose bodies were interred in the locality and whose spirits were anchored there (Gillespie 2002).

The engagement of the ancestors, conceived of as a collective totality rather than as individualized persons, in the production of the person prior to birth is suggestively hinted at by monumental images recorded on lintels over temple doorways at Yaxchilan (Tate 1992: 88–91; compare Proskouriakoff 1973). In these images, a female gendered individual evokes a floating serpent, sometimes explicitly named in accompanying texts as the co-essence (*way*) of a divinity or ancestor (Figure 3.3). From the open jaws of these serpents, human figures emerge. Some have been identified as ancestors. The occasion of at least one of the events at Yaxchilan is the birth of a young male heir. Because the woman acting was not the mother of the child, we can suggest that she is acting as a ritual medical specialist, or traditional midwife (Joyce 2001b: 125–126). It may be that these scenes reflect the divination of the co-essence of the child, or the provision of a co-essence for the child by ancestral figures.

The woman invoking the spirit may in other instances be intended to represent a mother. On a group of polychrome painted vessels (Figure 3.4), a reclining female wrapped in the folds of a serpent co-essence is depicted with greatly enlarged breasts (Reents-Budet 1994: 328). Although often described as sexualized objects of the desire of the old god emerging from the serpent, women with such enlarged breasts are normally depicted in small-scale Classic Maya art with suckling infants (Joyce 2002). Vessels with this imagery also have a painted text including the sign for "birth" (Macri 2001). This image may compress references to two aspects of the materialization of a Classic Maya person, the provision of the co-essence and the physical nurturing of the infant body, as aspects of birth.

While monumental art excludes images of female figures nurturing infants, this is a common gesture depicted among the three-dimensional modeled

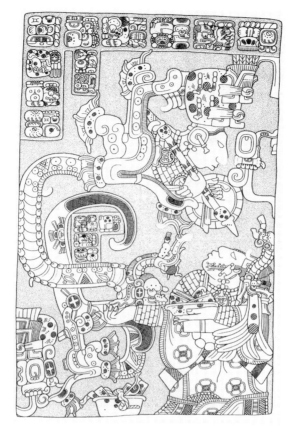

Figure 3.3 Evocation of a Classic Maya ancestral spirit through personified serpent. Yaxchilan lintel 25. Courtesy of Corpus of Maya Hieroglyphic Inscriptions, Peabody Museum, Harvard University.

Figure 3.4 Woman and serpent conducting Old God on Classic Maya polychrome vase. Photograph K5164 © Justin Kerr. Used by permission.

Figure 3.6
(top) Classic Maya figurine of woman grinding corn from Lubaantun, Belize. Courtesy of Norman Hammond. Used by permission. (bottom) Classic Maya figurine of woman holding child and pot of tamales, Altar de Sacrificios, Guatemala (Willey 1972: Fig. 34b). © President and Fellows of Harvard College. Used by permission.

Figure 3.5
Classic Maya figurine showing child suckling at woman's breast. Ulua Valley, Honduras. Photograph © Russell N. Sheptak. Used by permission.

figurines, made and used in noble households, that have been excavated throughout the Maya area (Joyce 1993). Female figurines are shown engaged in a series of activities that, together, embodied Maya children: suckling infants (Figure 3.5), grinding corn and presenting corn tamales (Figure 3.6), providing drink (Figure 3.7), and weaving the cloth that made up the final "social skin" of Classic Maya adults (Figure 3.8; Joyce 2001b). Through such performances, the nascent person was given substance. Provisioning children with food should be seen as more than a utilitarian action. Through sharing food, children and adults literally shared their substance, and became kin (compare Weismantel 1995: 694–695).

Young children's selves were further materialized through an overlapping sequence of actions whose traces are obvious in burials but are not the subjects of any representational media. The shaping of the skull, filing and inlay of teeth, and piercing and enlargement of holes in the earlobes for adult ornaments, are examples. Tattooing, a practice recorded among sixteenth century descendants of the Classic Maya (Thompson 1946, based primarily on Landa 1941: 89, 91, 125–126) and suggested by figurines from much earlier Preclassic societies (Joyce 1998), may have been an additional, unrepresented practice materializing embodied Classic Maya persons through the inscription of the surface of the body (compare Grosz 1994: 138–144). Just as cranial and dental modification and ear piercing substitute a culturally transformed appearance for the given stuff of the flesh, so tattooing would have substituted a cultural surface for

Figure 3.7
Classic Maya figurine of woman holding dog and ceramic vessel. Altar de Sacrificios, Guatemala (Willey 1972: Fig. 34f). © President and Fellows of Harvard College. Used by permission.

Figure 3.8
Classic Maya figurine of woman weaving. Photograph K2833 © Justin Kerr. Used by permission.

the physical skin that bound together the material and immaterial substances whose provisioning is recorded or hinted at. Under the conditions of tropical decay, skin itself disappears, and in images, clothing and ornaments cover much of the skin. What is left is never unambiguously marked as tattooed. Nor is there any clear depiction of painted patterns on bodies, despite the presence in a number of Classic Maya sites of stamps most likely used to decorate bodies. The foregrounding of skin as a subject in some images makes clear that it was conceptualized as a bodily boundary, a site of conjunction of bodily identity, and a medium for transformation from one state to another.

That the nature of skin mattered as part of the materiality of embodied persons is suggested by depictions of serpentine co-essences with patches of peeling skin (Figure 3.9). Many deities are identified by specific patterns on their skin (Taube 1992). Images interpreted as flayed skin masks, whether human or divine (Schele and Miller 1986: 50), testify to processing of skin as a separable part of the body (Joyce 1998). The malleability of skin is perhaps best illustrated by the loose boundary between images of male figures wearing animal skins and animal–human hybrids (see Chapter 5). As with the ornamentation of teeth, nose, and lips, it is possible that the lack of representation accorded to any marking of the skin is a consequence of the use of skin-marking practices to physically instantiate an otherwise immaterial aspect of the body. The immaterial aspect of the body most likely to be subject to such signaling on the skin may have been the animal co-essence itself.

Other immaterial aspects of the self may have been materialized through rituals of the life cycle. Names, recycled from previous generations, appear to

49

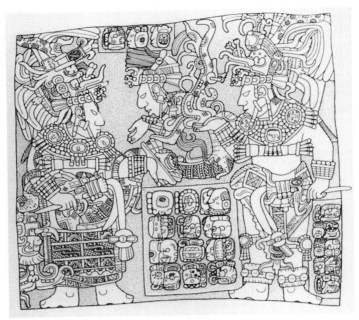

Figure 3.9 Skin of serpentine Classic Maya *way*. The body of the serpentine *way* winding behind the arms of the standing figures shows patches of skin marked with cross-hatched triangles, and areas without skin where parallel ribs inside the serpent are visible. Yaxchilan lintel 14. Courtesy of Corpus of Maya Hieroglyphic Inscriptions, Peabody Museum, Harvard University.

have been adopted at marked points in the life of the young men who later became rulers of Classic Maya sites (e.g. Tate 1992: 107, 138, 224, 275). The fate associated with the birth date, embodied in the calendrical birth name, may have been confirmed and, if necessary, adjusted (as it was among the much later Aztec) at rituals after birth (Monaghan 1998). Other rituals of transition, recorded for a few young men who later become rulers, are apparently associated with the adoption of specific regalia (Joyce 2001a: 120–132; 2001b: 121–122), extensions of the body that facilitated actions previously impossible for these persons (Figure 3.10). While we can document the adoption of ruling names on the part of some individuals first mentioned as children with other names, we do not at present know when and how such renaming took place. But it is clear that the names used in adulthood were a material part of the adult person, in the case of rulers, creating a form of consubstantiality with deceased predecessors, now ancestors (Gillespie 2002: 68, 71–72).

The labor of adults during childhood channeled the experience of the young person so that once they achieved adulthood, their experiences of the

Figure 3.10 Possible Classic Maya life cycle ceremony for young man. Palenque Temple of the Sun. Rubbings by Merle Greene Robertson. © Pre-Columbian Art Research Institute, 1995. Used with permission.

world reiterated those of their predecessors and ancestors (Joyce 2001b). The very buildings in which young persons grew to adulthood assisted in the materialization of a very specific set of ways of acting, moving, and being in the world (Joyce and Hendon 2000). Participation in the bodily experience of ancestors was an effect produced in the bodies of young people by their experience of the same architectural settings used by their predecessors (Gillespie 2002: 70; Hendon 2000).

Houses, raised on platforms, instilled in the developing person an experience of spatialized hierarchy that was echoed and reiterated in the visual relations of Maya art, where placement on upper registers marked focal persons (Figure 3.11). The asymmetric visual relations of people in house compounds formed by multiple raised buildings enclosing a courtyard enacted the kind of asymmetric visual or "perceptual field" that Houston and Stuart (1998) describe as part of Classic Maya personhood (compare Inomata 2001a). The provision of raised benches within the raised houses allowed ever finer experience of spatial hierarchy, as those seated on such benches commanded the actions of others who stood, squatted, or knelt on the floor, terrace, or patio

Figure 3.11 Classic Maya polychrome vase, showing height and frontal body as registers of rank. Duke University Museum of Art Museum no: 1980.116. Photograph K5353 © Justin Kerr. Used by permission.

Figure 3.12 Classic Maya noble residential compound at Copan. Multiple levels created through use of elevated stone benches, terraces, and stairways. Photograph © Russell N. Sheptak. Used by permission.

surface (Figure 3.12). The placement of many benches at right angles to the doorway ensured that those entering an occupied building would present a profile to the person seated on the bench, preserving another aspect of embodied visual hierarchy apparent in Classic Maya art, where central figures are shown with bodies frontal while subordinates are seen in profile (see Figure 3.11).

Connecting the courtyard-centered house compounds of Classic Maya cities were more or less formal raised paved roads. These provided a final architectural materialization of spatial hierarchy, as they formed radial patterns leading from scattered house compounds into a single, central, space—the palace of the ruling family (see Inomata and Houston 2001). Among these spaces, children of Classic Maya houses learned without words the way that relative status was marked by bodily deference. By the time a Classic Maya adult entered into formal life, they were thoroughly conditioned by the practices through which their bodies were materialized, transformed, and disciplined, and through which their person was given a soul, a destiny, and names.

Figuring Egypt

Bodily perfection is one of the most common visual and verbal tropes of Egyptian high culture. There is a clear gendered specificity in this bodily rendering and the conceptualization of aesthetics and beauty it implies. As Schafer pointed out (1986: 16) there was a vast transition from the corpulent images of women in Predynastic art to the classically slender images of women from the Old Kingdom onwards. This youthful ideal persisted over 2000 years with little variation. Woman assumed the image of a goddess, but any similarity of experience was irrelevant, and they did not enjoy comparable reverence or social treatment (Meskell 1999a). The vision for the feminine form was inherently sexualized and directed by the male gaze, whether in textual or artistic canons. In the Middle Kingdom Papyrus Westcar, pharaoh asks to go boating *with twenty women with the shapeliest bodies, breasts and braids, who have not yet given birth. Also let there be brought to me twenty nets and give these nets to these women in place of their clothes* (Lichtheim 1976: 216). As transparent as a fishnet dress itself, pharaoh's fantasy is male fantasy: women had to be youthful, shapely and free from the ravages and realities of childbirth. No specific stipulations were placed on the ideal nature of the male body. Since men were responsible for the constitution of such texts and iconographies, this should hardly be surprising.

In the strict artistic canon, the female body was distinguished by greater slenderness of shoulders, waist, arms, and hands, more rounded contours, a long slim neck, and a small head with finer facial features (Figure 3.13). If a man and a woman of the same height were depicted, the woman usually had smaller vertebrae and thus a shorter spinal column. This ensured that women were depicted with a higher small of the back, and longer legs in relation to her body height (Robins 1997: 251). In many iconographic instances the male is portrayed much larger than his female counterpart, to the point where reality is stretched, but the commentary on social relations is correspondingly more apparent (Meskell 1998b; Robins 1994). Female perfection was paralleled by male idealization, another form of fantasy in itself. Male limbs were shown well muscled, and biceps were indicated by a prominent bulge in the upper arm. Musculature of the lower leg was somewhat more schematic.

Male and female bodies were positioned in the strict guidelines of the artists' grid, a widely employed device in pharaonic times. There was an overt tension from an artistic viewpoint between giving the impression of covering the female body in some form of clothing, whilst still revealing the contours

Figure 3.13 Fowling in the Marshes, wall painting from the tomb of Nebamun, Western Thebes. Eighteenth Dynasty tomb now lost. Courtesy of the British Museum, EA 37977.

and undulations of the female form, the thighs, bottom, pubic area, breasts and so on. The front line of the rear thigh forms one side of the pubic triangle, giving definition to the female form. Female clothing and thus the female body were generally rendered restrictive, in direct contradistinction to the striding male figures, whose pleated and overly complex clothing allowed them movement, both literal and symbolic.

As in many cultures, the ancient Egyptians regarded cloth and garments as an important element in a person's life and a signifier of wealth and status. Cloth could operate as a form of currency: function as security for a loan, be sold, given away as a gift, or handed on from generation to generation (Vogelsang-Eastwood 1993: 2). Quality of cloth and decoration were the great social demarcators between individuals dependent on gender, status, age and ethnicity. Color was probably the key constituent. Elite individuals could use purchased dyed cloth, the extreme case being the garments found in the tomb of Tutankhamun (Vogelsang-Eastwood 1999). Others made do with colored threads interwoven into the linen fabric. Cloth and clothing feature prominently in tomb depictions. We find real examples included in tomb assemblages. Cloth and clothing figured heavily in economic transactions, and were resplendently fetishized in love poetry.

Clothing and dress were culturally loaded, especially for their sensual, erotic, and gendered characteristics. In the poetry now known as the Cairo Love Songs, love is metaphorized as the conjoining of a ring to the finger, or garments to the limbs for the female speaker and the fetishization of her clothing for the male protagonist: *I would be strengthened by grasping the clothes that touch her body, for it would be I who washed out the moringa oils that were in her kerchief. Then I would rub my body with her cast-off garments* (Fox 1985: 37). Later in the same poem the lover relinquishes any claims to status or control over her, saying *would that I were her Nubian slavegirl*—but the thing to notice here is that female servants could presumably enter private quarters and help with grooming and dressing. Such activities are often depicted in New Kingdom domestic iconography. For similar reasons the lover wants to be her washerman, a particularly low-status job, so that he might look upon and touch her personal garments, clothing here being fetishized as a site of desire. Love songs, connected with the popular Egyptian sentiment expressed as *to make the heart forget,* are written explicitly from a male perspective and gaze. The female subject is really an object, devoid of agency. Our male lover may envy the woman's servants, yet what he envisions is limited to his own erotic rewards: viewing her naked body, having intimate physical contact, and fetishizing her clothing (Meskell 2002: 130).

The highly sensual nature of the female clothing most often depicted, for example in New Kingdom tomb iconography, is not so easily matched in the quotidian world uncovered by archaeologists. Wrap-around garments, such as kilts, skirts, cloaks, shawls, and some dresses, consisted simply of a length of cloth. It may be possible to archaeologically identify larger linens used in female clothing as opposed to shorter male garments such as kilts, but much of the preserved clothing appears rather ambiguous. A second category was cut-to-shape garments like loincloths, bag-tunics and dresses. The basic shape was a triangle or rectangle, sewn at some of the edges and fastened with cords. These items do not show signs of being tailored to fit and there are no darts to indicate shaping (Vogelsang-Eastwood 1993: 6). This has obvious implications for the gendered iconography where women are often shown in revealing and tight-fitting dresses. The purpose in the iconography is to highlight the body. This is privileged over the accurate depiction of the garments (see Chapter 6). Such images are reflections of a desired, strictly canonical, world constructed by the male artisan (Meskell 2002: 162).

Like clothing, the sphere of personal adornment was heavily fetishized in New Kingdom Egypt. Bodily accoutrements of many kinds were accorded an extraordinarily high level of symbolic significance in social, ritual, economic and erotic domains. I have previously referred to much of this corporeal enculturation as embodied knowledge (Meskell 2002). It was not merely decoration but rather a personification or an extension of the bodily self. Much of the information we have about this sensual sphere comes directly from the material culture, but there are also representational materials. In Egyptian art we can apprehend reflections of sensory experience, and suggest that the olfactory and the visual were interconnected spheres. The iconic examples are hair scented with oil, women bedecked with flowers, the burning of exotic resins, and applied unguents. Egypt imported quantities of fragrant materials from abroad, from Punt, Arabia, and the Mediterranean. Unguents were particularly high-status and expensive commodities in which both men and women indulged. Many examples of expensive alabaster jars filled with ointment have been found in tombs, like those at Deir el Medina, and their expensive prices recorded in various economic transcripts. Unguent was applied to cult statues but was probably even more desirable for the living body. Spoons for dispensing the unguent were often designed in the shape of a swimming girl or semi-nude serving girl, with obvious sexual associations. The sexualized images of young women were further enhanced by the addition of other erotic signifiers such as ducks, lotus flowers, floral settings, and musical instruments.

Unguent was also depicted in tomb iconography in the form of cones worn on the heads of young women (Figure 3.14). There has been considerable discussion over whether wearing a tall lump of greasy perfume, melting over the top of one's wig was practicable or desirable. Depictions of unguent cones are unlikely to relate to real objects worn as they are illustrated. It is more likely that they represent the concept of aroma and all that it entailed symbolically. Culturally, certain smells had explicit erotic overtones especially when coupled with other signifiers such as hair, skin, make-up, breath and so on. Aroma was linked to drunkenness, festivities and sensual life. Gods such as Amun supposedly gave off a divine fragrance, evidenced in the tale of Hatshepsut's divine conception. In love poetry, the male lover is described as *my lovely myrrh-anointed one*, and the beloved describes herself as having a *bosom full of persea, my hair laden with balm* (Fox 1985: 15, 17). The use of perfume with all its ritual and erotic connotations ensured a good life. In its representation with the deceased, it indicated those who were blessed, justified and primed for resurrection.

In the richly scented world of ancient Egypt, perfume was used for personal attractiveness, adorning bodies and hair alike, in food and drink, for general intoxication, during festivals and funerals. It accompanied the deceased into the next world. Just as perfume was multivalent and value-coded, so too was hair an important visual cue inflected with meanings of status, gender and age, that also reinforced an elite vision of order. New Kingdom men and women made extensive use of wigs and hairpieces during life and in the mortuary realm. Women could supplement their natural hair or wear wigs over the top of it, whereas men tended to keep their hair short or their heads shaven. Elaborate hair made a woman sexually attractive, and was another signifier alongside the imagery of flowers, birds, monkeys, hip girdles and the like. It is also an alluring weapon attested in love poetry (Fox 1985: 73): *with her hair she*

Figure 3.14 Two women with unguent cones, tomb of Userhet, TT 51, Western Thebes. Courtesy of the Media Center for Art History, Archaeology, and Historic Preservation, Columbia University.

lassos me, with her eye she pulls me in, with her thighs she binds. According to iconography, specific hairstyles were worn for occasions such as childbirth and nursing, and different ones for festivals and feasts. The dressing and scenting of hair with perfumes and oils, the preparation of elaborate styles such as braiding, the iconography of grooming with female attendants, as well as the actual implements themselves, all suggest a kind of ritualized behavior that went beyond mere care of the self.

Treatments for skin included oil of various types, gum, powders, resins, honey, and milk. Kohl was also very important for men, women and children, having both symbolic and practical qualities. The bottles and containers that held such precious materials were owned by men and women alike and were molded and decorated in the most elaborate styles. Ornamental slate palettes for the grinding and preparation of eyepaint have been found from Predynastic times onwards, suggesting an inherent importance within Egyptian culture over the long term. The wearing and application of make-up was an erotically charged activity, as demonstrated in the Turin Papyrus (see Chapter 6), where a girl uses a stibium applicator and mirror. There are no immediate examples where men are depicted applying make-up in the same manner, yet this too could be simply an artefact of the artisans being male. Tattoos were another erotic signifier, apparently restricted to women, if one can take the iconography at face value. Importantly, goddesses and elite women were not depicted with tattoos (Meskell 1998b) in contrast to semi-nude singers, musicians, dancers and women of similar status shown in wall paintings, figurines and items of material culture. These tattoos may have been permanent or may have been applied like other make-up upon the body.

The accessories and paraphernalia of beauty held an exalted status within Egyptian material culture. Tweezers, razors, mirrors, pins, combs and their respective boxes and bottles were lavishly and symbolically decorated with a variety of materials. The sheer popularity of these items of grooming suggests that bodily maintenance was a time consuming and culturally necessary requirement that transcended any gender boundaries. While it may be the female regimen that attracted the erotic gaze in official iconography, it was also true that men performed many of the same bodily rituals and may have received a concomitant appreciation from both female and male viewers. That we can at least surmise.

Arraying bodies

The arrayed bodies of pharaonic Egypt have become synonymous in our own culture as icons of excess and eroticism, mutually constitutive elements of a civilized worldview we have construed from a familiar, contemporary perspective: "That sparkling finery and that make-up, those jewels and those perfumes, those faces and those bodies dripping with wealth, becoming the *objects*, the focal points of luxury and lust, though they present themselves as goods and as values, dissipate a part of human labor in a *useless* splendor"

(Bataille 1993: 141). While jewelry certainly possessed a sensual and erotic component, it was also replete with magical, ritual and personal inflections that cannot easily be separated into our own familiar taxonomies. Jewelry was worn all over the Egyptian body, with the notable exception of nose rings. Its wearing spanned the social classes from the very poor, as witnessed at sites like Memphis and Deir el Medina, to the elaborate embellishments worn by royalty. Jewelry, particularly necklaces and bangles, was often distributed as payment or honorific awards, and many of these episodes are shown in royal reliefs at sites such as Amarna. They were supra-economic payments as well as objects that signified rank and status.

Egyptian bodies could literally be covered from head to toe: diadems and circlets, hair amulets and jewelry such as gold bands. In the burial of the wives of Tuthmosis III we see striking examples of gold head-pieces, one of which consists of a cascade of gold cloisonné rosettes suspended by rings from an oval head covering (Andrews 1990: 109). These fantastic creations must have been difficult to wear and must have restricted movement, which may have been an important attribute of their use, not unlike the attire worn on royal occasions today. In the eighteenth Dynasty Theban tomb of Menna, his daughters are shown in impossible head-pieces consisting of many parts and levels with gazelle head protomes. These constructions may have been more symbolic than real, and extant matches in the archaeological record are absent.

Undoubtedly the most fantastic bodily adornment comes from the tomb of Tutankhamun (Figure 3.15): over 200 surviving pieces fashioned from a variety of techniques including cloisonné and inlay, granulation, repoussé and chasing, employing gold leaf and gold wire and solder, fashioned from numerous materials including gold, electrum, silver, bronze, iron, and stones such as amethyst, calcite, feldspar, lapis lazuli, serpentine, steatite, turquoise, resin, shell, faience, and glass (Reeves 1990: 152). It is supposed that tomb robbers stole many pieces of personal jewelry before they were catalogued. This speculation is supported by the discovery of a discarded piece of linen containing a number of rings. It has been estimated that some 60 percent of the jewels kept in numerous royal boxes were stolen. The jewelry ranges from the most elaborate gold working, as seen on the pectorals, to the plainest stone hoop earrings. Given the king's young age, one can only surmise the jeweled adornment that must have accompanied pharaohs such as Ramesses II to the grave.

Tutankhamun was buried with more than two dozen pectorals, collars and necklaces, placed on the body yet deep within the king's bandages (Figure 3.16). Several of the large collars were decorated with the motif of a falcon or vulture, so that the protective wings spread over the chest, in life and in death. One collar with a winged cobra goddess was crafted from sheet gold less than 1 mm thick; others reveal delicate inlaid faience. Necklaces showing evidence of wear suggest that they were indeed created for this life, not simply objects

Figure 3.15 Gold jewelry, bodily adornments and dagger uncovered on Tutakhamun's body in 1925. Below the gold death mask is a sheet-gold falcon, a resin heart scarab, a decorative apron, dagger with an iron blade and a gold serpent. Courtesy of the Griffith Institute, Ashmolean Museum, Oxford, EIB 14 1567.

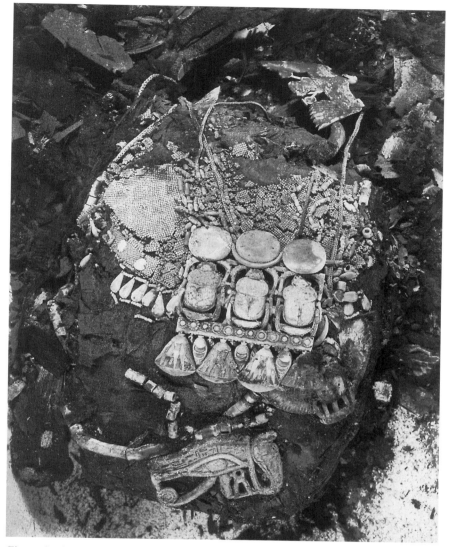

Figure 3.16 Pectorals and assorted jewelry uncovered in the wrappings on Tutakhamun's body. Courtesy of the Griffith Institute, Ashmolean Museum, Oxford, EIB 1 800.

that were crafted for the journey into the afterlife. Ornamental collars were popular both in life and in death for people of various social classes, and many examples survive in a range of materials. Simple examples could be made from semi-precious stones, faience beads or flowers, the latter having symbolic resonances of rebirth, sexuality, festivity and communing with the gods

(Meskell 2002: 152). Tutankhamun's pectorals were designed with large scarabs on solar barks. Others show the king himself with the deities Ptah and Sekhmet in a royal scene, or with Isis and Nepthys beside a djed pillar, symbolizing stability, surmounted either side by Tutankhamun's cartouches. Here the king is wearing the visual likeness of himself, replete with the power bestowed by visualizing his name. Many jeweled pieces like these pectorals spelt out the name of the king in various ways, imbuing each piece and the body of the pharaoh himself with divine power. It was said in Egypt that you *are* your name, so this doubling of the self was a form of corporeal reiteration. Tutankhamun wore, even performed, his name, over and over again in material form, as aesthetic adornment, as a signifier of wealth and status, and as ritual protection.

Jewelry could be said to personify the individual and enculturate the body: it literally completed the natural body. The burial of Tutankhamun is obviously an extreme example of that finishing process, but yet an instructive one. Along with his many pectorals and necklaces, Tutankhamun was buried with thirteen different bracelets. Some show no signs of religious imagery and appear to be purely decorative pieces. Iconographic renditions suggest that people could wear many pieces of jewelry together. How this would have affected the king's ease of movement can only be surmised. Perhaps the difficulty of moving with such extreme adornment was a significant aspect of royal performance.

In Tutankhamun's burials, there were bracelets with lapis scarab clasps, set in gold; another example with a large protective *wedjat* eye in carnelian; and another with an amethyst scarab set in gold and inlaid with hard stone. These show signs of wear and were found on the king's arms. Perhaps the most popular amuletic image was that of the *wedjat*, the eye of Horus after it had been extracted during a battle for divine supremacy. The right eye of Horus symbolized the sun, while the left was the moon, and the one generally considered to be removed. Both left and right eyes could be represented in amulets and they were often found on the dead body as well. The eye supposedly was sent by Horus to revive his dead father, Osiris, and thus became a powerful charm for warding off evil.

Tutankhamun was also buried with a series of bangles made from solid metal, although some may have served as anklets. One example made of ribbed ivory had inlaid metal plaques showing the king, depicted as a lion, killing an enemy. Here again the king's image served to decorate his own body, this time in the metaphorical guise of a lion, a potent symbol of kingship. Jeweled designs could easily spell out the name of the individual, since hieroglyphic characters were made of symbols such as the scarab and sun disc, in the case of Tutankhamun. He had a bracelet and pectoral ornament that spelt out his royal prenomen, Nebkheprure (see Figure 3.16), in a clever form of visual punning. Royal bracelets often show incised royal names and short texts on the inside of the piece. These may not have been meant to be seen but their ritual power would still be resonant to the wearer, with their constant reiteration of the name's potency.

Where the corporeal impact of such lavish jewelry and the constraints of the human body meet, is undeniably at the ears. Earrings became popular in the eighteenth Dynasty for men, women and children of both sexes, although it is traditionally women who are depicted wearing earrings. In some scenes boys wear earrings and circlets that are otherwise only worn by adult women. One theory is that the male earrings were discarded at puberty. But some adult men are depicted wearing thick hoops, such as Sennefer in TT92, and a prominent royal architect called Kha was buried at Deir el Medina wearing large gold earrings. After Tutankhamun's examination no mention was made as to whether the king's ears were pierced or not, but he certainly owned many pairs of earrings, mostly very large and ornate pieces. Some examples had bars that screwed through the lobe and must have entailed the maintenance of large piercings, as are implied by Classic Maya ear ornaments. These examples usually have floral, animal or god motifs and were constructed of many elaborate parts. They seem to be quite narrative and complex in their design. Others were large ornaments shaped like bobbins that must have stretched and deformed the earlobe through time. One pair was exquisitely crafted from gold and had three cascading levels of uraei, the last line being suspended by chains. This produced an incredible effect and must have framed the face in powerful symbols of gold.

Body modification is not something frequently or explicitly discussed by Egyptologists. However there is no denying that wearing the various styles of earrings that have survived entailed significant bodily alteration and enculturation (Figure 3.17). The huge plug earrings held in the collections of the British Museum must have entailed large holes in the ears, as would the large mushroom-shaped ear studs and circular reels. Each type was a very large, thick earring that would have entailed continuous stretching to make the large permanent holes. And although there are questions about gendered representations, one can see huge earrings protruding from heavy wigs on decorated coffin lids. At the urban site of Memphis, amongst the smaller dwellings, earrings were very common at various levels of the excavation, but were most popular in the mid to late eighteenth Dynasty and Ramesside Period. They were made from stone, faience, and copper alloy. Their ubiquity suggests they were very much part of New Kingdom bodily styles. It is unlikely that only women wore such items of adornment, even if this does present a challenge to the iconographic repertoire. At Memphis there was an enormous range of bodily adornment that was both ornamental and amuletic in nature. Scarabs, plaques, pendants, earrings and ear studs, bracelets, finger-rings and beads have been recovered from a small excavation area. Faience was the most popular material, because it was easy to produce inexpensively. White and red faience was regularly used for ear ornaments, while only variants of blue and green were used for pendants, bracelets and rings (Giddy 1999: 53). Such

Figure 3.17 Gold, silver, carnelian and glass jewelry from an undisturbed tomb Abydos, dated to the reign of Tuthmosis III, late eighteenth Dynasty. Courtesy of Liverpool Museum, N1993.0301.

colors were designed to mimic precious metals and stones, whether gold or turquoise. More specifically, pendants using the motifs of lotus, poppy or mandrake would have invoked the pleasurable associations of intoxication, festivity and sexuality.

Also excavated at Memphis were a large number of finger rings made predominantly from faience, and over a thousand beads. These were the poor imitations of expensive, elite jewelry worn by royals and courtiers. At the other extreme, Tutankhamun was buried wearing a series of large, double cartouche rings that bore his name in both gold and lapis lazuli. There were so many rings that they could not all be placed on the king's fingers and were simply placed nearby his hands. One intricate triple ring had a scarab complete with small gold figures emerging from it, deities on either end, and flowers on the shank. Underneath was inscribed with one of the king's names, marking it as a personal possession. Some rings had complicated bezels that turned. Thousands of rings from sites all over Egypt, such as Memphis, feature the names and titles of the reigning pharaoh, some in the shape of a cartouche, others in the shape of the scarab. This form of amuletic jewelry was circulated as heirlooms long after the end of a reign of a specific individual, complicating them as dating devices yet amplifying and enhancing their cultural potency. Jewelry, royal and otherwise, was also often re-used. In the tomb of Tutankhamun several pieces naming other individuals, such as Akhenaten, were recovered from the floor of the annexe. It was customary to include in the tomb something belonging to a relative, as a memento, whether you were a young pharaoh or ordinary individual like those from the community at Deir el Medina.

Extra-somatic selves

Some Egyptian jewelry types seem to be more gender-specific and may even pertain more precisely to age categories. Female sexuality is best perceived along an aged spectrum that included adolescent females, without the sharp demarcations in maturity or *rites of passage* than have been traditionally postulated (Meskell 2000a, 2000b). These experiences may have been reflected in the symmetry of bodily adornment: young girls are shown with the signifiers of female adulthood—earrings, circlets, and girdles.

Girdles are an interesting case in point in regard to gender. They are generally considered female objects in the New Kingdom but were, much earlier, defined as male adornments. While adult women of all classes were buried with girdles, they were not depicted wearing them in wall paintings. High status women wore chains of gold and precious stones around their hips. Some had detailed worked animal motifs such as leopard heads or fish, each suggestive of a specific female sexuality. Various examples had metal pellets inside these figurative elements that rattled which was also suggestive of female sexuality—this noise linked them with Hathor, goddess of sexuality. A class of singers, musicians and dancers who occupy a rather dubious social standing were shown often in nothing but a girdle. These do not look jeweled and were probably made from glass beads, strings of faience or shells that might also rattle. The cowrie shell was a popular amuletic adornment, emulating female genitalia and worn around the hips, particularly during pregnancy. All of these examples probably made a rattling noise that added to the sensory effect and warded off danger from spirits and demons. Significantly, Tutankhamun was also buried with a type of gold belt with a buckle bearing the king's name. So even though these items appear gendered female for the most part, we have to acknowledge that iconography and reality did not mesh uncomplicatedly.

Irrespective of age or sex, people wore amuletic jewelry, usually within close proximity to the specific bodily locale concerned. Magic was literally performed on the body. It might be possible to think of such amulets and body part doubles as extensions of the self, as part of the individual's personal magic known as *heka*. The repertoire of magical symbols and the means of attaching them to the body was extensive. Cylinders made from gold and precious stone, containing magical texts, were strung around the neck. Other ornate pieces, such as gold necklaces with apotropaic images of crocodiles, flies (thought to sting the enemy) and deities like Taweret, were worn around the neck. Fish-shaped amulets were tied to the hair to protect the wearer from drowning. Body parts, such as the eye, face, ear, tongue, hand, phallus, leg and so on, were also transmuted into amulets that were placed on the mummy to ensure bodily integrity, mimicking the living organs and their functions. Amulets could be applied to any part or orifice of the body. These sites of amuletic intensity were dangerous, liminal zones.

Douglas famously argued (1966) that the body is a model that can stand for any bounded system and its boundaries can represent any boundaries that are threatened or precarious. In many cultures bodily margins and orifices are specifically invested with power and danger due to their libidinal nature. These "libidinal zones are continually in the process of being produced, renewed, transformed, through experimentation, practices, innovations" (Grosz 1995: 199). Magical protection through the materialization of amuletic jewelry was just such an innovation. Perhaps the libidinal nature of Egyptian magic has been downplayed by traditional scholarship, although it appears to have operated at both subtle and explicit levels. Fluids and orifices feature strongly in Egyptian fears of bodily integrity (see Chapter 6). Psycho-analytic theory posits that sexuality introduces death into the world—both are inextricably linked, as are lust and horror. The rich presence of body ornaments that play on and enhance sexuality in Egyptian burials certainly suggest that here, sex and death were in a heightened relationship.

4

ANTI-CARTESIANISM

Anti-Cartesianism

Post-Enlightenment culture has its own very specific cultural formulation of the body. Its discursive embedding within the Western imaginary leaves little room for alternative visions. Numerous scholars, including Foucault, Lacan and Baudrillard, have dissected the Enlightenment notion of universal reason as an ethnocentric construct that serves to instantiate social relations of power while simultaneously undermining other modes of thinking or feeling. It occludes the plurality and heterogeneity of lived experience and cultural difference (Elliott 2001). Feminists and other scholars have also sought to challenge Cartesian thought (Gatens 1996; Grosz 1994; Hekman 1990; Lloyd 1993; Turner 1996), the dualistic frameworks for conceptualizing mind and body, reason and emotion, nature and culture. The richness of the Egyptian material similarly challenges these foundational claims and constitutes the basis for a pre-Cartesian model of the self which saw the multiplicity encompassed by the whole, rather than the dualistic and hierarchical binary construct, of mind/body. In New Kingdom Egypt, there was no division of body and soul, but rather a combination of physical and non-physical elements. Together they were called *kheperu*, or manifestations, and may be described as aspects or modes of human existence (Taylor 2001:16). The Egyptians also chose not to bifurcate the qualities of reason and emotional knowledge, since they considered both to reside within the domain of the heart. The heart was a fundamental storehouse that was left in the body during the processes of mummification so as to speak and represent the individual (individual identity, personality and biography) through the ordeals of judgment and the passage to the afterlife. In this inversion of the Western hierarchy, with heart valued over mind (which did not exist as a separate concept in a contemporary sense) we have a culturally specific example where the binary taxonomies of Western reason/ emotion and mind/body are challenged. More recent anthropological studies suggest that what "we" construe as "knowledge" might be linked with emotional and embodied cultural knowledges as well (Lock 1993; Lyon and Barbalet 1994; Strathern 1996).

As outlined in Egyptian sources, the heart was important to the individual during life and should be safeguarded and followed throughout life's course. The Instruction of Ani warns the individual—*do not vex your heart, he will return to praise you, when his hour of rage has passed. If your words please the heart, the heart tends to accept them* (Lichtheim 1976: 143). The heart was both a mimetic version of the self and an entity that retained its own agency, which could act on its own accord and even desert the individual in times of crisis such as emotional distress. It was a self-surveilling organ that kept the other senses in line: *Sight, hearing, breathing—they report to the heart, and it makes every understanding come forth. As to the tongue, it repeats what the heart has devised* (Lichtheim 1980: 54). The heart was vital in the sphere of death as previously outlined. Spell 26 of the Book of the Dead guarantees that *I shall have power in my heart, I shall have power in my arms, I shall have power in my legs, I shall have power to do whatever I desire, my ba and my corpse shall not be restrained at the portals of the West when I go in and out in peace* (Faulkner 1985: 53).

The body as the living person covered a multiplicity of aspects which survived bodily death (Meskell 1999a: 111–113). The most salient elements of the physical body were the heart and the non-physical entities *ka* and *ba*. Together with the name, shadow and personal magic, they were the key elements of personhood. None of the elements of the Egyptian self can be exactly interpreted as *soul* (although the latter could equally be read as an ambiguous term in contemporary society). The *ka* has been described as a series of relations and representations, but defies isomorphic translation. It was an animating principle or the life force of an individual that could vary in intensity over time. It was associated with vitality, virility and will-power, and was a phonetic parallel for "bull." The *ka* was the twin or double self that came into being at birth and was perceived as an identical copy of the individual. Depicted as arms upraised in the position of praise or an embrace, it lacked concrete form and required a furnished materiality, such as the *ka* statues frequently discovered in New Kingdom contexts. The *ka* signified reproduction, as demonstrated in the words vagina (*k3t*) and pregnant (*bk3t*), and formed the link between generations. The *ka* required sustenance in the form of food. The word *kaw* referred to food or nourishment, often provided in the tomb. While it required a physical form to inhabit in the sphere of death, the *ka* needed the freedom to access offerings placed by the living in the necropolis and the cemetery, the conjoining place where living and dead communed. The tomb was called *the house of the ka*. In spell 105 of the Book of the Dead the *ka* is entreated by the deceased (Lichtheim 1976: 123): *Hail to you, my ka, my helper! Behold, I have come before you, risen, animated, mighty, healthy! I have brought incense to you, to purify you with it, to purify your sweat with it.*

Several essential components of the individual survived the trials of death and continued into the hereafter: the *ka*, *ba*, the name (*rn*), the shadow (*swt*), and personal magic (*hk3*). The corporeal body had a tangible trajectory after death that was divisible or multi-faceted. Like the k*a*, the *ba* was linked closely to the body, retained much of one's individual identity and character, and depended on the physical body for existence. The *ba* is described differently according to whether it was linked to the gods, royals, or non-royal individuals. It is more than the personality alone, since non-human entities such as a door or even a town could each have its own *ba* (Assmann 1999: 20). Scholars still debate whether translations as self or soul are appropriate. We interpret the *ba* as a freely moving agent, representing the person, linking between the earthly world, heaven and the afterworld (see Figure 2.2). It was usually depicted as a human-headed bird that journeyed between the underworld and this world. The *ba* was known to leave the body in cases of extreme terror such as social isolation. In a well-attested text entitled the Dialogue of a Man and his *Ba*, the living man and his *ba* discuss their respective and opposing views about death. While the man longs for death and all it promises, his *ba* warns that the agony of death should be avoided till the last. The protagonist urges his *ba* to stand by him—a common wish found also in funerary texts—on his journey to the otherworld (Parkinson 1999: 152). In the sphere of death the *ba* had material needs just like the *ka*—bread, beer, and everything else that a body requires (Hornung 1992: 181). It offered another avenue for the individual to persist after death. It was able to eat, speak, drink and move, but always had to make contact with the material body. The capacity for free and unrestricted movement was central: it was the means by which the empowered dead could leave the tomb and travel. Through flight the *ba* bird could visit the living or access the gods in the sky. Deceased individuals, such as Paheri who was mayor of el Kab during the reign of Tuthmosis III (Lichtheim 1976: 17), called upon the *ba* specifically in the context of the tomb: *Your ba shall not forsake your corpse, your ba is divine among the spirits, the worthy bas converse with you, you join them to receive what is given on earth, you thrive on water, you breathe air, you drink as your heart desires.* We might consider that the pluralities of the person in ancient Egypt covered several facets: the materiality of the body, bodily being and spiritual associations, and in death, divine aspects.

The name also held the essence of a person's being and individuality. It was a medium through which one's existence was manifest and served to distinguish one person from the rest. One penalty for a serious crime was to have the name changed, such as from Ramose (*Ra is the one who gave birth to me*) to Ramesedsu (*Ra is the one who hates him*) (Taylor 2001: 23). Remembrance of the name was crucial. Popular funerary texts invoked passers-by to speak the name of the deceased, *making the name live*, as it were. In the interrogation text from the Book of the Dead, all about knowing the correct names of various deities, the deceased is not allowed to pass. It was crucial that the appropriate deities knew the name of the deceased and that their name was unknown throughout the demonic realm, since it could be used to have control over the individual. Remembering your name was key in the netherworld: knowing the names of the gods, having them know your name (as well as your relatives on earth who would commemorate you) and hiding that aspect from evil entities were all important (Zandee 1960: 179). Each image of the deceased was made more vital when it was accompanied by a hiero-glyphic text, the essence of the object being articulated with the name. The name was the special home of power (Forman and Quirke 1996: 33). Name, being, memory, and future were all intertwined.

In the Litany of Ra, the god is manifest in a number of bodies which are similarly his names and manifestations, and they are gods. The litany appeared on the funerary shroud of Tuthmosis III and on the walls of Ramesses VI's tomb in the Valley of the Kings, among other places. The heart and tongue have power over all other parts of the body: the heart thinks all that it wishes, whereas the tongue orders all that it wishes. The name is not a mere appella-tion, but a personality in itself. Thus the erasure of a name on a monument meant obliteration. The names of Ra are all embodied (Piankoff 1964): *Homage to thee Ra, supreme power, who gives orders to the time gods at their time! Thou art the bodies of Geb. Homage to thee Ra, supreme power, the great one of reckonings of what is in him! Thou art the bodies of Nut.*

After passing various obstacles the deceased individual might attain the status of a transfigured or effective spirit. According to the Instruction of Any, one should *satisfy the akh; do what he desires, and abstain for him from abomi-nation, that you may be safe from his harms.* There were other troublesome spirits known as the dangerous dead. These entities retained the lifetime sex of the individual: the dead were not sexed differently from the living. Female spirits seem to have been more feared. Within this schema the various elements of the person continued to exist, and an individual could ultimately adopt specific trajectories through time, benevolent or otherwise. Each of the aspects of the self retained the character of the individual (Assmann 1996: 80). It was because of earthly achievement that a person could aspire to an enduring place in the larger social memory. One could not simply rely on collective distinctions, such as elite descent or group membership—only indi-vidual achievements were of consequence.

Textually, the deceased likened themselves to the godly body, and to specific gods such as Re, particularly on the treacherous journey after death (Zandee 1960: 27–28). This deification of bodily parts also ensured the body's intactness and potency: *my hair is Nun, my face is Ra, my eyes are Hathor, my ears are Wepawet, my nose is She who presides over her lotus leaf, my lips are Anubis.* Such spells also underscore the culturally specific under-standing of the body, as a unity of separately functioning parts associated with specific qualities, functions and even deities.

Breathing and being

Breath and breathing were revered in pharaonic culture as integral to suste-nance, to communing with the gods, and being an active part of earthly life as

Figure 4.1 Limestone stela of Neferabu, showing the Opening of the Mouth ceremony in the left hand corner of the upper register, nineteenth Dynasty, from Deir el Medina. The text at the base is taken from the Book of the Dead. Courtesy of the British Museum, EA 305.

well as its transcendence. Representations of breath take the form of the life sign, or ankh, held at the nose or emanating from divine rays. The invisible became tangible, albeit through symbolic means. Breath equaled life. Since the living body breathed, the perfected, mummified body also had to acquire the function, through ritualistic practices performed by priests, usually referred to as the Opening of the Mouth (Lichtheim 1976: 120) (Figure 4.1):
My mouth is given to me, My mouth is opened by Ptah, with that chisel of metal, with which he opened the mouth of the gods.

Some seventy-five scenes representing the Opening of the Mouth ritual are preserved from the New Kingdom. In the Theban tomb of Sennefer we see a priest clad in a leopard skin performing a ritual libation and purification with the *nemset* jars. The water pours forth from the vessel and encircles both bodies, first Sennefer and then his wife, Meryt. A more detailed depiction appears in Rekhmire's Theban tomb including purification with liquids from *nemset* jars, purification with natron and incense, touching the mouth of the statue with the little finger, then with a sacred adze, polishing by craftsmen and then final delivery. It is striking that this particular ritual could be performed both on the mummy and on a statue of the deceased, signifying their parallelism as receptacles of the embodied self.

The third register of the scene in Rekhmire's Theban tomb displays ritual butchering, presentation of food offerings, the Opening of the Mouth ceremony with the ritual tool, and presentation of the deceased's statue to his son. This conferred power to infuse an image, generation after generation. Once the mouth of an image had been touched, that image could operate as the receptacle of the *ka* and could house the *ba*, thus providing the material entity for eternal life, as did the mummified body (Forman and Quirke 1996: 32). The Egyptian word for sculptor even refers specifically to the cult of the dead, *he who keeps alive* (Schafer 1986: 17). The word used for making sacred images, *ms*, was the same as that used to signify birth. Significantly this ritual almost exactly mirrors Hindu practice, specifically the awakening of the cult statue with an adze (Davis 1997).

The fourth register in Rekhmire's tomb shows his son, the Opening of the Mouth ritual with an instrument, touching the mouth with the little finger, a second slaughter scene, presenting the heart and haunch of meat, and a final Opening of the Mouth with the adze (Hodel-Hoenes 2000: 172). All of these acts and gestures ensure that Rekhmire could breath, that his mouth was symbolically open, after the actual sealing of the body during mummification rites. A fifth register shows the presentation of white garments, ostrich feathers, the *pesesh-kef* knife, then the offering of grapes and aromatics, and a final request for offerings. Both statue and mummy were rigid, impermeable and impenetrable beings, both potent and in need of breath that had to be symbolically constituted.

In the Book of the Dead, magical spells for Opening of the Mouth also sought to animate the limbs (spells 22 and 23), which was not pragmatically possible for the statue or the mummy of the deceased in its rigid form. Spells ensured that the heart was maintained within the body (spells 27 and 42), and that movement was allowed alongside free access for the *ba* and shadow, to and from the body (spell 92) (Milde 1991: 227). The *ba* needed to reunite with the corpse, an indispensable lodging. The shadow was usually illustrated by a dark outlined figure of a man positioned near the tomb edifice, clearly seen in the tomb of Nebenmaat at Deir el Medina (Figure 4.2). It too needed to be in close proximity of the transubstantiated body.

Other amuletic instruments and practices invoked the phenomenon of breathing in the Opening of the Mouth ritual, most potently the first breaths of the newborn infant. Amuletic *pesesh-kef* knives, made from obsidian or hard stone, harked back to the moment of birth when the umbilical cord was severed and the infant's mouth was cleared of mucus so it could breathe (Figure 4.3).

Figure 4.2 Wall painting from the tomb of Nebenmaat, TT 219, Deir el Medina. Photo courtesy of the IFAO, Cairo.

Figure 4.3 A series of *Pesesh-kef* knives in various materials. Courtesy of the British Museum, EA 8161, EA 18095, EA8164, EA 30848.

Just as the practice facilitated the ability for the newborn to exist amongst the living, the ritual enactment guaranteed the use of all the individuals' bodily facilities in the next world. This ritual mimicked birth, and its purpose was to take the newly reborn deceased through the transitions of birth and childhood so that he or she could be nourished by adult food amply provided in the Egyptian mortuary cult (Roth 1993). The ritual implements used created memory-laden links with the placenta, the severing of the umbilical cord, nursing, weaning, and teething.

The *pesesh-kef* knife was accompanied by an amulet known as the *ntrwy* blades, meaning the two gods. It possibly depicts two fingers that were used to clear the mouth at birth. These objects tend to also be found on the left-hand side of the pelvis, near the embalming incision. They also may represent the fingers of the embalmer, reinforcing the desire that the body should be seen as whole and impermeable, with all orifices sealed. Drawing on an Old Kingdom Pyramid Text, the *ntrwy* blades were used to split open the mouth while the *pesesh-kef* knife was used to make the king's jaw strong (i.e. ready to breastfeed), meaning that the umbilical cord had been severed. This birth scenario might also explain the practice of splitting the pharaoh's jaw in death (Roth 1993).

In other spells, two jars were presented: one empty and the other full of milk, explicitly called the breasts of Horus and Isis. Later in the ritual, weaning and teething are suggested by offering various soft and hard foods. The latter cut the teeth, and wine was offered to dull the pain. Though these associations originally derive from Old Kingdom texts, they continued into the New Kingdom ritual repertoire as evidenced in the Theban tombs of Amenemhet and Tutankhamun. Coming full circle, in the sphere of death one could look back to the moments of birth, the initial separation from the body of one's mother and the first imbibing of sustenance, milk emanating from the mother's body. These practices underscore the inherently corporeal nature of both practice and experience in the Egyptian context.

Before Descartes: breath/blood/bone

Ancient Maya texts make repeated use of couplets—poetic structures in which two terms are linked (Edmonson 1979: 12). These verbal tropes have provided analysts with material from which to construct an image of the ancient Maya as pre-Cartesian dualists. Closer examination of some of the key terms that might appear to support bodily dualism fragments this image, as triplets and even more complex cyclic structures link series of terms (Hanks 1989b: 15, 1989a). Breath, blood, and bone, are one such series of terms related to embodiment. Following through not simply their structural and symbolic, but experiential, relations, we can begin to explore an ontology based in continuity of embodied experience. The relational subject whose experiential materiality is foregrounded by these terms is one framed without sharp boundaries between nature and culture, human, animal, and vegetal, or present, past, and future persons.

Breath, blood, and bone were key bodily substances that extended personhood beyond the bounds of individual embodied subjects. Women repaired to sweat baths during pregnancy not only for their physical health, but as a means to continue the formation of their infants; sixteenth century accounts describe the sweatbath as "fortifying" the "droplet" forming the infant's body (Joyce 2001a: 156; Sahagun 1969: 151–152). The sweat bath itself may have been a source of substance, represented by the curls of steam, which emerged from the living body as breath. Breath and steam, like other transparent substances such as the smoke formed by burning incense, were transitory parts of the self. Breath moved in and out of the body. Captured in the body, the substance represented in images as scrolls provided a physical medium that carried vocal communication to the ears of other people (Houston and Taube 2000). The smoke rising from burning incense was figured as a connection between the living and supernatural beings, ancestors and deities (Freidel *et al.* 1991). Curls of vaporous substance were depicted around scenes of the visions or waking dreams represented in Maya sculpture by the serpentine *way*, the medium through which the dreaming person's spirit transcended limits of time and space, and around other figures that can be interpreted as the products of visions (Stuart 1984; compare Proskouriakoff 1993: 185–187).

K'ik', a substance shared by animals (as blood) and plants (as sap), was the material that gave the physical body its ability to move. In Maya mythology, not only the entire body but body parts were mobile, detached heads rolling along as long as they had not dried out (Gillespie 1991). The sap used to form the rubber game ball *k'ik'* gave the ball its motion. Burned as an offering of rubber or spattered on paper as an offering of blood, *k'ik'* could be converted into smoke, travelling the same pathway to gods and ancestors as breath (Stone 2002: 23–24).

The volatility of these substances can perhaps be better understood in terms of the experience Maya people had of conversions of matter in the environment in which they lived (see Harrison and Turner 1978; Pohl 1985; Rice 1993). The tropical lowlands where Classic Maya city states were located are hot and humid, but not uniformly so. For half of the year, from late spring into fall, the countryside experiences a rainy season whose intensity is the key to agricultural productivity. Beginning with scattered showers that coalesce out of an atmosphere thick with humidity, the rains gradually increase in duration and predictability until, by the end of the rainy season, daily showers lasting for many hours can drop so much rain that the water races over the saturated soil. Where rivers run across the land, in the southern lowlands, they fill with brown water rushing from even slightly higher ground, carrying sediment that falls out of the current when the rain-swollen rivers overflow their banks. The limestone plain of the northern lowlands does not support such surface streams, but there the rains flow over the ground, draining into lakes, sinkholes, and low-lying areas called *bajos*, at least some of these features being human modified and maintained. Throughout the area, as the overflow of water stretches out under the summer sun, it evaporates in visible curls of steam. Boundaries between land and water, solid surface and air, are difficult to fix in this volatile environment.

As the rains diminish, while the heat of the winter sun begins to decrease, the surface of the land, enriched by newly deposited soil, bursts into ever more exuberant growth. The difference in vegetation is subtle to eyes trained to the extremes of northern seasonality, with shades of green marking all seasons of the tropical landscape. But the rain-fed plants put on extra growth, sending out young shoots full of fresh sap. In the best-watered lands, a second corn crop can be planted at the end of the rainy season, and will grow over the winter months. Groves of trees, managed and harvested as cultivated stands in what Spanish observers saw as wild jungle (Atran 1993; McAnany 1995: 64–84), also put out new growth at this time, including flowers that will develop during the dry months into edible seeds and fruit. Around the end of the solar year at the winter solstice, rainfall normally stops again, and will not resume until after the spring equinox marks the sun's turn toward the north. So close to the equator, the seasonal round is not demarcated by great differences in the length of the day, but by the position of the sun on the horizon. The tropical light varies less in intensity than in clarity, as the disappearance of atmospheric humidity brings an intense bright blue color to a sky previously almost white with rain (Hunt 1977: 235–237).

In the dry season, the land's surface lies flat and hard under an equally flat and hard, blue sky. Even the water running through streams is clarified and subdued, as the streams traversing dry fields carrying little suspended sediment move most slowly and peacefully at their annual water minimums. The constant rushing noise of water that exists as a background throughout the rainy season ends, and is replaced by a hollow quiet. Nothing moves in the heat of the day, in the height of the dry season, in early spring, before the equinox. Nothing grows, as the seed plants in the fields dry and turn the overall green of the tropical vegetation slightly more yellow. Late in the dry season, when traditional farmers clear the fields they intend to sow with corn for the next harvest, the fires they set to consume the dead vegetation give off black smoke, more like the smoke of burning rubber than the steam, mist, and white smoke of native copal incense. After the fields are blackened, the farmers carefully plant individual seeds, traditionally carried in the fields inside *jicaras*. These are indigenous tree gourds (*Crescentia* sp.) of the type identified in Maya folklore with the skull of the dead Hero Twin hanging in the Underworld tree, waiting to spit on the body of the Underworld daughter, *Xk'ik'*, whose name can be glossed "she of the blood/sap" (Tedlock 1985: 113–115, 274, 328, 329; compare Ventura 1996).

While blood and breath created the distinctive substance of a living body,

76

bone linked the living to the dead. This solid enduring material of the body was removed from burials for secondary treatment. Often converted through carving into personal ornaments, bone could circulate over centuries until, in some cases, being redeposited in burials as heirloom ornaments (Joyce 2000b). Where breath and blood were inherently convertible to other substances, bone remained stable in essence despite physical reforming. Used as a material for personal ornaments, ancestral bone literally served to shape the bodies of descendants through practices of body modification.

Like breath and blood, steam and sap, bone was matter of everyday experience for Classic Maya subjects. Putrefaction in the tropical forest environment ensures that any animal that dies is quickly converted into relatively clean bone. As the flesh melted away from bone, it emanated stench—another of the immaterial substances linked to steam, scent and breath. Plant material also decays with a notable smell under these conditions, underlining the consubstantiality between plants and animals already signaled by their shared animating k'ik', blood or sap. As part of the process of decay, tropical insects carry away bits of flesh, recalling scenes from later Maya mythology of insects removing flowers from a guarded planting and bringing them to where the sons of the Underworld daughter waited for their magical overnight harvest (Tedlock 1985: 140–141). Viewed from this perspective, the bones left after the flesh of human subjects decayed would have been like plants stripped of their flowers, corn cobs with their kernels removed.

The white bone left after decay of the flesh was metaphorically likened to the white-feathered egret, named sak b'ak (white bone) through substitution of an egret for a bone in the inscriptions of Palenque (Lounsbury 1974, 1985, 1991; Mathews and Schele 1974). Feathers, with their hard quills that survive the immediate processes of decay, may have been seen as an external analogue to bone. Contrasting with the bright white of egret feathers were the green feathers most commonly depicted as part of Classic Maya costume, especially the lavish tail feathers of the quetzal bird (k'uk'). The feathers of the quetzal bird emerge from the headdresses depicted in Classic Maya art like the young shoots of vegetation with which they shared a name. In the heroic royal histories inscribed at Palenque, Lady Sak B'ak shares ancestral status with a lord whose name includes the quetzal bird, K'uk'. The pairing of white and green ancestral substances suggested by the plumage linked to these figures is echoed in the green jade mosaic mask, glued to the flesh of the Palenque lord interred in the Temple of the Inscriptions. The plaques of jade came to rest, after the decay of the body, against the white bone of the man's skull. These jade plaques were like permanent kernels of young green corn on the bony cob of an ear of corn, for Classic Maya the head of the supernatural patron of maize.

The bony skeleton and hard jade ornaments that formed the enduring remains of this buried person rested inside a stone container ornamented on all sides with images of ancestors bursting out of the earth along with fruit-laden trees (Schele and Miller 1986: 282–285). The image on the surface of

Figure 4.4 Classic Maya ancestral figure as human/tree hybrid. Detail of side of sarcophagus from Temple of the Inscriptions, Palenque, showing an ancestral figure bursting out of the earth, sprouting cacao fruit, as part of a grove of human/tree hybrids. Rubbings by Merle Greene Robertson. © Pre-Columbian Art Research Institute, 1995. Used with permission.

the container depicts a male dressed in the costume of the maize god (Taube 1985) falling into the maws of the earth in front of a fully developed tree which bears no fruit. The planting of the dead body in the core of this container, and the flourishing of ancestors emerging from the earth, powerfully suggest the identification of Classic Maya people with plants (Figure 4.4). Carved in the form of a royal bench or throne (Gillespie 2002), the container for the burial identifies ancestral bone as the seed promising prosperity to descendants seated on the throne.

The repeated placement of human remains within the core of benches, or in buildings in royal palaces, while lacking the pictorial annotation that makes the Palenque example so clear, would presumably have had the same implications for those who occupied the benches linked to the buried dead (Gillespie 2000, 2002). Like plants grown from harvested seed, the descendants of entombed ancestors were the enfleshed extensions of ancestral substance. Nobles lived surrounded by images considered to continue to exercise control over the visual field they permanently surveyed, traversing paths established by those entombed within the buildings they lived in, participating through shared names, fates, and animal spirit co-essences in the bodily substance of their predecessors, and wearing at times the same ornaments used by their predecessors or even ornaments made from the bones of the ancestors.

5

HYBRIDS

Border crossings

Diverse forms of cultural cross-codings have been constructed historically between specific deities, humans and animals. Egyptian and Maya examples are perhaps two of the earliest and most evocative. Within these societies certain individuals have been prepared to see capacities for agency distributed much more widely across many different categories of creation: humans, animals, spirits and the elements. These constellations disrupt and present a clear challenge to what Westerners have normally taken to constitute the properties of consciousness, self-awareness, and intentionality (Philo and Wilbert 2000: 16).

New Kingdom conceptual and representational spheres drew heavily upon the traversing of corporeal boundaries, specifically those between human and animal subjects and human and plant taxonomies. These imaginings were most evocatively played out in the portrayal of the divine and did not traditionally overspill into the representation of ordinary living individuals, animals or plants. While categorical blurrings are not unique to Egyptian culture, we are presented with one of the earliest preserved examples of this genre of border crossing. The bodily potentials of recombinant deities reveal Egyptian imaginings about the divine, specifically how the flexibility of the body and its figurations enabled a certain morphing of beings and things, incorporating the contours and essences of distinct typologies. Using Marx's terminology, every kind of organism is a "species-being" in a unique sense, possessing defining characteristics, and separable from all others (Morris 2000: 35). While Egyptian materials may seem arcane and distinctive, theorists from a range of humanistic fields are similarly excavating contemporary networks of human/animal relations. In tracing these topologies each of us highlights spaces and categories that ultimately constitute cultural difference in the formation of situated social relations (Philo and Wilbert 2000: 5). The heterotopic bodies of the divine offer other avenues to understanding the imaginative geographies of ancient Egypt, and might also hint at the constraining corporeal limitations that Egyptians themselves dreamed of overcoming. They reveal a lived and imagined world characterized by flux and permanence, with all the difficulties attached to confronting the promise and horror of change (Bynum 2001: 179).

This section examines the imaginative resources of the New Kingdom, specifically the morphisms between people, animals and things, and simultaneously underscores the conceptualization of Egyptian humanity. Contrary to Western Cartesian taxonomies, the Egyptians made different distinctions between animal, vegetable or mineral taxa, and saw all as manifestations of a generative power—the force behind the inexplicable. All participants in the Egyptian universe could appear as an outward expression of the divine. The gods were thought to inhabit all embodied forms, plants and minerals (Germond and Livet 2001: 12), although those quotidian entities were not worshipped in themselves. In Egyptian art the head of a deity might reflect the generic identity and quality of the deity, while the programmatics of bodily representation often determined how the body was shaped, specifically what activity or gesture was being represented. Given these principles, the human body could also be seen as a figurative solution for particular scenarios of representation resulting in visual hybrids. Far from practicing zoolatry, the Egyptians considered specific animals as manifestations of divine powers, mysterious forces and the active qualities of their universe. Their conceptual systems may reflect a deeply ingrained fear and fascination with the real and imagined borderlines between the animal and the human, the uncertainties posed by the wild landscapes that surrounded people and more pointedly, the possibilities of mixing or coupling humans and animals.

The tensions and preoccupations are familiar to our own society and many others. The issue is change—the fundamental fact that one thing can become another (Bynum 2001). Hybridity, metamorphosis and change were important intellectual concerns. Ordinary people were fascinated by change as an ontological problem, not simply birth and decay as evinced in the life stages passing, but the porous structures of gender, ethnicity and kinship that constitute identity and alterity.

From Predynastic times, approximately 3000 BC, it was possible for pharaohs to represent themselves in animal form. The Narmer and Battlefield palettes show the victorious Egyptians in lion and bird-of-prey form. The earliest kings of Egypt also took animal names such as Scorpion, Catfish, Kite, Cobra and so on (Hornung 1982: 105), perhaps assuming the potency and power of the animal world that surrounded them. From early in the Dynastic period it was possible to portray the gods in human form, suggesting an overlapping and porous connection between anthropomorphic and zoomorphic depictions of the divine and the royal.

Various Egyptian deities from the earliest depictions were either symbolically associated with specific animals, or manifested themselves in animal form, literally becoming embodied in animals, or their iconic representations (Morris 2000: 23–24). In many representations they were depicted as hybrids—a simultaneity of twoness made visible. This embodied a narrative form. These representations assumed that those with cultural knowledge knew the story associated with the image and had referents for its spiraling associations. These images were metaphoric. Ontological metaphors allow us to comprehend a wide variety of experiences with non-human entities in terms of human motivations, characteristics and activities (Lakoff and Johnson 1980: 33). From this point of view, the world is structured through metaphor, rather than metaphors simply operating as an embellishment or poetic device. Metaphors create new ways of conceiving of the world and they simultaneously destabilize and reveal it.

In the Early Dynastic period, Egyptian artists did not explicitly combine human and animal forms together within a single figure. Toward the end of the second Dynasty the first gods with animal heads appeared: Horus and Seth (Hornung 1982: 107). Eventually most of the major deities could be embodied and visualized in animal forms so that the lives of humans and animals were not only linked at the empirical level, but closely interwoven spiritually. One striking example was the deity Seth who was the archetypal dissembler: god of chaos, confusion and mummification. Seth was represented as a creature with a forked tail, a curved snout and tall, straight ears (Quirke 1992: 54). Many scholars have unsuccessfully tried to identify a specific animal in this image. It may prove more productive to view the god as a synthesis of distinct bodily features inflected with disorder itself. The fusion of animal head and human body is the most characteristic recording of the divine in Egypt. It represents a violation of category where contradiction and incompatibility were forced into existence. The opposite schema was mobilized within the Mesopotamian system: traditionally an animal body surmounted by a human head.

Symbolically such visual hybrids brought together the divine power manifest in animal form as a symbol, and visualized its potential influence through human agency (Germond and Livet 2001: 122). There is a rich corpus of possibilities within this representation schema. In the New Kingdom, for example, the goddess Hathor could be represented as a slim female with a pair of cow horns and a sundisc; a hybrid being with a female human body and the head of a cow; entirely in animal form as a cow (Figure 5.1); or as an isolated cow head with human features (Hornung 1982: 110). She could also appear as a lioness, a snake, a hippopotamus and a tree spirit. All these representational possibilities could exist side by side and were legibly understood by an Egyptian audience. Each is a possible manifestation of the deity or her specific personal attributes: maternal, wild, violent, unpredictable and so on. Egyptian iconography mirrored the agentic complexity and multifaceted nature of the divine. Significantly, the Egyptians did not equate the deity with the animal. It is misleading to think that they worshipped animals in any literal or reductive sense. Claude Levi-Strauss once defined religion as the "anthropomorphism of nature" and indeed many societies choose to animate and anthropomorphize animals, plants, objects, and landscapes. Particularistic essences and

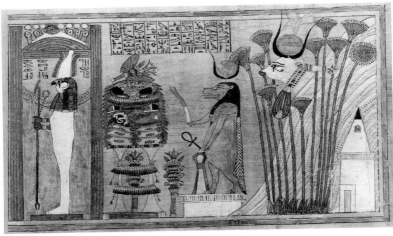

Figure 5.1 Detail from the Papyrus of Ani, showing Hathor as a cow emerging from the Western Mountain. Courtesy of the British Museum, EA 10470/37.

characteristics from the natural world were deemed salient and efficacious in the human sphere of New Kingdom Egypt. The frog goddess, Heqet, who assists mothers in childbirth, appears as a frog or in the form of a female body with a frog's head. The capacity of the frog to birth numerous offspring, and the various metamorphoses that ensued, undoubtedly influential in adopting that specific image of divine protection for a mother in childbirth. More unusual is Khepry, a deity with a male body and a scarab beetle for a head, the god of becoming, being and transformation.

The long tripartite wig worn by most gods disguises the bodily juncture and gives a seamless quality to the hybrid body. Even to the un/cultured Western eye these hybrids rarely create a monstrous visual effect. The major exceptions are those hybrid entities representing the liminal world. Bes and Taweret (Figure 5.2) could be described as grotesque deities, both to Egyptian and contemporary viewers. They combine multiple animal and human components—lions, crocodiles, hippopotami—aggressive animals that threatened and protected alike. Importantly, these composite deities were each the embodiment of spiritual agencies related to specific female bodily states of pregnancy, birth, child rearing and sexuality. None could be said to be aesthetically beautiful. Rather their corporeal monstrosity externalizes their internal power to protect. At the same time, it may also reveal the discursive male vision of visceral horror at the world of women. This may constitute a double reinforcement, since it has been argued that the very idea of species-crossing reveals anxieties over pollution and deep-seated fears of the female (Bynum 2001: 83).

Divinity was immanent in these living animal forms; they were all theophanies of the divine. As in contemporary Malawian society (Morris 2000: 29–30), while there is a clear ontological distinction between humans and animals, this does not constitute a radical dichotomy, since animals are thought to share many attributes with humans in having sociality, consciousness and subjective agency. The New Kingdom conception of both the divinity and the spirit world is essentially pantheistic, for both divinities and spirits manifest, or become embodied, as natural phenomena. In this context such a worldview is neither mystical nor animistic. In both Egyptian and Malawian society seemingly contradictory sentiments could be accommodated within a single cultural view: animals were regarded as necessary sources of food and assistance, they were symbolic vehicles that signified the qualities of the divine, and were sometimes hostile and antagonistic to human endeavor. The Judeo–Christian tradition has formed an unbridgeable gulf between the human and animal world, seeing and positioning humanity as inherently distinct (see Turner 1996). An interesting and powerful exception is the representation of three of the four evangelists in animal form: the ox for Luke, the eagle for John, and the lion for Mark. Yet only humans were made in the image of god, and thus animals are not personified in the manner of Egyptian culture.

Figure 5.2 Wooden cosmetic spoon with Bes handle. Courtesy of the British Museum, EA 5954.

What might it reveal that the divine took the form, or partial form of humanity? Did that mean ordinary mortals could assume a godly state of being? Individuals in ancient Egypt were not transformed into gods in death, but in a sense became deified ancestors who shared the realm of the gods. Upon the specificities of that existence, the texts are silent. Again, what might it signify culturally if the divine might also assume the appearances or associations of animal species—monkeys, jackals, birds, crocodiles, lions, and so on—

Figure 5.3 Akhenaten as a sphinx, from Amarna, eighteenth Dynasty. H. 56.7cm; B. 93.2cm. (Limestone) Inv. 1964.3. Photograph: M. Lindner. Courtesy of Kestner Museum, Hannover.

as they do in Egypt? In Genesis, God gives humans dominion over animals, but what of those cultures outside this order of things (Singer 2001: 12)? Would this suggest a democratization of power and agency, a destabilization of the taxonomic hierarchy that we are familiar with, or a separation of spheres where specific animals were understood relationally in specific discursive contexts, whether cultic, domestic or wild?

Like Egyptian deities, the pharaoh himself could be represented as a snake, falcon, sphinx (Figure 5.3) or criosphinx (ram-headed with a lion's body) that were all avatars of the king. In this way the corporeality of royal mortals approached the fluid and performative potentials of the gods. Egyptian representations may not be indications of true forms in a concrete sense, but characterizations of divine natures. That included the ability to traverse domains, and mortals could only access the gods in liminal spaces such as that of the dream world, in visions or in otherworldly contexts. Egyptian deities had the epithet, "rich in manifestations" or "lord of manifestations" (Hornung 1982: 125) and were commonly described in terms of many names, many faces, and many forms. The true appearance of the divine was not bounded by bodily contours but rather suffused with blinding radiance (Hornung 1982: 135). The bodily form of deities was considered hidden and mysterious. Only the deceased was thought to truly know the form of the gods. Priests might have also assumed the visual likeness of the gods' form, possibly by wearing masks. Little is known about such practices and only a few fragmentary masks have ever been discovered.

Figure 5.4 Wooden figure of a gazelle-headed protective figure from a royal tomb in the Valley of the Kings, Thebes, Egypt, eighteenth Dynasty. Courtesy of the British Museum, EA 50702.

Demonic and divine hybrids

Signifying the divine employed the now familiar stylistics of the hybrid being: the interchangeable and mutable corporealities of human and animal beings. A similar set of visual tropes was also employed for those demonic beings that inhabited the realm of the otherworldly, such as the eighteenth Dynasty statues found near the tomb of Horemheb in the Valley of the Kings. The monstrous gazelle-headed guardian demon painted in a black resinous substance (Figure 5.4), which was paired with a turtle-headed counterpart, is eerily menacing. Both bodies twist in a contorted position, lower halves in profile, upper bodies turned toward the viewer as if following their gaze, all-watching and all-powerful. The entire body of the turtle forms the head of one statue, unlike the divine wig that smoothes the juncture between body and head.

Both the turtle and gazelle were thought to be creatures of chaos, one inhabiting the marshy in-between spaces and the other the desert plains. Both were viewed as dangerous to the living and enemies of the gods, and thus were apotropaic when guarding the tomb of the dead pharaoh. Their efficacious hybridity was thought to protect the pharaoh in his journey through the dangerous terrain of the netherworld. In Egyptian thought the heads and specific attributes of deities were considered interchangeable (Hornung 1982: 118). In the Book of the Amduat a divine figure in human form has two

Figure 5.5 Details from the Papyrus of Huynefer, nineteenth Dynasty. Weighing of the Heart scene with Ammit. Courtesy of the British Museum, EA 9901/3.

protuberances in place of the head. He is the demonic binder—a frightening being who binds the damned in the underworld. Here the function of the entity, its particular purpose or torture, may act as a substitute for the head. This being is doubly monstrous since it operates in the liminal space during the judgment of the damned and is the harbinger of doom. Thus the divine and the demonic shared this potential to amalgamate and blend with other forms to create new bodily potentials and subjects. And while the gods assumed or integrated the forms of animals and plants in some cases, demonic beings could also conjoin with objects and non-living taxonomies.

In the representational spheres of New Kingdom royal tombs, demons in the netherworld were fierce and frightening amalgams of animal and human parts, specifically of those beasts considered frightening to an Egyptian audience. The artists re/produced this horror, although the cultural fantasy was contained within bodily limits (Schafer 1986: 34). The creature Ammit was such a demon (Figure 5.5). Known as *the devourer*, she was a composite creature gendered female combining the hindquarters of a hippo, foreparts of a leopard, and head of a crocodile. Similar to the combinations present in the deities Bes and Taweret, the beastly aspects of Ammit were each redolent of aggressive species and were ultimately connected to the female body.

Apart from human/animal hybrid couplings there were also evocative plant/human hybrids that became increasingly popular within New Kingdom culture. A striking visual motif of the Egyptian pictorial tradition is the tree-goddess, usually an incarnation of the goddess Hathor or sometimes Nut

Figure 5.6 Hathor emerging from a sycamore tree, pouring a libation over two peti-
tioners and two *ba* birds below. Possibly from Saqqara, nineteenth
Dynasty. H. 56cm; B. 59.5cm. (Limestone) inv. 2933. Photograph:
M. Lindner. Courtesy of Kestner Museum, Hannover.

(Figure 5.6). The hybrid assumed various bodily incarnations. All defy the
possibilities and known boundaries of the human form. In this popular
rendering the divine female body is emerging from a sycamore, the trunk itself
forming the lower half of this impossible body. Goddesses could reveal themselves in trees or in tree form or even suckle grown men from breasts growing
from the branches (Goldwasser 1995: 117). Notions of the bounteous fruit
tree mimics the spiritual nourishment of the individual. The doubling of this
bounty could take on further significance in a desert setting like Egypt where
trees themselves were scarce. In the Theban tomb of Kenamun, the deceased
wants to bask in the shade of her boughs, eat of her fruits and suck the nourishment from her breast as he is raised up into the sky. Sometimes the tree and
the goddess remain separate forms; at other times they are superimposed, and
in other examples the tree itself grows human features such as arms or a body.
In the tomb of Sennedjem the two images are conflated, yet still retain their
inherent differences, thus constituting a visual and ideational hybrid. The tree
and the body of the goddess have a conceptual equivalence, despite their
known taxonomic differences. Their oneness, reflected by their hybridity, is
the salient feature. Like all supra-human capacities, it has to be demarcated by
means of bodily difference. In contrast, human bodies remain locked in their

own limiting corporealities, only to be freed and capable of metamorphosis at the point of death. The human carapace, inflected with earthly constraints, needs to be shed before new somatic permutations are possible.

A salient feature of the plant/human composite is the connection to excess and fertility. A related set of images may be found with the category of Nile gods, referred to as fecundity figures, common throughout Egyptian art. Their associated sphere of imagery includes the diverse geographies of the human body, the water of the Nile and riverine plant life. These deities are composed of a human face with a divine wig and false beard. They have pendulous breasts, a large stomach and thick legs. They appear as feminized male bodies, wearing a girdle or belt that gives the appearance of nudity. Their heavy stomachs tend to spill over their belts and groin, in effect covering their genitalia (Baines 1985: 95) or the suggestion of genitalia. Some fecundity figures wear penis sheaths, so it has been argued that these entities were not likely to be eunuchs or sexless individuals. The position of the navel also indicates their massive corpulence and bodily difference when compared to other deified and human forms that were, by contrast, always slim, proportioned and perfect. The rendering of female versions of the Nile god was particularly problematic, since the artist was impelled to place corpulent images next to traditionally slim ones, so as to circumvent the problems raised by the female body's perfection. This reiterates the gendered imperative that the female form could only ever be a perfect form.

The body of fecundity figures could be depicted as waves or consisting of water (Baines 1985: 139), linking to concepts of fertility and life's cyclicality. Infrequently the body was painted red as at the Temple of Seti I at Abydos, but traditionally it was blue or green, as seen in the Temple of Ramesses II at Abydos. Blue symbolized water and its many associations, whereas green was the color of vegetation. Most of the figures carry water jars and are shown pouring, which further instantiates life and sexual fertility. The Nile gods were often paired and used to symbolize the unification of the two lands, representing upper and lower Egypt, alongside all the other dualisms of lotus and papyrus, and by extension they function as a cipher for the king. From the Egyptian point of view, the Nile did not come from terrestrial regions to the south of Egypt, but rather from the netherworld, and it communicated in some mysterious manner with the primeval water surrounding the cosmos that had emerged from it (Assmann 2001: 63).

Hybrid bodies are one of the clearest indications that we need to challenge our ontological assumptions in regard to the naturalness of boundaries between humans and animals. If we take seriously the premise that non-human animals participate in the same world and that they too have levels of awareness, agency, and intentionality (Ingold 1994), then we can begin to allow for different cultural understandings and conjoinings. Part of our dilemma is the rigid taxonomies that we have constructed and naturalized. While this construction is influenced by the organizing activities of the biological sciences, such taxonomies are questioned and revisited constantly by biologists themselves. We can see that the intellectual legacy of Cartesianism pervades the dualism of human/animal, as it does nature/culture, mind/body and the other bifurcations we seek to challenge in this volume.

Seeing double

Classic Maya texts and images record a plethora of animal/human hybrids that underline the disjunction between a contemporary notion of species boundaries and the extension of personhood across apparent natural disjunctures, including those between animals and plants. Even some objects are represented in Classic Maya art and texts as personified, having an identity, history, and even intentionality of their own.

The primary immaterial part of the embodied person, the *way*, "co-essence" or "spirit companion," most notably took the form of an animal (Houston and Stuart 1989; Grube and Nahm 1994). It has been suggested that most of the scenes in Classic Maya painted pottery showing groups of animals are actually representations of *wayeb*. Such animal figures are always marked as hybrids by the provision of ornaments like those worn by human actors (Figure 2.3). A few animals appear repeatedly as *wayeb*, some of them apparently the spirit companions of anthropomorphic supernatural beings such as the sun deity.

Anthropomorphic supernatural beings are, on close examination, often themselves marked as hybrids. They may have fish spines growing from their cheeks, or jaguar skin in patches on their bodies. Many supernaturals are marked as non-human by elaborations of their eyes (Taube 1992). The so-called "god-eye" replaces the round, central pupil filled in with black (typical of human figures), with a spiral, a square corner, or an off-center black zone (compare Houston and Taube 2000). Such elaborate marking of the eye recalls the central place vision plays in embodied experience, in particular, the non-reciprocal visual relations that provide the primary language of political domination. Seeing differently is the characteristic of gods and those like them. Bodily prostheses like the masks representing human/animal hybrids depicted on monuments at sites such as Calakmul, Copan, and Uxmal (Figure 5.7), or the jaguar mitts and boots worn by human/animal hybrids on polychrome pottery (Figure 5.8), enabled those wearing them to exhibit outwardly the bodily substance of otherwise immaterial animal spirit companions. In this way, not only did the represented visage, *bah*, establish the extension of individual identity (Houston and Stuart 1998: 77); it could also serve as a medium for consubstantiality.

The relation of human beings to animal co-essences was also inscribed in hybrid textual practices, particularly those of naming. An optional part of the identifying titles of Classic Maya nobles was references to their named *wayeb*. As Gillespie (2001) argues, sharing of names implied participation in the

Figure 5.7
Classic Maya animal/human hybrid mask shown in front of face, Uxmal stela 14. Courtesy of Corpus of Maya Hieroglyphic Inscriptions, Peabody Museum, Harvard University.

Figure 5.8
Classic Maya polychrome vase from Ulua river valley, showing jaguar/human with hybrid hand-paws and feet. Photograph © Russell N. Sheptak. Used by permission.

personne denoted by the name, whether that was a past human ancestor or a non-human co-essence. Animal names were repeatedly used as part of titles employed by successive Maya rulers, even when not explicitly marked as names of their spirit companions. The pair of ruling names used at Yaxchilan, Bird Jaguar and Shield Jaguar, are the most obvious example (Tate 1992). The use of animal names over generations suggests the possibility that ties between humans of different generations were created through their common consubstantiality with specific animal spirits, just as Monaghan (1998) suggests that ties through both the *way* and the birth date establish relations among humans. Among the most prominent animal/human identifications marked in royal titles used by the Classic Maya are links with the jaguar and the serpent. The textual logograph for *way* itself takes the form of a frontal human face half-covered by jaguar skin. The convention for representing the materialization of deceased ancestors and other non-material beings in Maya

90

Figure 5.9 Drawing of Classic Maya crocodile/human hybrid from Copan monument, showing hand–paw equivalence. Drawing by Annie Hunter, before

art is the body of an immense serpent, sometimes explicitly identified as a *way* linking a living human with others, presumably through their mutual relations to the same animal co-essence.

Spirit companions are not the only animal/human hybrids evident in Classic Maya representation, nor is hybridity solely a characteristic of the animal kingdom. Fundamental to the rich visual vocabulary through which Classic Maya sculptors located events they represented in time and space were animal/human hybrids commonly referred to as zoomorphs (Stone 1985). These monstrous animals, often exhibiting attributes of reptiles, could be named individually in texts. They can share the unnatural eyes of gods, and may wear ornaments of the kinds used by human actors.

Paradigmatic are the beings identified as the "earth monster" and "celestial dragon." Each is a quadruped, often shown with five claws on each extremity, blurring the boundary between human and animal (Figure 5.9). Earth monsters are positioned so as to embody the surface of the earth in Classic Maya compositions. Celestial dragons are laid out arching over doorways or forming upper frames or "sky bands" in the same or similar scenes. These representations imply that the earth and sky themselves were considered to be alive in the same way that animal/human hybrids were. Through the use of detachable signifiers that form part of the bodies of such animal/landscape hybrids, certain human beings participated consubstantially in the materiality of these aspects of the Classic Maya world, which might otherwise be considered inert or inactive. Like human actors, zoomorphs bear significant ornaments whose features can be read iconographically. The same ornaments are worn in certain

Figure 5.10 Classic Maya woman standing on earth zoomorph, with ceremonial bar. Naranjo stela 31. Courtesy of Corpus of Maya Hieroglyphic Inscriptions, Peabody Museum, Harvard University.

circumstances by human actors: the so-called "Quadripartite Head-dress" of the celestial dragon figures prominently as part of the costume or regalia of certain noble women (Robertson 1974). A serpentine form of the celestial dragon is carried as a ceremonial bar by male and female nobles (Figure 5.10).

What is perhaps the ultimate condensation of the hybridity between humans and landscape hybrids, achieved through the use of material extensions of the body, is provided by the formal costume worn by many noble women: an over-robe that represents a network of cylindrical beads (Bruhns 1988; Joyce 1999). The network surface pattern is identifiable with the conventions for depicting the skin of reptilian earth hybrids. In striking images from Chichen Itza, figures dressed in this costume lay recumbent with green, serpentine images rising up from them (Figure 5.11). In at least one case, the rising images are clearly plants.

A shorter version of this network garment that materially linked such anthropomorphic actors with zoomorphic hybrids is worn, with distinctive

Figure 5.11 Recumbent Classic Maya earth woman positioned above door, Upper Temple of the Jaguars, Chichen Itza. Photograph N30803 by Hillel Burger, detail of Adela Breton watercolor copy of mural, object cat. no: 45–5–20/15062. Courtesy of Peabody Museum, Harvard University, © President and Fellows of Harvard College.

Figure 5.12 Classic Maya bead showing warrior reclining, flanked on the left by a human/eagle/jaguar hybrid holding a trilobe motif symbolic of a human heart in its hand, recovered from the Cenote at Chichen Itza (Proskouriakoff 1974: Plate 43/6). © President and Fellows of Harvard College. Used by permission.

ornaments, by figures identified as representations of the supernatural maize plant and its human impersonators (Taube 1985; Fitzsimmons 2002: 124–126). To the extent that the Classic Maya actually shaped the skulls of children to approximate the elongated form of the maize cob head of the corn deity, living humans embodied a human/maize plant hybrid. Nor was such hybridity limited to this single symbolically central plant. In addition to hybrids conjoining maize and humans, Maya art also represents human/ flower and human/tree hybridity (Kurbjuhn 1985; Kolata 1984).

The ordinary status of people of corn was implicitly contrasted with that of persons who might participate in distinct forms of hybridity: the flesh-eating jaguar- and raptor-costumed figures that stand for warriors in Classic Maya iconography, represented in the carvings of Chichen Itza by their reclining human bodies juxtaposed to their animal alter egos devouring human hearts (Figure 5.12). The provision of costumes for warriors made of minimally processed products of the forest, animal skins, bird feathers, and bark cloth strips, demarcated a profound if transitory boundary in personhood between people of the forest and the inhabited towns, where woven cotton cloth was the norm.

The enactment of violent performances by costumed war dancers, the impersonation of *wayeb* in dramas, and the representation of maize and other hybrid supernaturals in rituals, all within the confines of the town, collapsed geographic distinction and counteracted the maintenance of boundaries between town and forest. When the prosthetic extensions of bodily materiality inserted through the ears of the living were shaped as flowers, the hybridity of human and plant was underscored. This hybridity was, like that of humans and their animal spirits, also consubstantial, as humans consumed plants and converted them into the substance of flesh. Classic Maya personhood is represented through hybridity as extending out to be coterminous with the physical world. Where are the boundaries of the person if the skin is not the edge?

6

PHALLIC CULTURE

Fluid economies

Many theorists, most notably Lacan (2001), have grappled with the concept that the personality could extend beyond the limits of the body and be constituted within a complex social network. Such a theory proposes that the identity of the human being could include elements well outside the biological boundaries of the body. Again this enters the realm of taxonomy and the hermeneutic limitations of language. In Egypt there was an extensive corpus of writing devoted to the power and potency of fluids, and concomitantly to the porous nature of the human body, especially at its border zones and orifices. As already suggested, this has an existential basis and speaks to the nature of being for both gods and mortals. In the beginning, the saliva of the goddess Neith formed the primeval water, while other entities, such as Apep, were brought into existence by being spat out. The world was literally formed with the ingredients of the contained body and the gods were masturbated into existence, spat out or cried out into being. Beings were produced from the body, manufactured by bodily process and exuviae, but were tacitly separable. In the New Kingdom Papyrus Bremner-Rhind (Allen 1988: 28), the god Atum states:

> *For my hand, the fact is that I acted as husband with my fist,*
> *I copulated with my hand,*
> *I let fall from my mouth by myself,*
> *I sneezed Shu and spat Tefnut.*
> *It is my father, the Water, that tended them, with my eye after them since*
>   *the time they became apart from me*

Divine bodily secretions of the gods, tears and sweat specifically, were then consumed by other gods and literally became *self-sustaining* substances. The gods ate themselves. Their secretions had special values; in fact anything from the divine body was deemed productive. In the Coffin Texts, Shu claims *I, in fact, am Life, son of Atum—It is from his nose that he bore me, it is from his nostrils that I emerged* (Allen 1988: 23). According to the Papyrus Salt the

95

tears of Horus touched the ground and olibanum sprouted; the blood from Geb's nose sprouted pine trees. Both were divine resins. From the tears of Shu and Tefnut terebinth resin was also formed. The tears of Ra on contact with the earth changed into a bee that then produced honey and wax. The sweat of Ra's body turned to flax and could be transformed to cloth, while his spit, which he vomited, produced bitumen (Meeks and Favard-Meeks 1997: 70).

Significantly, these bodily residues were required for the mummification process, specifically for that of the first mummy, Osiris. These substances were the extension of the original embodied creation, kept active in a form of circulation, like an endless kula ring of fluids. Anything extra-somatic (parts or substances that detached or emanated from the divine body) were imbued with concomitant power, although the outcomes of their corporeal agency were often deleterious. In the story of Isis and her father Re, the aged sun god was prone to dribbling, causing his spittle to drop on the ground. Isis collected and fashioned this substance into a snake that then bit Re, his own fluidic potency used against his divine person. Magic itself was a form of energy that could be swallowed or consumed or eaten; it was said to be *in the body*.

Just as the gods had fluid beginnings, so humanity is said to have arisen from the divine tears. The Egyptians referred collectively to "mankind" or "people" as *rmt*. From the New Kingdom onwards this term extended to non-Egyptians as well. It has an existential punning reference to humans as coming from the tears, *rmit*, of the creator god's eye (Meskell 2002: 58). Unsurprisingly, this act has a sexual substrate, since the eye and the penis, tears and semen have a conceptual and mythological link (te Velde 1967: 55). In the story of Horus and Seth, divine semen plays a powerful role in determining the right to rule and the difference between right and wrongdoing. Seth attempts to penetrate Horus, although the latter catches Seth's semen in his hand. When he shows it to his mother Isis, she immediately cuts off his hand and throws it into the Nile. She then takes the newly produced semen of Horus and places it over the favorite food of Seth, the lettuce, which itself produces a milky semen-like substance. Seth eats the lettuce and becomes pregnant. At a tribunal of the gods, Seth uses his penetration of Horus to claim that he has done *a man's deed* to him, and as such Horus cannot rule. Horus retorts that the gods should call upon the resting place of the divine semen. As they do so, Seth's semen is shown to reside in the Nile whereas Horus' semen is implanted in Seth's body. The divine seed asks, should I come out the ear? Should I come out the top of his head? And indeed it does the latter, appearing as a golden sundisc. Horus is proclaimed right, and Seth wrong (Lichtheim 1976: 220).

The myth illustrates various beliefs about the permeable body and the fluid self. The word for poison and semen is the same in Egyptian language (te Velde 1967: 45), and so an intelligent audience would have noted the pun. For the Egyptians, demons were thought to enter through orifices and openings such as the ear or eye. These were breaks in the field of containment and therefore susceptible. Magical papyri tell of spells to drive out the poison of the god, goddess or dead man or woman (Pinch 1994: 82). Linked to this fear was a notion that the two sides of the body had different qualities: the breath of life enters into the right ear and the breath of death enters into the left ear (Nunn 1996).

New Kingdom Egypt had a libidinal economy in its ritual superstructure, evidenced by the well documented discourse pertaining to bodily fluids and boundaries. Magic coalesced in the body of the magician, but it required conscious manipulation through spells and rituals. Many of these practices relied on the materiality of the body and particularly its bodily substances— saliva, blood, and excrement. Magic was said to be *on the mouth* and this oral dimension involved spitting, licking and swallowing. There were over twenty words for spit/spittle: it was a generative force that could create gods, kings, demons, plants and animals (Ritner 1993). Saliva was creative and sexualized. There was a psychological pairing of spittle with semen and the mouth with the vulva. Spittle had both positive and negative connotations: it conveyed purification and healing, conducting evil away from the body, but was also viewed as waste and corruption. Medico–magical spells were written on the flesh then licked off. Other texts were written on papyri then burnt, ground up, dissolved in water and drunk so that the power of the spell was ingested. Spells could be recited and then spat over the site of a problem. Deities, like Maat—goddess and personification of cosmic order—could also be painted on the tongue. Power was transmitted through fluids. They were animated and empowered substances, becoming efficacious around bodily boundaries, orifices and surfaces.

Fatal fluids

Bodily fluids retained the powerful essence of the gods, and even of pharaoh. Yet certain fluids were dangerous. Semen and blood were considered unclean and menstruating women were ritually impure. Menstrual blood might thus be used as a repellent. The *tyet* amulet, probably linked to menstruation, resembled a girdle or sanitary towel, and was made from red stone. Like saliva, urine was considered as both cleansing and destructive. Following Mary Douglas, some pollutants may be perceived as expressing general views of the social order. This suggests that sexual contact was dangerous, the threat expressed through contact with sexual fluids. It was men who were most at risk, reflecting the sexual asymmetry of Egyptian society. The urine of a pregnant woman was especially potent, with life-giving properties. An ancient Egyptian pregnancy test consisted of having the woman urinate on young plants: if they grew, she was pregnant; if they died, she was not. Mother's milk, either human or animal, was positively power-laden. It was regularly used in medical prescriptions. If a woman wished to know whether she could conceive she drank the milk of a woman who had borne a son: if she vomited she either was, or would soon be, pregnant (Pinch 1994: 82). Fluids were powerful, almost independent entities that seeped from the innermost regions and secret parts of the body (Grosz 1995: 196).

Predominant magical ingredients consisted of menstrual blood, animal blood, and animal dung. Human detritus such as saliva, hair or nail clippings could also be used. Exuviae can be considered the products of the abject body that exist in a borderline state, signaling danger and vulnerability (Grosz 1994: 187–210). According to Gell (1998: 104), exuviae sorcery worked "because of the intimate causal nexus between exuviae and the person responsible for them. These exuviae do not stand metonymically for the victim; they are physically detached fragments of the victim's 'distributed personhood' … beyond the body-boundary." Egyptian pharmacopoeia illustrates an extensive use of blood and excrement: there are nineteen words for different types of excrement cited in the papyri. A substantial portion of the Coffin Texts feature the deceased's denials of drinking urine or eating excrement, usually seen as a metaphor for chaos or the world turned upside down. Following Mary Douglas, Kadish (1979) argues for an extended meaning: it is an explicit statement by each individual about choosing to be part of the moral order of the universe. The deceased states (Kadish 1979): *What I doubly detest, I do not eat. What I detest is excrement; I do not eat it. Faeces, it does not enter this mouth of mine.*

These imaginings and phantasies must have haunted the Egyptians, since they figure so prominently in the fabrications of the afterlife and its trials, but also in that other fundamental liminal space, the dreamworld. Some literate Egyptian men possessed what scholars have termed Dream Books, which followed a formulaic structure and sought to provide meaningful interpretations and portents based on the composition of dreams. One such book belonged to a man called Qenhirkhopshef, a scribe at Deir el Medina, who handed the book on to his descendants (Gardiner 1935: 12). Here there is a section devoted to desires and anxieties over drinking certain fluids—blood, milk and urine:

> *if a man sees himself in a dream*
> *drinking blood*   *good; putting an end to his enemies*
> *if a man sees himself in a dream*
> *drinking milk*   *good; a large meal will come to him*
> *if a man sees himself in a dream*
> *drinking his own urine*   *good; eating his sons possessions*

The cultural cadences are probably lost to the modern interpreter and no emic explanation for the symbolism has ever been discovered, if indeed it existed. The principles behind the interpretation are often unclear but seem to resemble those of magic practice, such as, like affects like or one thing suggests its opposite. These practices connect to Mauss's (2001 [1950]: 15) two laws of magic: the law of similarity and the law of contiguity. On a superficial level one might deduce that drinking blood and vanquishing one's enemies has a direct link. In the Pyramid Texts, spell 1286, the followers of Seth are tortured and killed, their hearts ripped out and their blood drunk (Walker 1996: 151). The practice of cannibalism, whether solely mythical or possibly factual, underscores the Egyptian conviction that destruction of the body ensured eternal annihilation. Even a theoretical consumption of the other could betoken one's own victory and corporeal prowess. The paralleling of milk with a large meal might speak to the common associations of fertility and nurturing. As outlined in Chapter 5, Hathor and other tree-goddesses were depicted suckling adult men in afterlife scenarios. The relationship between drinking one's own urine and consuming the possessions of one's sons is more difficult to understand. Given that drinking urine was one of the most despised fears of the realm of death, it would be expected to augur unfavorably for the dreamer.

Closely connected to the circulation of fluids was the power of smell, especially of the divine aromas that emanated from the godly body. In the Book of Caverns, the mummy of Osiris with its phallus erect is placed in the deepest recess of the netherworld. Spell 78 declares that *Horus came from the seed of his father when he was already putrid*. The blessed dead were thought to inhale the fragrant odors of the veiled putrefaction of the divine corpse so that they might live (Hornung 1990). In fact there are numerous spells to assure the deceased's breathing on the journey after death, especially breathing air amongst the watery depths of the netherworld. This reverie of divine decay is juxtaposed against the enormous cultural anxiety over the decay of the human body, its putrefaction and its ultimate return to a fluid state. The nightmare of mortal decay and those entities that would devour the decomposing body is revealed throughout the Book of the Dead. Spell 17 promises to *deliver me from this god, who seizes souls and licks that which is rotten, who lives on offal and is in darkness and obscurity* (te Velde 1967: 55). Spells were written for the deceased that specifically stopped bodily destruction at the hands of Seth during the seventy-day period of embalming. Death was an enemy that brought physical disintegration and loss of bodily control, the soft tissue being particularly susceptible to liquefaction, which is another reason why the process of mummification was so essential—it rendered hard, material, and object-like the fleshiness and fragility of the body. There was an explicit concern over bodily fluids, such as sweat, and with the dead body's loss of integrity through the presence of maggots. Sensual descriptions of death are common, and the Egyptians were not inhibited from writing about the smell of the decaying body, the disintegration by parasites, the rotting of flesh, mutilation, the eyes perishing and so on (Meskell 2002: 183). This horror was reconciled, even remedied, by practices such as embalming and evisceration, even if only at a heuristic level.

Phallic culture

Applying a psychoanalytic perspective to ancient culture obviously requires various caveats. Theoretical applications cannot offer conclusive answers to understanding Egyptian art and, given the insights of hermeneutic theory, such a reductive reading would be a fiction, or at least a misreading. However, this does not erase the utility of the psychoanalytic perspective. It offers another theory of viewing, or an additional perspectival point. What would phallic culture look like? How might it represent itself in various cultural forms and institutions? In Egyptian existential writing, phallicism was there at the point of creation. Masculine sexuality was the driving force that generated, and kept the generative force of the world active in perpetuity.

Evidence from Egyptian cosmology and iconography demonstrates a strongly contoured sense of phallocentrism, so that one might argue that a term like phallic culture might be appropriate. Castration was represented on royal monuments as the ultimate sign of power over the bodies of one's enemies, suggesting bodily anxiety around this ultimate act of violation and dissolution (see Chapter 8). A modern viewer's reception of these images will be informed to some degree by the inescapable influence of psychoanalytic theory on modernity. This does not undermine its utility for re-thinking the Egyptian material, although it was not a template the Egyptians themselves would recognize.

The primacy of the phallus was determined at an early stage as the key determinate of difference: the visible, physical penis. Of course, the penis is not the same as the phallus that inhabits the cultural sign of power. In Lacanian theory, the phallus offers the only possibility of grounding an endless yearning for completion, and functions as a structural concept that is an absolute guarantor of all meaning. Yet it has long been recognized that the phallus has no status in reality, certainly not in the actual male organ. Signifiers are arbitrary and have no tacit value, the phallus being no different. From this perspective, it occupies a spurious position that lacks any substantive justification for the power it confers. It is an empty symbol of castration and loss—a sign which only gains its meaning from the fact that in patriarchal societies those who bear the phallus (represented by the penis) have the power to define all other meanings, and therefore the material power to dominate (Minsky 1995: 154).

The structural concept of the phallus, supposedly derived from the ancient emblem of power, simultaneously undercut by the fear of symbolic castration, provides the fulcrum upon which all other meanings are premised, even if precariously. Yet while the phallus designates the agency of symbolic authority, its crucial feature resides in the fact that it is not *mine*, nor the organ of a living subject, but a place at which a foreign power intervenes and inscribes itself onto my body. Its status as a signifier means that it is structurally an organ without a body, somehow detached from the body (Zizek 1996: 109–110). Its semiotic power creates chains of meanings: "having" and "not having," positive and negative, power and lack, masculinity and femininity, invoking all the other binaries that many cultures have used to categorize and differentiate reality.

What is instructive for feminist and subaltern scholars are the epistemic repercussions that follow a challenge to the reification of the phallus. If its status is deemed false and arbitrary, then so are all the other oppositions modeled on the binary meanings of the phallus and the lack, "masculinity" and "femininity," by which we structure our world. Thus male identity is rendered unstable, founded on an erroneous calculation of power, prompting the use of power to coerce female desire and reinforce male desires (Minsky 1995: 160). Ancient Egypt was essentially patriarchal and succumbed to aspirations for male dominance in the representational and social sphere, to circumscribe female sexuality. Nonetheless, our sources reflect a certain ambivalence toward male sexuality. There are worrying ambivalences, such as the celebration of male genitalia as signifiers of power, phallic intimidation, sexuality and fertility, juxtaposed with the trend against male nudity in the representational arts, in strict opposition to the portrayal of women. This gendered difference reveals a concern for the elite status of clothed men, in contrast to women's inherent sexualized representation. Despite what many scholars have argued for decades, Egyptian eroticism is not exclusively tied to fertility, fertility symbolism or even mutuality, since these characteristics are often at odds with creation myths that describe how mankind arose from an act of masturbation, spittle or tears of the eye—all fluids emanating from the autonomous, deified, male body.

In the well worn theoretical ground laid out by Mary Douglas, the issuing of bodily fluids—such as spit, blood, milk, urine, faeces, sweat or tears—transgresses and traverses the boundaries of the body. Ideas about demarcation, separation and transgression impose a system of symbolic order on an inherently messy or disruptive experience (Douglas 1966: 6; Williams and Bendelow 1998: 27). When corporeal matter is out of place different cultures call on ritual or myth as means of protecting the vulnerable margins and threatened borders of the physical body and the broader conceptual embodied world. The human body thus lies at the juncture between ordered and disordered realms.

In psychoanalytic terms all traces of the natural body must be erased: it must be clean and proper in order to be fully symbolic, it should endure no gash other than that of circumcision, equivalent to sexual separation and/or separation from the mother (Kristeva 1982: 71). Bodily orifices, seepages and flows were imbued with fear and sometimes disgust in ancient Egypt, yet were also redolent of opportunities for magic, power and wholeness. Demons could potentially enter through bodily orifices and openings such as the ear or eye: breaks in the field of containment were susceptible, like the notion of the female body's leaky borders so deftly critiqued by feminist theorists. Kristeva argues (1982: 71) that neither tears nor sperm have the negative connotations of menstrual blood or excrement. The ancient data challenges this formula, since semen occupies an ambivalent status, its name having the same phonetic value as poison.

Psychoanalysts have long sought to understand the dream world, specifically as it relates to the sexual core of individual personality and embodied social relations. The ancient Egyptians similarly regarded the realm of sleep as an arena for prophetic reflexivity. While there was no culture of therapy or analysis in antiquity, texts known as Dream Books reveal the linkage between dreams of a sexual nature and the fate of the individual. The Ramesside Dream Book (Gardiner 1935: 12) is formulaic in style, androcentric in focus, and phallic in obsession. All is written with a male reader in mind. Strikingly there are no equivalent prognostications for the female subject.

> *... if a man sees himself in a dream*
> *His penis becoming large*   *good; it means his possessions will multiply*
> *copulating with a*
>   *female jerboa*   *bad; the passing of a judgment against him*
> *copulating with a woman*   *bad; it means mourning*
> *seeing his penis stiff*   *bad; victory to his enemies*
> *copulating with a kite*   *bad; it means robbing him of something*
> *shaving his lower [ ]*   *bad; it means mourning*
> *seeing a woman's [ ]*   *bad; the last extremity of misery upon him*
> *uncovering his own backside*   *bad; he will be an orphan later*
> *copulating with a pig*   *bad; being deprived of his possessions*
> *drinking blood*   *bad; a fight awaits him*
> *copulating with his wife*
>   *in daylight*   *bad; the seeing of misdeeds by his god*

At face value, the possession of a large penis clearly ensured a good outcome, whereas an erection symbolized defeat, presenting a clear contradiction. Yet to the Egyptian reader, the results may have in fact more to do with wordplay than the visual image the text conjures up (Parkinson, personal communication). While the meaning and symbolism of the interpretations are obscure, we know that word games in Egyptian culture had more significance than simple punning: they revealed multiple levels of religious meaning (Assmann 2001). More transparent and potentially didactic is the aversion to bestiality and the general undertone of misogyny in the text: sexual relations with both women and animals will lead to ruin.

Phallic power also inhabited Egyptian fantasies of death and the hereafter, and men expressed fears about losing their potency after death. One formula states *my sperm is the sperm of this one and the other. As regards everyone who will know this spell, he copulates in this land by day and night* (Zandee 1960: 61). Sexual functionality was key in the afterlife, at least as defined in male texts, as was the ability to procreate. Sexual activity was as necessary in the afterlife as air, water and nourishment. It was integral to being in this life and the here-after. In the Book of the Dead, spell 175, sex is actually privileged over the traditional foods of bread and beer, and thus functioned as a sort of total sustenance. Again these texts coalesce around the male subject, with no adequate female counterpart. In the few instances where the Books of the Dead were copied out for women, the text mimics the male reading, and nothing is changed to account for a female subject position.

Myths of becoming

The place of the phallus has assumed iconic status in our own culture, as it did previously in ancient Egypt, albeit with variant, culturally specific resonances. With the emergence of phallic culture, the phallus became a cipher with polit-ical valences and assumed an equivalence with sexuality. Moreover, it mirrored the virtualities of symbolic exchange and delineated the emergence of a political economy of the body (Baudrillard 1993: 116). Closer examination of Egyptian language underscores its potency as a multivalent signifier. The hieroglyphic determinative of the phallus, or the phallus issuing liquid, is used in a number of thematically related words signifying masculinity (penis, foreskin, semen, urine, donkey, male and husband), sexual power (to become erect, impregnate, beget, bull, virility) and aggression (rape). The words for semen and poison were simi-larly written. Phallic associations of violence and poison were juxtaposed against fertility and sexuality: all could be construed as signifying power.

In medical texts the word penis was written as *nfr*, phonetically the same as good or beautiful, written with the regular *nfr* sign plus the phallus determi-native. The word for the sun's rays, *stwt*, was also associated with male sexu-ality: *sti* to eject or impregnate, and *styt* for semen, all derived from the verb "to shoot" (Troy 1986: 18). The Egyptians deployed many puns expanding on these associations. For example, the word *qmꜣ* can mean "spear" or "throw," as in the throwstick in depictions of fowling scenes (see Figure 3.13), but can also mean "beget," "create," or "ejaculate." The root of the verb *sti* ranges in meaning through odor and scent as well as the action of pouring and other connections with water. The root, *sti*, could mean to "beget," "produce," or even "sow" and was written with the determinative of the phallus issuing fluid. From Middle Kingdom times onwards these verbs certainly sounded the same and must have been metonymic verbal puns. Within Egyptian culture there was a clear linkage between scent, fluids, phallic sexuality, and creation.

At the heart of phallic culture were originary stories that explained human existence, as outlined in Chapter 2. While there are various local accounts of becoming, or origin myths, each of them has a phallic substrate whether in the act of masturbation or in the exuding of bodily fluids. In the evocative Heliopolitan myth, Ra-Atum, the original father, brought the world into being, *he took his phallus in his fist and made sweet ejaculation from it, and the twins, Shut and Tefnut, were born* (Hare 1999: 111). Later accounts erase this primeval act of masturbation, suggesting that Atum sneezed or spat his offspring into being. In Coffin Texts 76, Shu states, *I was not built in the womb, I was not tied together in the egg, I was not conceived in conception. My father Atum sneezed me in a sneeze of his mouth* (Allen 1988: 18). Atum's purpose, in the first account, appears to be sexual pleasure, not parenthood. His act is one of singular desire, without need of a female partner, and his progeny are accidental: they are a supplement to his autoerotic intent. In this account, his semen produces the air god, Shu, and moisture goddess, Tefnut. Brother and sister have sexual intercourse and thus create Nut, the sky goddess, and Geb, the earth god. In iconographic representations, the earth was always conceived of as masculine, which is a direct challenge to the stereotype that most religions feminize the earth or have female earth deities.

In contrast, Egyptian earth gods are male, as depicted in the tomb scenes of Ramesses IV: Geb, the predominant earth god; Tatenen, who symbolized the weary earth; and the mysterious Aker, a primeval deity in the form of a double-headed lion (Forman and Quirke 1996: 128). Papyri depicting creation show the earth thrusting up to meet the sky, personified by the goddess Nut. Geb signified their sexual union with his penis erect, ready for penetration (see Figure 2.1). Yet Geb and Nut were physically separated, which meant that Geb had to fellate himself. In the twenty-first Dynasty papyrus of the Chantress of Amun, Henuttawy, the earth father god Geb is shown performing oral masturbation beneath the ithyphallic figure of Osiris, representing the night sky (Parkinson 1999: 170). In other accounts Nut and Geb embraced so tightly that nothing could exist between them and their own conceived children could not be born. Shu forced Geb and Nut apart, holding the sky goddess high above the earth, so that her body formed the starry heavens. She then gave birth to Osiris, Isis, Seth and Nephthys. According to this narrative, the universe came into being through autoeroticism and was sustained through sexuality. We should view these different texts as syncretic accounts rather than competing theological narratives that seek to explain the transmission of matter from a single source to multiple realizations in the world (Allen 1988: 36). Each originary account represents a monadic state of becoming, a closed system of operation, that erases relations with others, specifically females.

Accounts that Atum spat, rather than ejaculated, as the first act of creation transfer sites of creation from phallus to mouth, and transform the bodily efflux, representing the first of a sequence of substitutions whereby the phallic body is displaced in favor of different conceptions of creation (Hare 1999: 116). But various accounts suggest that it was semen, not saliva, that Atum spat out. The Bremner-Rhind Papyrus states: *I clenched my hand being alone … I used my own mouth* and further *after I acted as a husband with my fist, my heart came to me in my hand, ejaculation being fallen from my mouth* (Allen 1988: 30). There is a lack of temporal continuity in myth making in literary form, so that, in the Memphite Theology, the other gods (the Ennead) are described as teeth and lips in this mouth. This grounded and intensely phallic self-begetting is erased in other accounts, in preference for a more conceptual framework of creation.

The phallic body and human existence were intimately tied from the outset in ancient Egypt. What might it signify to remove the female role in conception, birth and indeed genesis, especially in view of the sophisticated gynecological knowledge the Egyptians possessed? A certain fascination with the vigor of male sexuality, a belief in the procreative power of the male organ, a reflection of gender supremacy, or a recognition of phallocentrism in and of itself? This celebration of phallic being was not loaded with the sexual guilt or moralistic overtones that pervade Western culture, as evidenced by the Egyptian word for orgasm, _ndmmt_, which emanates from the root for sweet.

Phallic worship was an integral part of Egyptian religion, linked to deities such as Osiris, Ra, Min, Bes (see Figure 5.2) and the baboon god, Baba. Many of these phallic deities, including Baba, Min and Seth, do not represent fertility gods. Rather, they represented sexual power itself. Gods like Seth did not father offspring, so integral in Egyptian culture (te Velde 1967: 55). Phallicism was central to mythological accounts like that of the murder and dismemberment of Osiris, the miraculous re-assembling of his body by his wife, Isis, and his ability to father the god Horus through impregnating Isis after his death. In this account, the phallus was severed along with the other limbs and scattered far and wide. Various representations show Isis in the form of a bird mounting the erect phallus of the dead king as he lies on his funeral bier.

This evocative myth has made a lasting impact on the Western psyche. In _Écrits_, Lacan (2001) himself used the myth as central to a psychological paradigm triangulated among the phallus, the subject, and the signifier. The modern subject attains self-knowledge through discovering, recovering or uncovering the phallus. It is not simply the notion of emasculation or the phallus itself, but that of the substitute or replacement (from penis to phallus) that is so powerful (Hare 1999: 221). The phallus becomes the site of rejuvenation, as well as of sexual pleasure and of course, progeny. The fragmentary corporeality of Osiris is likened to the fragmentation of the signifier. It is also a reminder of death and bodily destruction, which diverges from other phallic cults. Lacan was drawn to the Osirian myth as portrayed by Plutarch, yet still in the Egyptian version there was a similar concern over the loss of body and the phallus. What was clearly Egyptian was the fear of bodily dismemberment and the fragmentation of the self at the transition to the next world. Hare concludes that the phallus should not be read here as the site of loss or emasculation, but rather a site of pleasure, agency, sovereignty, dominion and presence itself.

Phallocentrism was an integral component in Egyptian mythology and cosmology. Returning to the story of Isis and Osiris, the scenes of the impregnation of Isis, such as in the Temple of Seti I at Abydos, depict Osiris recumbent with an erect penis. Isis transformed herself into a hawk or kite to conceive Horus from the body of her dead husband. The penis of the male deceased in its mummiform state was bandaged to simulate Osiris in its erect state. This linked the dead individual with the deity and his potential for resurrection just as the inanimate corpse was aligned to the potent corporeality of the ithyphallic god. All of this could be symbolized by the posthumous erection of Osiris. Hare (1999: 147) has posited that Egyptian culture was composed of a "web of relations that suggest fecundity and fertility, love, dominion, and stability through the conspicuous physical spectacle of the erect phallus of god."

The most evocative example of this must be Min, who is one of the earliest documented gods of the Egyptian pantheon. He was associated with the desert, specifically the regions around Coptos and Akhmim. Usually shown in a wrapped or undifferentiated state, his body is completely encapsulated save his upraised arm and erect member, both painted blue or green to symbolize their fecund state. Mimicking Osiris, the divine body of Min appears as if arrayed in the white linen of the mummy's bandages, signifying his inviolable power. Traditionally represented on a plinth, his legs can never move. He is more statue than being; only his phallus is active (Figure 6.1). It is likely that he was originally conceived of as an apotropaic deity who employed phallic intimidation—a suggestion reiterated by his characteristic threatening gesture of the upward arm. There are close parallels to contemporary Mesopotamian deities that show the same arrangement of features, phallic form, upraised arms and so on. His ascribed aspect of fertility may have been a secondary overlaying. Like Seth, Min was associated with the lettuce, believed to have had aphrodisiac qualities since its juice was considered to emulate semen. As we have seen, the lettuce figures heavily in the myth of Horus and Seth and their sexual encounter. And finally, through his emblematic iconography, scholars have argued that Min is linked with the door bolt, signifying the protection of a temple or sanctuary: the door bolt was similarly a metaphor for the phallus (Wilkinson 1991/2: 115).

In the New Kingdom, Min was equated with Amun and was given the epithet, *Kamutef*, "bull of his mother" (Romanosky 2001: 415), namely the one who impregnates his own mother so that she literally births him in an eternal cycle of becoming. Min was a key player in the rejuvenation and sustenance of the king's power to rule. This is evidenced in repetitive splendor at the temple of Ramesses III at Medinet Habu where the image of Min in his various manifestations is resplendent over the walls. He appears as the deity himself and as a cult statue in procession, all equally erect. A similar suite of images adorns his temple within the Amun enclosure at Karnak, showing an erect Min at his own festival, his statue being ferried on covered processional carrying poles. At this temple various gods, including Amun-Re, are shown emulating Min's ithyphallic shape. Many of these images were selectively damaged, the phallus being the object of purposive mutilation. A similar fate befell the images of the deity at

Figure 6.1　Limestone stela of Huy with his son Seba, showing Min with the Syrian goddess Qedeshet and Canaanite war deity, Reshep. From Deir el Medina, Ramesside Period. Louvre C. 86 N.237. Photo by Lynn Meskell.

the temple of Seti I at Karnak. There is a small graffito of Min on the northern wall, showing a crudely drawn figure with an enormous phallus. Practices of addition and erasure were enacted in the iconography of Min. Phallic spectacle was part of a lived experience, rather than simply representational, and the image had potency in and of itself. Subsequently, many of the images of phallic gods in Egypt have been defaced over the centuries for many reasons from prudery to magic. Coptic defacement of ithyphallic gods in Luxor temple is well documented (Brand 2000: 98). Some of the stone was probably slowly removed since even the dust from the representation conferred the power of an aphrodisiac. The power of these images continues; pharaonic statues have long been regarded in modern Egyptian culture as the embodiment of fertile vigor.

Relevant to the discussion of Egyptian phallic culture is the title given to New Kingdom queens in the cult of Amun, where they were known as the god's wife and more explicitly, the god's hand. This harks back to the phallic act of Atum, who masturbates to create Shu and Tefnut, and so on. Since the word for hand is grammatically female it was an easy extrapolation to personify the hand as a goddess (Robins 1993: 153). By the eighteenth Dynasty this term was usually associated with Hathor, goddess of sexuality, and was thus doubly sexual in resonance. How it was manifest ritually is unknown. However the queen's responsibility was probably to stimulate the god sexually to simulate the creation myth and its cyclical maintenance of the universe. Sexual union was a means of renewal, free from the moralistic connotations of Western religious systems. From a Lacanian feminist perspective, sexuality and indeed subjectivity are tied to language and culture, a prime example being the Law of the Father (Elliott 1994: 130). Through cultural and mythic media in Egypt, as with contemporary culture, asymmetrical power relations between men and women were reproduced. Yet as feminist theorists have underscored, the psychic forces that underpin patriarchy are not inevitable; they can be altered and transformed. Constructions of femininity rely on a series of suppressions and displacements of the social and political forces that structure gender difference (Elliott 1994: 117). In Egyptian culture those forces transcended the living world and permeated the realm of the netherworld.

Just as the origins of becoming were premised on the phallic body, the transition to the next life and its perpetuating cyclicality was linked to masculine sexuality. This is vividly illustrated in the tomb of Ramesses VI from the Valley of the Kings. One vignette from the Book of the Earth shows an ithyphallic deity issuing sperm towards a child below, who is associated with the rejuvenated sun (Figure 6.2). The accompanying text suggests that sperm (itself considered fiery) procreates flames—a phenomenon that can be both positive and destructive. Another figure called "the bloody one" takes the burning sperm and distributes it amongst the damned. Derrida (1987: 73) too has spoken of burning semen, like lava destined for nowhere. Creation and destruction exist together in the moment. This phallic male is called "he who conceals the hours" and his phallus is bound to the goddesses of the hours by dotted lines which go forth from him to the father/sun anew (Hornung 1990: 85).

The dead would identify themselves with the phallus of the hyper-phallic deities, Ra, Min, and Osiris, yet the Coffin texts outline how the dead threaten to bite the phallus of Re and Osiris (Behrens 1982: 1018). On the tomb ceiling of Ramesses IX, also in the Valley of the Kings, male bodies springing to life symbolize resurrection and rejuvenation, their legs apart, phalluses erect. In various vignettes a trio is shown facing the same direction, two erect males either side of a female. The effect is striking. The non-phallic body is in line to be penetrated in the midst of this demonstration of male sexual vigor. Other related scenes show the deceased, the majority of which are male individuals with the genitals clearly demarcated, raising themselves from their funerary biers. The dead identify with the role of the begetter, but more specifically with the semen of the god himself, the fluidic result of the sexual act (Troy 1986: 26). The double function of begetter and begotten is a constant process of reaffirmation and constant rejuvenation. Through this rich iconography the phallus and its seminal trace exist in a nexus of significations extending the power of the father, whilst promulgating the threat of violence, pollution, and danger (Hare 1999: 111).

Figure 6.2 The One who hides the Hours, Book of Caverns. Section of a wall painting, tomb of Ramesses VI, Valley of the Kings (Piankoff 1954: 339).

Horus and Seth: phallic relations

Phallic relations were instantiated in myth, funerary iconography and literary narratives, the most famous being the Tale of Horus and Seth alluded to above. Versions of the story had long-lived popularity over the centuries and were well known in the New Kingdom. Contained within the myth are prime examples of male sexual aggression, power and same-sex relations. Moreover, it is inflected with a belief in the power of semen and the force of impregnation, doubled with the fear of transgression of gender boundaries. Undoubtedly those who listened to the story had never seen a pregnant man. Yet the possible specificities of the mythic bodies should not so easily be dismissed. The tale rests on a substrate of phallic intimidation, sexual aggression, male rape and incestuous desire, whereas female desire and corporeality are notably absent.

To briefly recapitulate the story: Horus and Seth are battling publicly for power (some might say the inheritance of the Father), specifically the throne of the now dead Osiris, and have been brought before the gods for resolution. After various tricks and bodily transformations, Seth tricks Horus into staying the night with him. In the twelfth-Dynasty version of the literary Tale of Horus and Seth, Seth says to Horus: *How lovely is your backside! Broad are*

109

[your] thighs. This is a play or parody on the ritual greeting *How fair is your face.* Seth's attempts to have sex with Horus appear to be intended to humiliate him, but in this account are a source of pleasure for Seth, described as *sweet to his heart.* It is an act of desire for Seth, not simply an attempt to exert power over Horus. He then attempts to rape Horus who evades penetration and catches Seth's semen in his hands. Horus runs to tell his mother, Isis, who advises him if Seth makes any future overtures to say *it is too painful for me entirely, as you are heavier than me. My strength shall not support your strength* (Parkinson 1995: 71). At the sight of Seth's semen, Isis cuts off the hands of Horus and throws them into the Nile—a form of symbolic castration or dismemberment. This is reiterated in spell 113 from the New Kingdom Book of the Dead. Isis magically replaces his hands and then masturbates Horus until he ejaculates, placing the sperm into a jar. The sperm is placed on Seth's favorite patch of lettuce, which he duly eats the next day, and is thus impregnated.

Later, Horus and Seth appear before the court of gods again to challenge the right to kingship. Seth vocally claims the right since he declares he has done a man's deed to Horus, on which the gods revile the latter. Horus calmly denies the claim and suggests that it is in fact his seed that impregnates Seth. After much arguing, Thoth calls forth the semen of Seth, which is subsequently shown to be in the Nile. No one present seems surprised at the thought of Seth ejaculating into the Nile (perhaps this act could also be read as a doubling of the fertility concept). Thoth then calls forth the semen of Horus, which as a surprise to almost everyone present, emanates from Seth's head as a luminous disc. Since this is deified bodily fluid, and thus sacred, Thoth appropriates the disc, placing it in his own divine crown. The transference of semen from Horus, to Seth, to Thoth is intriguing—a virtual circulation of fluids within the most sacred political economy. Horus successfully claims his place as rightful heir, assuming the place of the father in what must be seen as the original Freudian family. Even leaving aside the incestuous arousal between mother and son, there is the pseudo phallic penetration of Seth by his nephew.

Embedded within various versions of the tale is the suggestion that Horus not only steals Seth's semen but also perhaps emasculates him, so that the real and symbolic are combined. Despite the variations of this myth over time, all retain the overt homosexual element. Horus loses his eye, Seth his testicles—a tacit sort of parallelism: eyes, blindness, semen and testicles are all linked (te Velde 1867: 33–34). In psychoanalytic terms there are strong parallels between eye and sexuality, made famous by writers such as Freud, Lacan and Bataille. Just as Seth's finger thrusts out the eye of Horus, the phallus of Seth attempts to penetrate Horus, and liquid issues from the eye (Bataille 1986: 36). In texts of the Opening of the Mouth and the ritual for Amenhotep I, the bolt is not referred to as a finger, but the phallus, of Seth. Finger and phallus are thus interchangeable. In the ritual of Amenhotep I the offerings are called

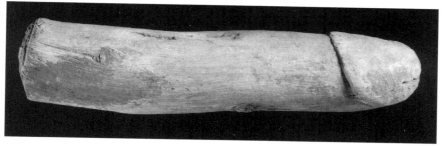

Figure 6.3   Wooden phallus from Deir el Bahri. Courtesy of the Ashmolean Museum, Oxford, 1926.401.

eyes and testicles, harking back to the story of Horus and Seth. By giving them back as offerings, harmony can be restored (te Velde 1967: 49–50). Tears and semen are also parallel: the ejaculate of Atum is often transmuted into the tears of the divine creator. This should not be surprising since the Egyptians thought that semen (or poison) flowed to the head. Other texts attest to the association of rape with afflictions of the eye and head, so that one can construct an economy of fluids and orifices. In a culture dominated by dualism, the asymmetrical power or oneness of the head also paralleled the oneness of the phallus.

Archaeologies of the phallus

Phallic culture inflected various levels of social life in New Kingdom Egypt, from the explanatory narratives of originary myths, to common votive phalloi (Figure 6.3) deposited at local shrines, and satirical papyri parodying sexual acts. The phallus occupied the status of privileged signifier, joining the role of the logos and the advent of human desire. As to why the phallus has such power, Lacan argued it was the most "tangible element in the real of sexual copulation" as well as the most symbolic in the literal sense of the term. By virtue of its turgidity it also serves as the image of vital flow as it is transmitted in generation (Lacan 2001: 318–319). Egyptian phallicism was materialized in the everyday, a salient reminder that sexuality infused many aspects of ordinary life, challenging our notions of the discrete taxonomies and sexual semantics that characterize modern Western culture.

Phallic objects modeled in clay, wood and stone were common votive offerings in the New Kingdom at sites across Egypt at Deir el Bahri, Deir el Medina, Mirgissa, Timna and so on. For prudish reasons the early excavators failed to properly document these finds. However, they collected them nonetheless. Related votive objects defy classification, such as naturally formed, phallic-shaped stones. At Deir el Medina the nineteenth-Dynasty scribe Ramose offered a votive in the form of a stone phallus attached to a plinth dedicated to Hathor in the vicinity of her temple (Pinch 1993: 235). At Deir el Bahri many basket loads of wooden phalloi were found, whereas only three were officially recorded archaeologically. Those many examples now in museums are roughly hewn from acacia wood, approximately 12–20 cm long, and some have traces of red paint. That paint signified potency and ritual power, but also may have indicated the fleshiness of the male member. Many are carved in enough detail to show that they represent circumcised organs, and on one a scrotum was attached. Male figurines have been recorded from the settlement at Memphis (Giddy 1999: 48). One clay example appears to have been wheel-turned, finished by hand and painted red. These objects of material culture, clearly venerating specific aspects of the male body, are votives prepared in service of a female deity, Hathor, goddess of sexuality.

Hathor has many epithets, such as Lady of Drunkenness and Lady of the Vulva. She was also known as the Hand of Atum, literally the one who stimulated the god through masturbation, and was consequently associated with the semen of the sun god. The offering of phallic objects to Hathor relates to overall fertility, whether agricultural or human, and may relate to cures for impotence as well, given Hathor's mythic activities as a sexual stimulator. They may have also functioned as a cure for childlessness: both men and women could have been donors. It seems likely that their donation was linked to specific festivals like the Beautiful Festival of the Wadi, and that they were removed by priests after they had accumulated. At the time of discovery they literally covered the floor (Pinch 1993: 244). Phalloi were offered by a wide cross-section of social strata in Ramesside times, yet there was a fundamental difference between the representations of sexuality in ritual life versus funerary art. Neither displays intercourse in a formal context. Ritual isolates a body part that operates as a multivalent signifier. Displays of sexual organs were probably considered apotropaic. This harks back to the myth of Hathor distracting her father, the god Re, through display of her own genitals. Min and Hathor may have been worshipped as male and female sexually generative gods, so the same sort of offerings would have been appropriate for both. However, it is clear that many more male genitalia were donated than female.

Hathoric imagery pervaded many objects of material culture, specifically those that positioned the female body as a site of spectacle. The most iconic example of that performative spectacle, coupled with the overt display of the phallus, is located within the Turin Papyrus (Figure 6.4). In a series of vignettes on one side of this New Kingdom papyrus, numerous men are shown with outrageously enlarged genitalia, engaged in various performative, acrobatic sexual activities. Similar images of graphic sexual intercourse have been preserved on ostraca and in graffiti. In the West what is sexual is largely what is defined by men, in terms of their own sexuality. Perhaps this is also true of Egyptian culture, and that what we witness as onlookers is almost akin to that of the pharaonic male gaze—without the intrinsic cultural knowledge of erotics. We can approach this only at a base level, by recognizing nudity or gross sexual cues, while much of the imagery's sexual specificity is elided. Sex and sexuality

Figure 6.4 Scenes from the Turin Papyrus, redrawn by Lynn Meskell (see Omlin 1973).

should not be viewed as mutually exclusive categories. In Egypt the situation was far more complex (Derchain 1975), or alternatively, has been far less theorized (Meskell 2000b).

The Turin Papyrus is a striking example of a culturally specific erotic canon. In one section of the papyrus we have a series of sexual encounters performed, and in another, a series of humorous depictions where animals adopt human gestures and roles—where monkeys, lions and donkeys play musical instruments. This unique papyrus depicts a series of sexual encounters between short, aged men and young, hyper-sexualized females. We cannot say whether it is simply a pair of individuals represented in a series of vignettes or a number of people. Some scholars have suggested these scenes represent a brothel, although no material evidence of such a place has come to light, and it is uncertain what one would look like archaeologically. One interpretation posits a satirical slant on a key Egyptian myth: the nightly travels of the sun before the dawning of a new day and its attendant discourses of rebirth and resurrection (Assmann 1993: 35). This is bolstered by the inclusion of the world-turned-upside-down motif so popular with the Egyptians: mice attacking cats, birds attacking cats, mice in chariots led by lions and dogs and so on. Another episode inverts a bed scene—the woman on the bed and the man under it, whereas traditionally it would have been the opposite. Egyptian beds were single rather than double, reinforcing their place as status objects rather than sites of duality and mutuality.

In the parodic sexual scenes, several patterns can be identified (see Meskell 2002: 136–139). First, men are shown with inordinately long penises resulting in a comical bodily imbalance. Sometimes these penises have added red detail signifying potency, ultra-masculinity and the deity Seth. Without respect to the male's stature, short or tall, the penis remains wildly out of

113

proportion. They protrude from beneath each man's kilt, yet none is shown completely naked in the sense with which we are familiar. Perhaps this phallic exposure, clothed but not clothed, was itself considered erotic. Second, the women adopt acrobatic poses in the throes of sexual intercourse, whereas the men do not. Women are depicted bent over, standing on one leg with the other in the air, upside down, over a chariot, and posed against a sloping wall or ladder. A single vignette suggests a woman appears to be taking a dominant sexual role, where she mimics the bodily posture of the sky goddess Nut over the top of her male counterpart. The erect male emulates the god Geb, representing the earth, who literally penetrates the sky. The woman retains her idealized divine body shape, whereas the man is balding. The enormous power of the phallus in this regard is an example where the penis is deployed as the phallus, from an anatomical body part to the locus of power and prowess. In the case of this vignette, it is literally the power of creation and all life stemming from that originary act.

It is possible that erotic genres existed for men, such as the revealed male phallus always hinted at, and obscured by the pleats of the kilt, yet in general the subtleties of Egyptian eroticism elude us. It is likely that the young, muscular, beautiful bodies represented in Egyptian art were enough to be considered sensual by both male and female viewers. Although these inflections are rare, they are reiterated in the form of tales and love songs. In the Chester Beatty Love Songs, a young woman gazes inadvertently upon her lover's body (Fox 1985: 74): *My brother is at the watercourse, his foot planted on the riverbank. He prepares a festival altar for spending the day, with the choicest of the beers. He grants me the hue of his loins. It is longer than broad.* This vision of male bodily perfection, broad, square shoulders, narrow waist and defined musculature in the limbs—the triangular physique—has subsequently become the pinnacle of corporeal desire within modern heterosexual and queer schemas. Egypt arguably offers one of the first canonical formulations for this vision of maleness that was then adopted by neighboring cultures and, through Classical cultures, even embraced in our own contemporary culture.

In contrast to our reading of the male body, there was an explicit erotic semantic which inflected almost all representations of women. While female sexuality was ever present visually, it was not tacitly the subject of discourse, except for the topos of the "dangerous and seductive woman" popular within didactic texts and stories. In contrast, male sexuality seems to be a thing of fascination in mythological and narrative accounts. And unlike the signifier of the phallus within hieroglyphs, the female breast and genitalia do not appear frequently, and the glyph for the female genitalia is usually replaced by a similarly shaped glyph picturing a body of water (Hare 1999: 137).

With few exceptions, Egyptian iconography depicted women at their physical peak. In general, New Kingdom female representations are commensurate with the renderings of the Turin Papyrus. The normativity of female representation across genres prompts us to question the stereotypes of women set forth in commonplace imagery. First, there is no equivalent female voice or gaze to reflect back or give the semblance of equivalence or mutuality. Second, these women bear all the visual cues signifying sexuality or even identification with Hathor herself: lotuses, hip girdles, make-up, kohl jars, musical instruments, convolvulus leaves, *menat* necklaces, and mirrors (Meskell 2002: 136). Women in this construction might thus be construed as interchangeable, lacking the individual contours of personification. Third, these images sexualize and commodify women through their construction as visual subjects. The tobe-looked-at aspect of the female subject is not mirrored by the Egyptian male. She is rendered passive and inactive in all spheres. She is not shown as producing or contributing for the most part, yet she is there to be consumed, visually and erotically. In Freud's formulation of sexual difference, masculinity is associated with individuation, agency and desire while femininity implies passivity, lack and the object of desire (Elliott 1994: 116). Woman occupies the site of spectacle—an object to be viewed and a literal vision of beauty. She is the locus of visual pleasure, sexuality, lure and gaze (de Lauretis 1984: 37). This is well illustrated in the Turin papyrus: a woman, passive and disinterested, applies her make-up, legs astride while underneath her a phallic man holds her thigh and the edge of a vessel that is inserted into her vagina. She seems unperturbed—a passive receptacle in every way.

The papyrus was crafted by a literate man for other men's viewing pleasure, perhaps by one of the scribes at Deir el Medina. It fits well within the schema set out by Bakhtin (1984) to analyze humor and parody in the Renaissance and Middle Ages. His study converges upon the symbolic iconography of the grotesque body and its sexual functions, which finds its ultimate display in sexual intercourse. These representations were in flagrant contradiction to formal Egyptian literary and artistic canons. New Kingdom visual culture was remarkably homogenous, particularly in elite settings such as temples and tombs. In both cultures the body was ideally a finished product where all apertures were closed, and conception, pregnancy, childbirth and intercourse were not appropriate subjects. The papyrus, together with the sexual images on informal ostraca, transgresses formal decorum and the social rules that dictated the boundaries of the body and sexual representation. This is reinforced by the somewhat stylized and fragmentary texts that accompany the illustrations: next to a woman we read, *your phallus is in me, see, you don't bring me a good reputation.*

We should factor in a good deal of visual pleasure for specific viewers, and we can be certain that only educated males could have read the accompanying text, although they may have read them aloud in a performative setting. Part of the pleasure of this text may have been derived from shattering convention and taboo, being able to hold and own this sophisticated satirical piece and unrolling the papyrus slowly to reveal and titillate in a visual striptease. The fundamental substance of psychical life is enjoyment, which is inextricably linked to the notion of lack (Zizek 1991). Fantasy is the very dimension of libidinal enjoyment, spinning off in both pleasurable and painful directions, compensating for the empty space of the self.

Apart from the more explicit renderings of female sexuality already discussed, it is important to recognize that sexuality was pervasive in Egyptian society (Meskell 2000b; 2002). As in many cultures, sexuality did not exist as a separate sphere and there was no word for "sexuality" in Egyptian language. Our classifications of heterosexual or homosexual were not instantiated within Egyptian discourse; there were names for practices rather than people (Parkinson 1995). It is unproductive to hold to Western categories when Egyptian ones were so culturally different and fundamental to a more contextual understanding of social dynamics. Judeo–Christian sentiments might radically erase the connections between religion, ritual practice and sexuality or the possibilities of sexuality in the next life—but the Egyptians lacked such a framework. Various scholars within Egyptology have interpolated fertility, rather than sexuality, into discussions surrounding images of the female body in Egyptian art. In some contexts the two domains are clearly inseparable, such as tomb paintings of specific female kin. Yet they could also operate as exclusive domains of desire, as evidenced in the Turin Papyrus, where sexual pleasure is the primary objective.

Clothing desire

The phallus is something lost and forever out of reach. It is not simply the penis, it is that plus the idea of lack. And the lack points to something beyond itself. As something missing, the phallic object is best represented as something covered or concealed. These tenets are evocatively exhibited in the elaborately clothed male body of elite art and the gendered differences between male and female iconographies. The focus is specifically on the covering and revealing of the genitals and the use of linen as a status signifier to elaborate, reveal or conceal the gendered body. We need to disentangle reality from representation. In reality, the amount of cloth worn was dependent on both the means and status of the wearer. Decoration was enhanced by elaborate pleating, fringing and the assembling of different garment types. For men, there were sash kilts that covered the waist to the knee, as seen in the Theban tomb of Huy. This type of kilt was often worn over more elaborate garments such as a long kilt or bag tunic, so we should envisage a layering of cloth and clothing types for men. Kilts were often worn with loincloths as well. Most garments tended to wrap around the body and fasten at the front, made of a single piece of rectangular fabric. One notable exception to this gendered rule is the representation of field laborers, boatman or workers of a lowly status, whose bodies were not the site of culture or power, but rather closer to the disempowered, overtly sexed bodies of women and children (Meskell 1998b). Representations of these men can be found in the lower registers of various New Kingdom Theban tombs belonging to elite men, such as the sculptor

Ipy: they belong in the frame so as to detail daily life and to outline the social hierarchies of the day, for those who were served and those who performed the service.

Gender identity is formed through a privileging of the visible, of having or not having the phallus. Males are able to assume phallic privilege since the image of the penis comes to stand for sexual difference. Lacan argued that the phallic signifier was chosen because it was the most tangible aspect of sexual intercourse and salient image of the vital flow transmitted in generation. Thus masculinity is constituted as phallic and femininity as non-phallic. Masculinity, constructed around the sign of the phallus, ultimately confers power, whereas femininity is constructed through exclusion from the symbolic realm of power. Importantly for the Egyptian context, Lacan suggested that femininity exists outside of language (excluded from the value of words), culture, reason, and power (Elliott 1994: 132).

These gendered characteristics of visibility become apparent when one compares, for example, the numerous relief scenes of Akhenaten and Nefertiti. Nefertiti's pleated garments expose her genital

Figure 6.5 Wooden statue of an official with elaborate pleated clothing. Dated to the later part of the eighteenth Dynasty. H. 29.2 cm. Courtesy of the British Museum, EA 2320 (Robins 1997a: 142).

region to view, whereas Akhenaten's are covered in layers, even if the artist tries to achieve the effect of transparency. Linen was usually rendered white in the tomb scenes, but in the eighteenth Dynasty there is a tradition of darkening the linen in areas, usually coupled with pleating, as in the tombs of Menna and Nebamun, that together could suggest an overlaying of fabric. In representational terms, men were traditionally depicted wearing billowing and heavily pleated garments on their monuments, stelae and pyramidia, such as the pyramidion of Ramose or on the tombs' walls, such as those of Sennedjem. As

the nineteenth Dynasty progressed the male costume became more ostenta-
tious with excessive pleating, with male skirts becoming more triangular, volu-
minous and unrealistic (Figure 6.5). And while Egyptologists have noted the
stylistic changes there has been little comment on the significance or salience of
this obvious gendered difference. Representationally, these garments successfully concealed the phallus while drawing significant attention to it as a site of
power.

Representing elite men entailed complete coverage of the genital area,
whereas it was the reverse for female subjects. To prevent rendering the
male tunic transparent, additional skirts and kilts are often worn in
conjunction, so as to render the entire genital area opaque. This is well
illustrated in the Theban tombs of Userhat, Menna, Sennefer or Nakht. In
the tomb of Rekhmire the owner is shown wearing a long kilt denoting his
rank, extending from the armpits to the ankles, covering his entire body
(Vogelsang-Eastwood 1993: 60). More commonly, various garments were
simply depicted as overlapped, tunics, kilts and sashes, as in the tomb of
Sennefer. He also wears heavy and elaborate gold jewelry, a double-heart
amulet, gold bracelets and large earrings. His wife, on the other hand,
wears faience equivalents, rather smaller and less obtrusive. Despite the
frequency of touching gestures, she assumes the subordinate role. Both are
youthful and in perfect physical condition, yet in several scenes Sennefer is
shown at least twice the size of his wife, Meryt. In one she sits on a platform
at his knee embracing his lower leg. In another she is seated on a much
smaller chair also at knee height to her husband. Again his bodily adornment overshadows hers. In a third scene she is shown presenting Sennefer
with a tray of elaborate jewelry with amuletic associations, each made of
gold and precious stones. In another she offers him unguent, a lotus collar
and flowers.

Women's clothing as literally uncovered in the archaeological record
proves to be rather different from the iconographic tradition. Most women
probably wore wrap-around dresses, loosely wrapped twice around the body
with an open end of cloth placed to one side, allowing sufficient material for
moving. More complicated wrap-around dresses were also worn, with a
variety of different methods for tying. There was also a bag tunic, a long
version worn by men and women, and a shorter version reserved for men.
Numerous examples of these clothes have been found in settlement sites
(Deir el Medina, Amarna) and in tomb contexts (Deir el Medina, Valley of
the Kings, Kahun). Clearly, these styles would have covered the body, yet
the tendency in artistic representations is to reveal some measure of the body
underneath. For women of all ranks and ages through Egyptian times the
sheath dress was worn, described as a tube of material being fastened at one
shoulder. No such examples have been found archaeologically. They would
have been almost impossible to wear or move around in and it would have
been impossible to conduct the sorts of bodily postures and movements

portrayed in the tomb paintings in such a garment (Vogelsang-Eastwood 1993: 160).

Representational schemas in Egypt privileged the clothed male body, arrayed with significations of status and power, while deprivileging the overtly sexualized and revealed female body. While psychoanalysis suggests that sex makes a difference to the kind of body image and subjectivity available for the subject, this difference is explained in terms of a binary structure (active:passive, presence:absence) that always cedes power and primacy to the phallus and male sexuality (Grosz 1995: 36). Since there was no autonomous representation of women in Egypt, and no self-representation by female artisans, they were denied a position congruent with, or independent of, men. In our own culture we recognize that such a disparity demands a new use of language, new representation and new forms of knowledge capable of articulating femininity and women's specificity in ways different from those of the past. Egypt was one of the earliest cultures to represent and thus materialize these corporeal inequities, ultimately reinforcing social difference in the real. It is important that scholars recognize the temporal limits of these constructions and the grounding of contemporary body politics in an ancient past. A presentist approach to gender difference elides the origins and longevity of phallic culture and the pervasiveness of an Egyptian imaginary.

Bodies, beauty and desire among the Classic Maya

Scholarly views of Classic Maya sexuality are remarkably uniform, whether we consider studies from the first half of the twentieth century or those of the new millennium. The public monumental art that dominates the visual and textual record for the Maya is characterized by decorous bodies, typically with tightly controlled expression of emotion (Houston 2001). As Andrea Stone (1995: 194–197) has noted, uncommon, overtly sexualized images painted on the walls of the caves of Naj Tunich are characterized by extreme violations of the canons of representation of the body in monumental art (Figure 6.6). An ejaculating figure squats in an awkward three-quarters frontal pose, face shown in unusual frontal or three-quarters view. Another stands with shoulders twisted at an angle, face peering back over the shoulder. These unusual images stand in stark contrast to the assumed ideals of Classic Maya society.

A long tradition links Tozzer's (1957: 111) claim that phallic images were elements introduced by invading foreigners with Houston's (2001: 213) statement that the Classic Maya "found the display of genitalia repugnant or distasteful." At first glance, the apparent suppression of sexuality in Classic Maya art contrasts markedly with Egyptian materials. But this characterization belies the homoerotics of much of Classic Maya visual representation, in which the bodies of athletic young men are on display for an audience that often is pictured as a single, politically dominant, male (Joyce 2000d). The imagery of

119

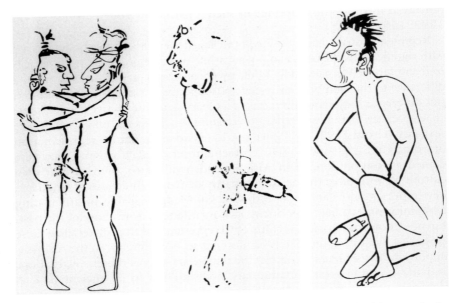

Figure 6.6 Classic Maya cave drawings of sexual encounters. Naj Tunich petroglyphs 17, 18, and 20 from *Images of the Underworld: Naj Tunich and the Tradition of Maya Cave Painting* by Andrea J. Stone, © 1995. By permission of University of Texas Press.

ballgame playing, dancing, and warfare that predominates in courtly art provides a basis to explore the visual representation of young men's bodies as pleasing to other men. Tracing erotics of the male body suggests that phallicism was in fact by no means foreign or distasteful to the Classic Maya.

As many scholars have noted, the majority of the figures depicted in Classic Maya monumental art can be identified as males. When figures identified in texts as women are depicted, their bodies are draped in clothing that reduces bodily contrast with male figures, with whom they share gestural language, hair treatment, and body ornamentation (Joyce 1996, 1999). The concealed bodies of women contrast remarkably with the bodies of the male figures who dominate in Classic Maya pictorial images.

A striking image from Yaxchilan (see Figure 2.11) underscores the contrast. Here, the focal figure, indicated by the frontal position of the body, is the woman kneeling on the right. The head and hands that emerge from her draped brocaded garment and beaded collar and cuffs are the only traces of her body visible in the image. Even her hair is tightly bound into a tail pressed against the back of her head and shoulder. The male figure facing her, depicted in profile on the left, has an astonishingly exposed body by contrast. The belt and loincloth he wears leave his legs exposed to the hip, with beaded ornaments below the knee drawing attention to the curve of

120

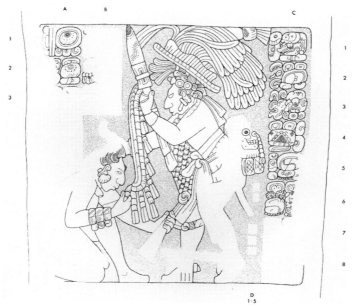

Figure 6.7   Classic Maya male lord gazing down toward a noble man he has captured. Yaxchilan lintel 45. Courtesy of Corpus of Maya Hieroglyphic Inscriptions, Peabody Museum, Harvard University.

thigh and calf. A cloth cape draped over his shoulder allows an expanse of chest and most of the arm to be visible. The opposite arm, turned so the inside faces the viewer, is even more exposed, with only a cuff of beads at the wrist breaking the line of the flesh. His hair is loosely bound with a headband, pulled up at the crown of the head into an unruly topknot emphasized by a sheaf of feathers. The careful delineation of the toes and side of the foot enclosed in jaguar-skin sandals reinforces the fleshiness of the male figure, when contrasted with the concealed body of the woman he faces.

The male body exposed in Classic Maya images is most typically juxtaposed with other males in multi-figure scenes from which even cloaked women are absent. In monumental art, such multi-figure scenes are often those of captors and prisoners. While captives may be depicted almost nude, stripped of most body ornaments, they are depicted as carefully and sensuously as their captors. The latter often share with the captives who kneel before them a body left exposed by minimal clothing, despite much richer ornamentation. On a monument from Yaxchilan (Figure 6.7), the captor standing on the right grasps the hair of the kneeling captive in a gesture of domination. The captive touches the trim hanging from the captor's shield in one hand, and the knotted cloth strip at the bottom of the captor's cotton "armor" with the other. The two bodies are interlocked, connected by the bodily prostheses,

121

Figure 6.8 Classic Maya battle scene. Bonampak mural showing idealized battle scene in which elaborately costumed male warriors engage in hand-to-hand combat. Painted on the wall opposite the doorway of a room located on a raised platform, most likely a reception hall like those represented on contemporary pottery vessels. Photograph N26979 by Hillel Burger, detail of copy painted by Antonio Tejeda, object cat. no: 48–63–20/17560. Courtesy of Peabody Museum, Harvard University, © President and Fellows of Harvard College.

Figure 6.9 Classic Maya titles of a Late Classic ruler of Copan, Honduras, with penis title at the extreme right.

shield and armor, that prepared the captor for participation in warfare. The prisoner in fact is named (as are other prisoners) as the captor's *b'ak* ("bone") marking the captured male as an extension of the captor's hard bodily substance.

In battle scenes painted on polychrome vases, which mirror the extraordinary mural preserved inside a building at Bonampak (Figure 6.8), body contact between captors and captives is accompanied by connections mediated by the ultimate military prosthesis, the long spear, determinative of battle in both pictorial images and texts (Schele and Miller 1986: 209–221). In the narrative sequence presented in the murals of Bonampak, blood flowing from the wounds on captives' bodies prefigures the blood the captors produce by piercing the penis in post-battle rituals. This linkage would have been underwritten for a Classic Maya viewer by the knowledge that the word for young man, *xib*, like the warriors shown in battle, was also the word for penis (Bricker 1992).

In texts, *xib* is represented by a pictograph of a penis and testicles. The same visual elements formed the core of a title displayed in the inscriptions of many of the rulers of Classic Maya sites (Figure 6.9). Far from suggesting that the display of the penis was distasteful, these textual references underscore an implicit phallicism with which much Classic Maya visual imagery played (Joyce 1999, 2000d). The clothing that covered male genitals worked to draw attention to them as much as to deflect attention from them.

The single item of costume routinely depicted on the near-nude bodies of male figures is a loincloth distinguished by a long frontal apron. Ornaments added to the basic loincloth emphasize its status as a metonymic reference to the male genitalia it covers. The most formalized ornaments consist of a belt with a central mask with three pendants in the form of axe blades, like the blades of axes shown in decapitation scenes (Joyce 1999). Markings on the loincloth and ornaments along its sides identify the loincloth with the world tree, the *axis mundi*, at the center of the Maya image of the cosmos (Schele and Miller 1986: 77).

This conflated representation of a decapitated head (mask) at the top of the world tree (loincloth) recalls a Maya tale, recorded after the Spanish conquest, of Hero Twins who were decapitated after losing a game against the lords of death (Tedlock 1985). In this story, the head of one of the twins, placed in a tree in the underworld, spits on the daughter of a death god, impregnating her. While the text that has survived in full dates at least 800 years later, images in Classic Maya art suggest that there were earlier versions of such tales in circulation (Reents-Budet 1994: 275–278; compare Coe 1997). The personification of the penis as a headless manikin (or a manikin with a penis instead of a head) in variants of the written sign for *xib* makes explicit the underlying identification of the penis and the head in unambiguous Classic contexts (Closs 1988). For a Classic Maya audience versed in early versions of stories of Hero Twins in the Underworld, the presence of an effigy of a decapitated

Figure 6.10 Classic Maya male figure piercing penis with bone awl, Yaxchilan lintel 17. Courtesy of Corpus of Maya Hieroglyphic Inscriptions, Peabody Museum, Harvard University.

head, located at the groin, above an image of a cosmic axial tree, would have echoed the identification of the male penis covered by the loincloth with the still potent skull of the deceased mythic hero.

The equation of spittle and semen implicit in the identification of the penis as a decapitated head is suggestive, in light of bloodletting practices recorded for Classic Maya men and women. Male bloodletting appears to have preferentially been embodied in the perforation of the penis (Thompson 1961; Joralemon 1974; Schele and Miller 1986). The corresponding practice for women was the perforation of the tongue—an action that identified the woman's tongue with the male penis (as noted by Joshua Bell in an unpublished paper). Visual images of male and female bloodletting emphasize these correspondences. A lintel from Yaxchilan (Figure 6.10) shows a male figure, seated holding a pointed bone awl directed towards his groin. To his left, a kneeling female figure draws a rope through a hole in her protruding tongue. Students introduced to this image, confused by the visual imagery, have been known to identify the action as fellatio, because of the way the female and male bodies are juxtaposed. While this identification itself is literally erroneous, it recognizes a potential in the pose that links the male sexual organs and the female mouth or head.

124

This association is more generally evident in other images showing female figures engaged in drawing ropes through a perforated tongue. In such images, the woman kneels in front of a standing male (see Figure 2.11). The gaze of the female figure is routinely directed toward the male groin. Andrea Stone (1988) argued that such images represented sexualized postures of submission. The visual relations in these unusual images of males and females together underline the fact that in Classic Maya art more generally, the bodies of young males are presented as objects for the gaze of other, centrally posed, male figures within the picture plane, and of male and female viewers of these works (Joyce 2000d, 2002).

In monumental art, the visual engagement of male viewers with a visually surveyed male body is clearly illustrated by the abundant imagery of captors and their captives. Similar scenes are featured in the multi-figure compositions painted on polychrome vases, made and used in the palaces of ruling and non-ruling nobles. Polychrome vases foreground the experience of vision itself. Because cylinder vases wrap continuous scenes around the exterior of the vase, they allow isolation of a focal figure, often presented in frontal view, seated on a raised platform or throne (see Figure 3.11). Within the image, the focal person gazes at other figures, grouped together on the remainder of the pot, standing on lower terraces or groundlines. Each face of a cylinder frames different groups of figures. Often, the additional figures form all-male groups engaged in vigorous action. They play ball games, leaning with one knee on the ground as they brace to return the bouncing rubber ball to other young males. The male figures take part in battles or dance-dramas re-enacting battles, leaning over to capture prisoners, turning towards each other.

The bodies displayed in such scenes are doubly the focus of the gaze of others: both of focal figures, usually male, in the painted scene, and of the patrons and users of the vases themselves. Many painted vessels display scenes of the kind of court life in which painted pottery vessels were used, including images of painted vessels resting near enthroned males (Reents-Budet 1994). Such vessels served as a kind of exemplary mirror for the experience of life in palaces, reflecting back to those who used them the idealized relations among actors who were primarily male.

The dances, battles, and ball games engaged in by all-male groups painted on polychrome pots were the occupations of youths who lived together in young men's houses in Maya cities at the time of the Spanish conquest (Joyce 2000d). In multiple late Classic sites in the northwest Maya lowlands, buildings that can be identified as possible young men's houses share imagery of dancing and ball-playing. Many of these buildings are distinguished by phallic ornamentation, including three-dimensional sculptures of erect phalli up to 3 meters long (Figure 6.11). As part of their experience, groups of young men living together in such spaces were engaged in testing the limits of their physical skill. They did so in the presence of glorified images of youthful male potency.

The absence of women in such all-male scenes records a homosocial

Figure 6.11 Classic Maya monumental sculpture of phallus. Miscellaneous Sculpture 1, Acanmul. Photograph 40–9–277. Carnegie Institution of Washington, object cat. no: 58–34–20/72680. Courtesy of Peabody Museum, Harvard University, © President and Fellows of Harvard College.

environment, if not explicit same-sex desire. The presence of male viewers watching the groups of youthful active males on many vases, and the implied gaze of the male owners of such vases, suggests that same-sex admiration, at a minimum, was part of courtly life. A polychrome vase shows on one face a frontal ruler seated on a raised throne, his eyes directed to his right. The apparent focus of his gaze is a scene in which two young men are engaged in penis perforation, a common male group activity on other pottery vessels (Thompson 1961; Joralemon 1974). Andrea Stone (1995: 143–146) has identified the sole erotic scene from Naj Tunich cave involving two figures as likely an image of male–male sex. Coupled with the absence of images of sexual relations between young males and females, the predominance of homosociality and same-sex visual relations suggests the likelihood that the experience of young men was one of sexualized admiration for their male peers.

At the same time, where female figures are depicted in monumental art, they also exhibit the same visual orientation toward the exposed bodies of youthful males as objects of admiration and arguably of desire (Joyce 2002). Reciprocal sexualization of the female body in monumental art is absent, or extremely uncommon. Houston (2001) reports an unpublished monument from Tonina depicting a naked woman engaged in some form of sexual encounter, which he interprets as a rape following a military victory. While a sexual act, such a violation would represent an act of aggression, not an instance of desire.

Small-scale representations of female bodies, especially in the form of three-dimensional figurines, routinely depict more explicit bodily sexual characteristics that are covered up in monumental art. But here again the exposure of the female body may be less concerned with sexuality than other embodied experiences (Joyce 1993, 2001b, 2002). The majority of the attention given to the female body in small-scale figurines and pottery vessels is lavished on careful depictions of breasts. These often support suckling infants (see Figure 3.5), suggesting that an alternative bodily experience—that of the connection of mothers and children—would have been the context for the original viewing audience.

The most commonly accepted erotic images involving females are in fact images in which an elderly male or an animal reaches out to touch an exposed female breast (see Figure 3.4). There is a long tradition in Maya studies of characterizing the female figures in such compositions as lewd goddesses (e.g. Schele and Miller 1986: 143–144; Taube 1989b: 367–371; Schele 1997: 53–55). These characterizations rely on a variety of indirect arguments, including identification of the persons depicted with characters in much later myths, and characterizations of cross-species sexuality as "bestiality."

The specific characteristics of these images suggest that the onus is not on the female, whose pose is usually as serene as in the least erotic of monumental images. Instead, it is the male figures who are depicted in ways that divorce them from the apparently desireable image of decorum. Male animals in these scenes may display an exposed erect penis. The elderly males are depicted as wrinkled, pot-bellied, and bald—the inverse of the characteristics of the youthful idealized male body. These male figures might best be identified as burlesques (Taube 1989b)—figures of fun that police the boundary of acceptable action by male subjects (Joyce 2002).

It is unlikely to be an accident that these marginal figures invoke animal hybridity—a boundary of embodied being that we have encountered in other aspects of Classic Maya personhood. The permeability of embodiment that the fluidity of blood, semen, tears, and other effluvia mark so strongly in the texts available for New Kingdom Egypt, unequalled by any extant Classic Maya sources, is most clearly indicated in Maya visual culture by the representation of the exteriorization of the part of the self represented in animal form, the *way* or co-essence. The fluid boundary of the self is also, paradoxically, indicated archaeologically by the transformation in death of some body parts and bodily prostheses into objects that persist through time and so extend embodied being beyond the limits of the skin and the skin ego. The transformation of subject to object traces another of the unstable frontiers of the ancient self in both New Kingdom Egypt and Classic Maya cultures.

7

SUBJECT TO OBJECT

Transubstantiated bodies

Textually and archaeologically, we can apprehend constructions of the embodied Egyptian self through the material world. In the New Kingdom, images and objects operated as personal biographies for the individual and through mimetic processes. Individuals could be represented or doubled through statuary, images and wall paintings. Mimesis can be read here as the nature that culture uses to create second nature, in this case the living body. This second nature is foundering and highly unstable, spiraling between nature and culture, essentialism and constructionism, forging new identities and offering dramatic new possibilities (Taussig 1993: 252).

An evocative example of this creation of a second nature is the Egyptian practice of mummification, in itself a type of transubstantiation. The dead individual represented an Osiris—a dead, but deified, being capable of being reborn in the next world. In corporeal terms, the body of the living subject, through a series of bodily processes, becomes an object—at the nexus between the living world and the next, a type of artefact in and of itself.

The mummy has always held a rather liminal status, in pharaonic and contemporary culture. It exists as the physical remains of a human being while being transformed by technology into an/other sort of product. The body in death and its partibility is a major focus—explicitly, how bodily organs acted metonymically for the entire person. In death, the body was a plastic entity that had to be manipulated before its successful entry into the next world. The bodily self and the existence of the person were inseparably tied together. Destruction of the body meant a double death. The unique characteristics of the individual and his/her narrative biography also persisted beyond death.

Subject to object

The specificities of the Egyptian climatic setting ensured heightened preservation of the physical body. Under ordinary circumstances the hot, dry sand was enough to retain a lifelike integrity and appearance of the body, evidenced by various Predynastic burials. This set of natural factors undoubtedly influenced perceptions of the possibilities for the embodied self in death and the potentials of a certain personal trajectory. Central to this ideology was an obsession with preserving the living body through and beyond the zone of death, coupled with an attendant dread of physical decay.

Decomposition of the corpse is a source of anxiety that lies at the heart of many cultures, past and present. Hence the materiality of the dead must be manipulated and made perfect in appearance. In Egyptian language, bodily decay was referred to as *transitoriness, to consume, to dry up, to perish, to become maggoty, to go bad, to flow away*, and *to smell* (Zandee 1960: 56–60). Decomposition and decay void the corpse of its signs and its social force of signification. It de-personifies the individual, leaving it as nothing more than a substance. For the community, the process reinforces the fragility of life and the existential terror of its own symbolic decomposition. One interpretation posits that the Egyptians sought to deny or defeat death through artificiality. Through elaborate bodily rituals and preparations the elite sought to evade the unbearable moment when flesh becomes nothing but flesh, and ceases to be part of the embodied whole.

The decayed body was an abject sign of mortality in this world and subsequently the afterlife, and of the non-divine status of the individual. Through time-consuming practices of enculturation the "natural" body with its biological realities had to be transcended through mummification and sarcophagic practices (Baudrillard 1993: 180), resulting in a very specific form of transubstantiation. But this is not the "body as artefact," so prevalent in the archaeological theorizing of British prehistorians: in an Egyptian context the body becomes objectified and transmuted into the divine. The former approach diminishes human agency and intentionality in the process of death and transformation, reducing the body to a system of signs. The latter extends being and potential embodiment.

Death and its attendant rituals were anchored in physicality. They were not simply contingent upon arcane ritual practices that inhabited the ethereal or otherworldly. Mummification was tantamount to preservation of the body through its violation. The human body was never considered naturally divine and thus required substantive modification or construction. Egyptian mummies aspired to a perfectly preserved (and embellished) image of the deceased, transmuting the body into a simulacrum of itself. The transubstantiated body *was* the person, the self, and yet only a remnant of its earthly being. At the point of death, the motionless body becomes a thing, now deprived of the capabilities of living individuals: *the eye is blind, the ear is deaf*. Magical spells were required to explicitly bring those functions back to the corpse, to make the dead body akin to its living counterpart. A series of oppositional spells invoke the tensions of sensual life compared to the rigidity and perishability of the dead body.

While the mummy—material, visible—bore the trace of the individual, and preserved the identity, it was scarcely readable (Derrida 1987: 43). It was not a matter of continuing the life-like body, the original subject, but of transforming it into another sort of object altogether. It was eternally self-referential, yet only a trace, a trace soon to be lost, at the interstices of subject and object. To paraphrase Thomas Mann's (1978: 510) description of Egypt "… your dead are gods and your gods dead." But immortality was progressive, passing from limited to eternal survival. Immortality was also democratized. In the New Kingdom the possibilities for the afterlife were extended to more non-elite individuals than in preceding dynasties—another reason why this book focuses on this specific period of history.

The materiality of death

Our information about pharaonic mummification largely derives from post-New Kingdom documents, since it may have been taboo to record such transformative practices throughout the pharaonic period. Herodotus wrote about mummification in its extreme form: the brain was removed through nostrils, an abdominal incision was made and the cavity cleaned, washed, and filled with aromatic substances. Removal of the brain by breaking the ethmoid bone and employing a long metal tool that liquefied the brain became a popular practice for elite individuals in the eighteenth Dynasty. The body was held upright to allow the fluid to drain out of the nose. Alternatively, it could be removed through the eye socket (Taylor 2001: 53).

Ideally, the body was placed in natron and covered for seventy days. Natron is a known drying agent. Frankincense was employed to anoint, perfume and conceal the smells of bodily degradation. Following this period of transformative stasis the body was washed, linen strips were cut and prepared with gum, and the transformed body was then wrapped. Alternative practices were possible in the New Kingdom. Specific wealthy families chose not to have their kin eviscerated. Some opted for simple wrapping of the body that further retained its lifelike qualities (Meskell 1999b). Some measures involved keeping the internal organs intact; others dissolved them.

Another strategy involved inserting cedar or juniper oil into the body through the anus and then preparing the body in natron (Ikram and Dodson 1998: 104). Afterwards, the oil was drained and the dissolved internal organs left the structural integrity of the body intact. Flesh and bone retained the lifelike quality of the person in death, while the removal of the intestines guaranteed its preservation in the face of natural decay. Spell 154 from the Book of the Dead attempted to stave off decomposition and is inflected with carnal sensuousness (Faulkner 1985: 153):

> *Such is he who is decayed; all his bones are corrupt, his flesh is slain, his bones are softened, his flesh is made into foul water, his corruption stinks*

and turns into many worms ... who kills the body, who rots the hidden one, who destroys a multitude of corpses, who lives by killing the living ... You shall posses your body; you shall not become corrupt, you shall not have worms, you shall not be distended, you shall not stink, you shall not become putrid ... I will not become worms, I have not decayed, there is no destruction in my viscera, I have not been injured, my eye has not rotted, my skull has not been crushed, my ears are not deaf, my head has not removed itself from my neck, my tongue has not been taken away, my hair has not been cut off, my eyebrows have not been stripped, no injury has happened to me. My corpse is permanent, it will not perish nor be destroyed in this land forever.

Apart from the elaborate fabrication of the body there was an explicit concern to render the borders of the body impermeable and to safeguard the dangerous zones that exposed the individual to external supernatural threat. The cranium, nostrils, ears, and occasionally the anus were coated with resin and, for wealthier individuals, the abdominal incision was covered by a piece of metal, sometimes gold, and in some cases the opening was sutured. Priests and embalmers actively sealed all bodily orifices and inevitably made the body whole again after the violation of evisceration.

The final product was a newly crafted corporeality, hermetically sealed, free from imperfections, orifices, openings or fissures that might allow demonic forces to seep into the body and thus, the self. Following Kristeva (1982: 102), the body must bear no trace of its nature in the realm of death: it must be clean and proper in order to be fully symbolic. To confirm its otherwordly status, it should be presented as free from earthly disfigurement where even the mark of the embalmer is masked. Only that of circumcision can be celebrated. Any other mark would be the sign of belonging to the impure, the non-separate, the non-symbolic, and the non-holy.

According to later accounts by Diodorus the embalmer responsible for the visceral incision traditionally ran away while being abused and stoned by his fellow workers, perhaps as a means of magical aversion of the negative repercussions of violating the body that the Egyptians still considered anathema (Taylor 2001: 54–55). It was a necessary, yet abhorrent duty enacted at the most dangerous and liminal point of the lifecycle. Egyptologists have suggested that the embalming tent, often referred to as the place of rejuvenation, was placed adjacent to the tomb's opening (Frandsen 1992), sometimes designated as a door. The place of embalming literally functioned as a portal between one state of existence and another.

While many cultural practices were instantiated to deflect the force of death, the difficulty lay in reconciling the abhorrence of bodily intervention with the explicit requirements of fabricating a new type of body through artificial means. The numerous spells for bodily integrity in the Book of the Dead

(Faulkner 1985: 64) attest to this inherent tension between a desired divinity and the visceral phenomenology of putrefaction:

> *Spell for not putrefying in the realm of the dead*
> *Weary, weary are all the members of Osiris!*
> *They shall not be weary, they shall not putrefy, they shall not decay, they*
> *   shall not swell up!*
> *May it be done to me in like manner, for I am an Osiris.*

While the Egyptian body was partible and its very fragmentation was a necessary prerequisite for wholeness, some body parts were privileged sites—a form of gestalt for the individual. Most importantly, it was crucial to keep the heart within the body, although sometimes it became loosened through the process of removing the viscera. In dire circumstances substitute hearts could be placed within the body's cavity. Wrapping the heart separately, as a mimetic copy of the individual, was also a powerful practice.

The embalmed viscera sometimes took on the visual likeness of the human mummy. They were deposited in the canopic jars or *jars of embalming* that possessed the zoomorphic heads of deities known as the *sons of Horus* who kept the internal organs preserved in perpetuity. As simulacra of the dead person the canopic jars could act as substitutes for the body itself—another example of the Egyptian predilection for mimesis and doubling. The canine Daumtutef held the stomach, the baboon god Hapy kept the lungs, the falcon deity Qebehsenuef guarded the intestines and the human-headed Imsety, the liver.

In elite burials fragments of skin or organs that were separated from the body were treated and wrapped in the same way as the intact body, suggesting that all flesh denoted an embodied constituent of the person. These body products were buried near the tomb. This practice might explain an enigmatic object known as the *tekenu*—an amorphous bundle with a human head, which is represented with the coffin and canopic jars in the tomb procession (Taylor 2001: 63). Even the implements that had close contact with the body of the individual were ritually important and integral to the burial. This accords with evidence from baby burials at Deir el Medina: here placentas (known to represent the twin self and a powerful spiritual force), viscera, bodily residues, fabrics covered with blood, and flints used in cutting the umbilicus were buried alongside fetuses, neonates, and infants (Meskell 1994).

In Egypt, notions of death operated within both monistic and dualistic ideologies simultaneously. The monist perspective regarded death as a necessary condition for eternal existence whereas a dualistic one recognized death as the enemy of life and something to be feared. The first is based on religious reflection, the second grounded in the materiality of death and personal experience of the natural world. The Egyptians freely wrote about their fears of existential loss and bodily disintegration. Death was described as a robber and an enemy. It could also be likened to horror, an affliction and sleep (Zandee 1960).

Techniques of the body in New Kingdom culture, both in living and mortuary spheres, were elaborate, with a great measure of overlap between the two domains. In death the corporeal presence of the person had to resemble the ideal living state, devoid of all physical shortcomings or effects of aging. Missing limbs could be substituted and numerous prostheses have survived. Extreme care was taken to give the body a lifelike appearance even after bodily damage or loss of parts, using wood and other artificial substances. Other individual imperfections could be addressed through cosmetic procedures. Balding could be remedied by interweaving additional hair, hair and nails could be hennaed, black detail could be used for hairlines and eyebrows. Pieces of linen with eyes drawn upon them were placed over the eyes, since the eyes desiccate very quickly during mummification. Onions could also be used over the eyes, as well as in the ears and nostrils, possibly because of their shape, their disinfectant properties or because they were believed to stimulate the deceased to breathe in the next life (Ikram and Dodson 1998: 121).

Wrapping the body in linen also secured its completeness. Linen wrapping provided the body with a type of all-over amuletic protection. Linen was also extremely expensive and signified status and prosperity in this world and the next. While linen was necessary for preserving the body, the dead nonetheless desired to free themselves from their bandages as reiterated by numerous spells: *cloths unfolded, ties loosened, bandages opened.* Mummies in the eighteenth Dynasty were wrapped in numerous layers of linen and full shrouds, with their extremities wrapped separately before enveloping the body entirely. From New Kingdom times onwards, special wrappings were made, rather than using cast-off cloth and garments, although poorer people would have still employed these more inexpensive materials. Decorated shrouds were also utilized at this time and draped over the coffin, sometimes reproducing the perfected likeness of the deceased, as in the case of Sennefer (Meskell 1999a). In the twenty-first Dynasty, mummification techniques were further refined with a focus on re-fleshing the mummy with artificial substances and painting it to look lifelike, countering the earlier preoccupation with dehydrating the body. Embalmers were known to have restored the royal mummies of earlier generations. However, it is unlikely that such reverence was extended to ordinary people.

Wrapping, in the sense of making hidden, was perhaps considered a sacred act in itself, bestowing a mystery and sanctity to the body. The actual process of embalming and wrapping was undoubtedly considered a low-status occupation in itself. Great pains were taken to wrap the penis separately and to make false genitals if they were in any way damaged or lost as might occur when tombs were violated. In the case of Tutankhamun, the penis was bound separately and the scrotum was flattened against the perineum.

Amongst the dense layers of amuletic linen were placed real amulets, worn by living and dead alike, usually inscribed with protective spells. The body of

Tutankhamun revealed in excess of 140 amulets strewn throughout his linen wrappings. Amulets in the form of papyrus stalks and those made of faience or green stone symbolized regeneration and fertility. A headrest amulet, *wrs*, was placed under the head so as to prevent its loss or theft. Spell 43 from the Book of the Dead states (Lichtheim 1976: 121): *The head of Osiris shall not be taken from him, my head shall not be taken from me! I am risen, renewed, refreshed.*

Objects of material culture, even small mass-produced ones, were thought to have eternal efficacy, much like the power of crosses, effigies of the saints and rosary beads in Christian practice and belief. Performative aspects were central to the passage between worlds. During the wrapping of specific limbs a priest would recite spells of reanimation for the next life. This represented one of the most potent and powerful moments in the bodily transformation. A vigil was probably held while the body was being mummified, and various rituals were performed to enhance the person's forthcoming travels through the netherworld journey. This too may have operated as a safeguard against the deceased using his transfigured power malevolently against the living, especially relatives. For the elite, the body was transferred to the tomb on a sled drawn by oxen in a solemn funerary procession. The son would perform the necessary rituals. Mourners followed, usually portrayed in the scenes as women, gesticulating and wailing, wrenching their garments and heaping earth upon their heads. Their hair is loose and wild, mimicking the chaotic and emotional state of their bereavement and loss.

External treatments were just as important as physical ones. There was a clear focus upon visual display, elaboration and radiant perfection. Coffins (Figure 7.1), masks and cartonnage were mimetic doubles for the self that promised to persist beyond the realm of bodily death with its ever-present threat of decay. Elite funerary masks used gold foil and inlay, as in the case of a woman named Satdjhuty (Figure 7.2). The black background of the coffin was symbolic of resurrection, whereas the gold leaf represented the golden flesh of the gods— something ordinary individuals desired to attain. Since gold never corrodes it carries the double promise that the fleshed body remains incorruptible after death (Robins 1997a: 146), while the feathered motif signifies the protective role of Isis and other deities. The woman Satdjhuty was undoubtedly of high status and was probably in the service of queen Ahmose Nefertari (Russmann 2001: 204). The funerary mask conferred a divine status on the deceased, and specific facial features of the mask were associated with divine beings, alluding to the deceased's link to Osiris and Ra. Thus the whole construction bestowed upon the individual possibilities for rebirth.

In the New Kingdom open-work mummy boards feature cut-out deities, and additional bands were sewn onto the wrappings, so that the mummy itself came to mimic the external appearance of the coffin, doubling and re-doubling the image of the individual. Open-work cartonnage became more elaborate to match the intricate decoration of multiple coffins. The whole assemblage was covered in flowers and wreaths, as we see at Deir el Medina and in the Valley

Figure 7.1
Inner gilded coffin of the Theban priestess Henutmehyt, nineteenth Dynasty, from Thebes. H. 188cm. Courtesy of the British Museum, EA 48001.

Figure 7.2
Funerary mask of Satdjuty, an elite woman probably from Thebes. Painted cartonnage with gold leaf. H. 52cm. Dated to the early part of the eighteenth Dynasty. Courtesy of the British Museum, EA 29770.

of the Kings. With these flowers and wreaths come all the associations of communing with the gods, of divine smells and their regenerative force.

The coffin, as a material object, harks back to the myth of Osiris. Seth discovered the exact measurements of his brother, made an elaborate box that only Osiris could fit, and lured him to try it out for size. When he was inside, Seth secured the lid and threw it into the Nile, rather than placing it in a tomb. Inadvertently, Seth's actions assured Osiris eternal life since the coffin ultimately guaranteed continuous preservation and existence (te Velde 1967: 83). The body of Osiris was later dismembered and dispersed, and numerous spells were needed before Isis and Nepthys could reunite the body parts, underscoring the Egyptian preoccupation with partibility as a route to wholeness.

The coffin stands as a regenerative structure—a time machine that defies the limits of the earthly life cycle and promises eternal being. The goddess Nut, depicted arched above the deceased on numerous coffin lids, was also integral to its materiality and power, signifying the daily cycle of the sun reborn through her body as a parallel for the deceased. Nut is the vehicle or womb that births the deceased in a spiral of new becomings. For the Egyptians the living body's cycle was likened to the cycle of the known universe and existence itself. They employed artificial methods to construct this object-like body. This is reflected linguistically in the distinct words for the living body (living form or appearance) and that of the corpse (embalmed body, mummy, or the body after the performance of specific rites). Yet it was not the living body itself that was expected to become life-like again or physically active. Rather the body provided the place of conjunction for all the physical and non-physical elements of the person, such as the *ba* and *ka*. The survival of the body allowed the reunion of all these elements and was thus critical, but not sufficient (Taylor 2001: 16).

Being and non-being

Perhaps the most perilous tension for the Egyptians, and their concept of personhood, was the possibility that earthly being could be forfeited at the time of death, leading to an eternal state of non-being with all its concomitant horrors. Being and non-being were formed in a fraught opposition that was most ardently felt in discussions surrounding death. Euphemistically, the notion of dying was expressed in verbs such as *to land, moor, pass away, go forth, go far* or *to go away*. Hence death itself was expressed as journeying. It remained one state of being along the spectrum of existence. Ultimately, the place of death in Egypt is an ambivalent one, permeated by fears of the realm of non-existence and yet full of the promise of rejuvenation. Both stem from the same domain. One cannot have rebirth without death, despite the associated dangers and fears. Non-existence was an absolute reality (Hornung 1982: 182) and creation was only possible through non-existence, this twilight world with abundant perils. Existence needed constant regeneration in the form of ongoing performative acts and spells, for the living and the dead. The specific Egyptian construction of enduring being was full of tension and ambivalence; it was not portrayed as an ecstatic triumph, but rather as a sober experience.

The idea that personhood is dispersed through time and space is a component of innumerable cultural institutions and practices. It may find its first elaborated expression in Egypt. Temples, ancestral shrines and effigies, tombs, memorials, sacred sites, and so on all facilitate the extension of personhood beyond the confines of biological life via indexes distributed in the milieu (Gell 1998: 223). Much of our information for this extension of being in the hereafter stems from what we know as the New Kingdom Book of the Dead, although that name would not have held meaning for the Egyptians. After the reigns of Tuthmosis III and Hatshepsut, papyrus copies of the book became widespread, and two other major texts, the Litany of Re and the Amduat, first appeared in the surviving record (Forman and Quirke 1996: 116).

In the Book of the Dead, the famous judgment scene depicts the deceased's heart balancing on huge scales, against the feather of truth, representing Maat (see Figure 5.5). If the heart, as a metonym for the individual, proved heavier than the feather, it was fed to the monstrous hybrid creature Ammit, and the individual was assigned to oblivion. Written spells on papyri, tomb walls and upon individual coffins helped the deceased individual pass through the difficult terrain of the underworld where bodily violence and destruction were an ever-present threat.

The materiality of ancestors

Classic Maya mortuary practices pursued different goals from those of Egypt. No practices attempted to counter decay of the flesh, which was probably inevitable in the tropical forest environment. The body interred soon became a body in pieces. Subsequent re-entry of tombs, clearly attested at sites such as Caracol (Chase and Chase 1996), allowed for removal of skeletal elements and bodily ornaments. This would have been sacrilege, endangering the survival of the individual in the Egyptian context. But, for the Maya, the personhood of the buried individual clearly persisted despite the clear evidence for such secondary burial treatment, for circulation of selected skeletal elements, and other practices that might be taken as evidence for an objectification of the body antithetical to its continuity as a signifier of an ongoing embodied life (Gillespie 2001, 2002). Deceased individuals are depicted in monumental sculpture engaged in interactions with their living successors and descendants, and their agency continued to be acknowledged in texts long after their death. What is distinct in the Classic Maya case is the understanding of the relationship between bodily integrity and selfhood. For people who identified invisible substances as fundamental parts of the materiality of the self, the disappearance of the flesh appears not to have held the horror that characterized the Egyptian attitude towards the partibility and putrefaction of the dead body.

This is not to say that death had no terrors for the Classic Maya, nor is it to ignore the fact that their highly elaborated funerary rituals were at least in part cultural works undertaken to counter the threat posed to society by the death of the individual person. But the imagination of that loss must have been profoundly different from that in the Egyptian tradition. While it is difficult to resist seeing ancient practices as evidence that attitudes toward death are universally reflections of natural processes, the threads we have been

unraveling offer material for another view of death. Through mortuary treatment, the Classic Maya dead did not simply enter another stage of existence.
Instead, they became a different kind of being—one we inadequately comprehend as an ancestor. Immune to the passage of time, able to traverse barriers
between different planes of existence, ancestors continued to participate in the
life of their descendants, without the obligation of work, without the burdens
of the flesh. Reduced to their durable essence, ancestors could even participate
consubstantially in the personhood of descendants or successors who used the
ornaments that had been extensions of their personhood, or made new ornaments of their ancestral bone (Joyce 2000b). The circulation of the enduring
parts of embodied persons, re-used over centuries, resulted in a blurring of
any boundary that we might presume should have existed between clearly
recognizable burials and caches that provide our main evidence of other
formal ritual practices (Becker 1992; Chase and Chase 1998).

Although texts clearly record the dates of mortuary ceremonies and give
some hints at the actions carried out (Fitzsimmons 2002), we have no lengthy
accounts from Classic Maya texts to match the Egyptian sources that describe
burial rites and treatment of the body. Instead, we must primarily rely on
other material evidence (Coe 1988; Hall 1989; Ruz 1965; Welsh 1988). That
evidence documents great diversity in burial treatment, with many individuals
simply laid out in midden deposits. At Copan, such simple treatment was
accorded a disproportionate number of women and children (Storey 1992;
Hendon 1991). The same may be true at other sites, such as Seibal, where
formal, recognized tombs were overwhelmingly occupied by males
(Tourtellot 1990).

Whether in tombs, more formal burials, or midden deposits, Classic Maya
burials were typically not separated from domestic spaces (McAnany 1995,
1998). Burials were incorporated under the floors of residential structures,
sometimes inside or below the benches recognized as both day-time seating
areas and night-time sleeping platforms. Other burials were placed in tombs
located below stairways leading up to raised houses, so that successors would
walk over the dead every day. At many sites, tombs were located in the court-
yards that formed the central workspace in house compounds. The locations
of some of these burials were obvious, the cut through the previous surface
materials not patched, perhaps as an aspect of the affirmation of knowledge of
the place of the dead by members of the group (Hendon 2000).

From this perspective, burial in funerary temples, while striking, is somewhat misleading. It suggests a separation of the place of death from the space
of everyday life which is actually atypical. Indeed, Classic Maya burial temples
and the plazas marked by historical monuments to which they are adjacent
may actually best be thought of as extensions of royal residential compounds
(Joyce 2001a, 2001b), the palaces that are expanded versions of the house
compounds of lower-ranking nobles and commoners (Inomata and Houston
2001). Burial temples and monumental plazas are always physically adjacent

to residential structures of the highest-ranking nobility, and are integrated in cosmologically symbolic layouts with residences of nobles (Ashmore 1989, 1991). When Classic Maya people buried their dead, even in tombs located under temples, they placed them in the fixed space of the residence of a group, unlike the separation of burial that characterized New Kingdom Egypt. The location of Classic Maya burial was apparently the space of the social group of which the deceased had been part, allowing a continuing relation with the living. As McAnany (1995) and Gillespie (2002) have emphasized, the dead buried in house compounds remained part of the social group, with a new embodied status as a physically immobile, hard core of imperishable ornaments and bones from which more transitory bodily substances had wafted away.

We can take the most elaborate tombs documented as exemplary of the most complex funerary treatment practiced by the Classic Maya. In carefully excavated early Classic burials from Rio Azul, Guatemala (Hall 1989), the body of a buried noble was laid out on its back on a mattress stuffed with kapok, the fibrous material from inside seed pods of the ceiba tree sacred in Maya cosmology, with which male nobles were ritually identified. At Rio Azul, as at other Maya sites, the body was placed on a structure that recalled the built-in benches in residences, the place where artwork shows living people sat during the day and where archaeologists presume they slept at night. Thus the bodies of deceased group members were laid out as if they were asleep, the state of being during which the animal spirit companion (*way*) could leave the body of the living and roam between worlds. Gillespie (2002) has suggested that this structural equivalence indicates that the dead were thought of as being like sleepers, with spirits free to roam at will.

At Rio Azul, like many other sites, burials included numerous pottery vessels, some definitely containing traces of foodstuffs, notably the bitter chocolate used in Maya ceremonies (Hall *et al.* 1990). The vessel forms most common in burials, cylinder vases and wide tripod plates, contrast with the bowl forms more typical of food serving in residences. At the Sepulturas noble residential neighborhood at Copan, remains of cylinder vases and tripod plates were more strongly associated with shrines than dwellings, indicating that they served in distinctive ritual practices within these household compounds (Hendon 1991). This link between shrines and tombs suggests that mortuary ritual included special libations, not simply a mortuary feast at the time of burial or provision of food for the dead. The carving or painting of texts on Classic Maya serving vessels, especially those placed in burials, identifies them explicitly as intended to contain a few specific foods: *atole*, a corn gruel; *tamales*, steamed corn dough stuffed with meat; and above all, *cacao* (Reents-Budet 1994: 75–83).

The symbolic significance of cacao, remarkably not fully explored as yet, may have made it especially appropriate for mortuary ritual. Cacao was central to social exchanges that created connections between different families through marriage (Gillespie and Joyce 1997). Cacao beverage, depicted as a red liquid, may have been equated with blood flowing between intermarried families (Henderson and Joyce 2002). Cacao pods, growing directly from the trunk of trees, would have been understood to contain *k'ik'*, the liquid shared by plants (as sap) and humans (as blood). The action required to produce liquid cacao, drying seeds, toasting them on a comal, and grinding them on a metate, mimics the preparation of maize for consumption. The dry seeds of cacao shared the dry property of bone, but mixed with water, could be whipped up into a blood-colored suspension. This final step, of mixing ground seeds with water, was used with corn to create a gruel. It was also the fate of the bones of the temporarily defeated hero twins claimed as mythical predecessors by Maya elites (Tedlock 1985). Having lost a rubber ball game with the lords of the land of the dead, these twins were killed by exposure to heat in an oven, their remaining bones ground up and thrown into a river. There, the apparently inert bone dust of the twins reconstituted itself in the form of monstrous catfish, the first of several forms these trickster heroes assumed.

Mortuary offerings of a drink produced through the same processes would have experientially represented the promise of continued physical existence through the incorporation of bone in the bodies of successors. Indeed, Fitzsimmons (2002) has recently demonstrated how maize itself, its processing, and consumption, were intimately related to death and mortuary practice. He identifies a term used in inscriptions at Copan that characterizes a successor as "peeling" or "slicing" the bones of an ancestral ruler, in conjunction with the placement of relics from his tomb in a cache below a new monument. Fitzsimmons relates this unique text to a monument from Tikal that depicts ceremonial actions taken with regard to a skull and bones, and notes that, here, the monument cache actually contained human bones and a cranium. Arguing that Maya rulers were conceptually related to the ears of maize, he suggests that defleshing of ancestral bones was equated with the processing of maize cobs as part of a general relationship between eating maize and eating death (Fitzsimmons 2002: 68–71, 76–78).

In addition to elaborate food-serving vessels, Classic Maya tombs also enclosed vessels described by archaeologists as incense burners. Similar vessels are recovered outside tombs, including from funerary temples at sites like Palenque (Taube 1998: 453–454). Textual references to a mortuary ceremony glossed as *muknal* describe incense burning as a central action (Stuart 1998; McAnany 1998; Gillespie 2001: 90). The provision of offerings of burned incense at tombs and funerary temples may have been another reference to dissipated bodily substances of the class represented by scroll motifs.

Some Maya texts specify that the substance burned was *pom*, a word used today for the translucent white resin obtained from the copal tree. As a form of running sap, *pom* would have been named with the same word as blood. It dries into a solid, just as blood does. But this resin can be transformed through fire into a transitory, transparent substance perceived by smell instead of sight. The finally triumphant hero twins of Maya mythology used burned incense to reanimate the dry skull of their father, defeated, decapitated, and hung in a gourd tree, restoring its capacity of ordinary sight and extending this to prophetic vision (Tedlock 1985). A central ritual action depicted on many Classic Maya monuments shows a living person dropping a stream of solid drops of a substance identified explicitly in some texts as a form of incense. In some of these scenes, the living actor is either shown or described as being in contact with the spirit companion of a deity or ancestor. It is possible that these historical rituals, through the use of a volatile substance, enact a reanimation of the dry bones of ancestors like that recorded in the later myth.

Copal may have been considered a kind of sustenance more suitable for less solid beings (Taube 1989a, 1998: 446), including ancestors, who retained their non-material and hard parts but left behind the flesh that had required constant replenishment through meals in life. Copal incense was shaped into forms similar to corn tamales, placed in serving bowls, and thrown into the waters of the Cenote at Chichen Itza (Ball and Ladd 1992; Coggins and Ladd 1992). This formal equation of copal resin balls with corn tamales, reinforced by representations of "donor figures" at Chichen Itza holding serving vessel forms with visually ambiguous copal/maize dough hybrids (Krochock 1998) is particularly interesting. Tamales were produced from a wet corn dough, made by grinding corn kernels whose hard dry character was altered by soaking them in a lime-water bath. The soaked kernels were then ground and shaped into balls that concealed other food substances, forming a kind of flesh wrapper around hidden cores. This sticky wet corn dough was then transformed into a solid form by exposure to steam.

Like the bodies of prenatal infants given substance as their mothers took steam baths, the solid form of the tamale owed its nature to a combination of solid and vaporous substances. Perhaps we should consider the prominence of corn tamales in texts on funerary ceramics less an indication of their significance in everyday cuisine, where they would imply a routine investment of exceptional effort, than of their symbolic suitability for use in ceremonies marking transitions in the life course, as is the case in Postclassic ritual texts (Bricker 1991; Bricker and Bill 1994). Funerary practices involving copal resin and tamales would have resonated with the experience of other bodily practices and understandings of bodily transformations appropriate to the context. A close connection between the transformative action of burning incense and the processing of human bodies is underlined by the use at Chichen Itza of a human skull as an incense burner (Moholy-Nagy et al. 1992).

While not treated in any way to retard decay, bodies in Maya tombs were provided with elaborate costumes, often including complete masks that ensured that a double of the living features was preserved. Such mask faces (bah) sometimes were attached directly to the flesh of the dead person, and at other times replaced entirely a head removed for use or disposal elsewhere.

The removal of bones from Maya tombs apparently was not uncommon, and some tombs were clearly re-entered and the bones moved. At some sites, such as Caracol, Belize, tombs were used by groups, and the gradual addition of new bodies was accompanied by consolidation of the bones remaining from previous interments (Chase and Chase 1996). Bodily integrity was less important for the Classic Maya than the extension of bodily connections into the future, achieved through the use of bones by living people, including as body ornaments (Joyce 2000b).

The most complex burials in Classic Maya sites were completed by raising new construction over the interred body (Coe 1956; Chase and Chase 1998; McAnany 1998). These new constructions range from rebuilt, amplified residences, marked out as the predominant house in a multi-family group through new construction, to funerary temples, sometimes accompanied by freestanding historical monuments recording death and mortuary ceremonies. Based on such inscriptions, the time elapsed between death and the final mortuary rite was often quite long, averaging more than a year (McAnany 1998: 289). Gillespie (2001) suggests that the construction of new buildings must be seen as a project through which the surviving group incorporated the physical remains of the dead individual, transformed into an ancestor, in the household. Hendon (2000) points to evidence at Copan that the location of even relatively less elaborate burials was deliberately left marked within the space of the household, by leaving an unpatched hole in plaster.

Far from being concerned with placing the dead body safely in a different space, separated from the living, Classic Maya burial practices seem concerned with creating an indelible set of markers of the location of this immobile member of the extended group. Shafts to tombs, like the main burial in Palenque's Temple of the Inscriptions or a deep shaft described for Copan's Structure 11 (where the prior existence of a disturbed tomb is suggested by recovered materials), are other examples of the construction of features connecting the spaces of everyday life with the places of the dead in Classic Maya sites. The thick caps of chipped stone noted in some sites, including Rio Azul, that are so obvious that archaeologists can use them as marks of burial sites, could have served the same mnemonic function for people in these ancient communities (Hall 1989; Coe 1988).

The Classic Maya dead, in short, remained part of the community, in a materiality transformed by natural processes of decay that left the solid substances and the non-material essences of the embodied individual intact. Through the extension of the person by the construction of monuments, described as the *bah*, mask, face, or double (Houston and Stuart 1998), the durable materiality of the deceased person could assume an even more imposing presence in the lives of successors. The constant awareness of the buried dead in house compounds, achieved through placement in the midst of the daily round, while more subtle, would have had the same effect (Hendon 2000; Gillespie 2001, 2002; McAnany 1995, 1998). The disembodied presence of the ancestors would also have been constantly marked by Classic Maya naming practices, in which names carried by predecessors were adopted in adulthood by successors.

In Classic Maya texts the subject is represented by strings of signs usually glossed as the name of a specific historical person. These strings of signs consist largely of categorical signs, titles. The signs used to denote a person changed over time and varied from context to context. This raises the question of the nature of naming itself as a means through which a person is formed as a subject. Maya "names" can be viewed as instances of interpellation (Althusser 1971: 127–188). The most distinctive signs, those usually described as the "personal name" of the rulers, are regularly used repeatedly within the ruling line of particular sites, and sometimes over larger areas. The adoption of a name associated with an ancestor who was a living presence, often with a known physical resting place in the house compound, made living persons consubstantial with the dead (compare Stuart 1998: 395–396; Monaghan 1998). When the person referred to as Chel-te in his youth exercised his authority as ruler of Yaxchilan as Shield Jaguar, one of a pair of circulating rulers' apellations, he did so in part as the living embodiment of his predecessor. Death was no bar to the continuity of Classic Maya personhood.

The record in some Classic Maya texts of projections of dates far into the future (even beyond our current time), from this perspective reflects an understanding of the meaning of mortality that is far different from that exemplified by ancient Egyptian texts. Just as the hoped-for visions of the future were distinct, so too, the nightmares that haunted the consciousness of Classic Maya and ancient Egyptians were distinct, and clearly rooted in their distinct embodied experiences of personhood and its risks.

143

8

SHADOWS

Hellish visions

It has long been recognized that the Egyptians conceived of, and graphically illustrated, the first visions of what would later be deemed *hell* in Christian theology. And while there was certainly an otherworldly concept of heavenly existence for the worthy, it was not visually or textually represented to the same degree as its nefarious counterpart. Fantasies of fear and deprivation have always captured the imagination; the worst of society's most fearful punishments and tortures multiplied exponentially and lasting in perpetuity, demonic creatures expert in the performance of cruelty, and the ultimate reversal of the natural, knowable order of things. Long before Dante's *Inferno*, the Egyptian Books of the Netherworld (Book of the Dead, Amduat, Book of Gates, Book of Caverns etc.) crystallized those expressions of dread, that all coalesced around the limits of the embodied self. There are potent elements of familiarity between ancient and modern cultures even in these existential moments.

Judgment after death is first known from Egypt, a concept depicted in the weighing of the individual's heart on the scales against the concept of right order, personified as the goddess *Maat* (see Figure 5.5). These scenes of judgment and the hellish moments afterwards were first represented iconographically in the eighteenth Dynasty. This elite vision of the abyss and of torture in the royal tombs was set against common images of the life hereafter in the chapels of private tombs which showed scenes of drinking, dancing, feasting and all the signs of luxury and indulgence.

Time was reversed in the underworld, which paralleled the dead's experience of their living world in reverse. The underworld was subterranean and hierarchically structured with the gods, pharaohs and the blessed dead enjoying sublime status, as well as those that were damned. Places such as the Field of Reeds and Field of Offerings were the abode of the blessed dead where they could harvest grain and flax for their eternal sustenance (Forman and Quirke 1996: 182). In contrast, the condemned were exposed to horrific tortures in the underworld where events and actions happened in reverse, such as walking backwards and upside down, faces turned backwards, eating excrement and so on. Enemies of the gods were trapped and slaughtered like animals. Textual descriptions are replete with the imagery of torture and imprisonment, all enacted against the limitations of bodily survival. Death was commonly portrayed as full of horror and fear, and the place of the dead was signified by the presence of evil snakes, demonic entities including the *Mistress of Fear*, *Master of Terror*, *Frightful One*, *Mistress of Trembling*. The place of death was replete with roaring, wailing and trembling.

The afterlife could take two forms. The netherworld was subterranean, dark and horrific, while the Egyptian concept of "heaven" was a starry and idyllic realm where one conjoined with revered deities. Death did not mean a step out of time into eternity—it represented the transition to a new existence or what might be termed an interstitial realm. The deceased remained within time and experienced new lifetimes in the underworld. The fortunate individual participated in the daily orbit of the sun, which formed a temporal and spatial link between this life and the hereafter (Hornung 1992: 66).

But the passage to the hereafter was fraught with uncertainties. The underworld, so vividly described in the Book of the Dead, could prove to be a place of nightmarish destruction for the unworthy person. It was described as *completely deep, completely dark* and *completely unending*. It was a place inhabited by forces that destroyed everything on entry and that knew no bounds in their destructive imagination. Decapitation was only one of the bodily tortures inflicted upon the damned (Hornung 1992: 99–101). As previously discussed, the destruction of the body similarly meant the dissolution of the *ba*, *ka* and other constituents of the self and hence all possibilities for eternity. Those individuals faced oblivion and non-existence.

Fire, burning and bodily destruction feature prominently in this nightmarish imaginary. In one scene from the Book of Gates, the ninth hour, we encounter the serpent that breathed fire upon the condemned (Hornung 1999: 41), while other scenes illustrate fire-filled pits or the Lake of Fire, filled with burning red liquid. In the Book of Caverns, also reproduced on the walls of royal tombs, knife-wielding demons heat cauldrons in which the deceased and all their constituent parts (human heads, hearts and flesh) were dissolved, physically and spiritually, resulting in a state of non-being that the Egyptians considered as anathema (Figure 8.1). Hearts, souls and the personal magic of individuals could be devoured. Frequent images of roasting and cooking again invoke the human fear surrounding cannibalistic practices. Bodies were frequently inverted in this realm of chaos or were dismembered.

The Egyptian vision of hell was an unquenchable fire, auguring the Christian construction many centuries later. The tongues and eyes of demons spat fire, as did their knives. There were serpents who exhaled poisonous breath. In scenes from the Book of Caverns the damned are shown with torches where their heads should be—a perpetual corporeal punishment (Hornung 1990: 156). In the tomb of Ramesses VI a vignette shows four of the damned

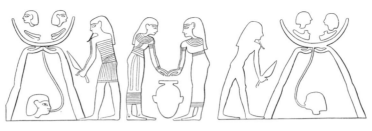

Figure 8.1   Illustration from the Fourth register of the Book of Caverns in the tomb of Ramesses VI, showing heads and hearts in the pits of fire, from Piankoff (1954: Fig. 125).

assaulted by fire-spitting serpents, two men pierced by arrows while the other two are bound at the arms and similarly helpless. A body reduced to flames symbolizes the absolute negation of physical existence, perhaps the most terrifying image to portray in an Egyptian context. These forms stand in direct challenge to the edifice of the tomb that served to guard life, and the dead. The threat of the all-burning annuls itself: the body reduced to cinders, that dusty theme of humanity, the immemorial image decomposed from within, a metaphor or metonymy of itself, a lost memory of what is no longer here (Derrida 1987: 31). One has to question why pharaohs chose to represent these vivid images? Perhaps they served as an apotropaic warning that the king knew what existed, the threat of terror, but knew no fear of it—a display of his divine knowledge, for knowledge is power.

Burning was especially feared as it meant total damnation since the body's materiality was totally destroyed. The Books of the Netherworld show heads, hearts, corpses, souls and shadows thrown upside down into boiling water, while serpents and demons stoke the fire, spewing their own flames into them (Figure 8.2). Consumption by fire was a known earthly punishment, both while the victim was alive and also after death (Leahy 1984). Hundreds of clay figurines near the fort at Mirgissa depicting bound prisoners were burnt in a kiln, then buried or nailed to the walls of the fort. A similar fate awaited traitors or foreign enemies (Pinch 1994: 93). This torturous treatment effectively erased all bodily trace and subsequently any chance at attaining an afterlife. The total destruction of the body was the ultimate damnation.

This action has the significance of a sacrifice, of an offer by which the flames void the individual's bodily existence (Derrida 1987: 46). This stands in complete opposition to the idealized treatment and transfigured reality of the blessed dead. A fire-breathing serpent *who burns millions* carries out her tortures while Horus speaks before the dead (Hornung 1990: 156):

> *The blade of vengeance is for your bodies;*
> *Death for your souls,*

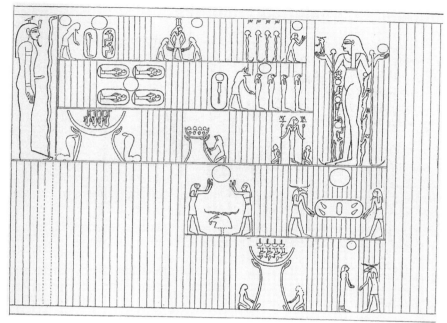

Figure 8.2   Illustration from the Fifth register of the Book of Caverns in the tomb of
Ramesses VI, showing inverted beheaded bodies, dissolving flesh, *bas*,
heads and hearts in cauldrons, from Piankoff (1954: Fig. 14).

Darkness for your shadows
The block for your heads.
You never lived, you are turned about,
And you rise not, for you stumbled into your pits,
Whence you escape not, nor are freed.
The serpent's flames are for you
And the fire of this goddess is for you ...
The dagger of the goddess is in you,
Tearing your bodies asunder.

Mutilation and violence

Apart from the horrors of fire, the threat of torture and bodily pain occupied a
primary position in the pharaonic imaginary of the hereafter. Spell 17 from
the Book of the Dead attempted to save the deceased from

> *those who deal wounds, the slayers whose fingers are sharp, who deal out*
> *pain, who decapitate those who follow after Osiris; they shall not have*
> *power over me, and I will not fall into their cauldrons;*

and also to save them from

that god whose face is that of a hound but whose skin is human, who lives by butchery, who is in charge of the windings of the Lake of Fire, who swallows corpses, who controls hearts, who inflicts injury unseen .... Save me from that god who steals souls, who laps up corruption, who lives on what is putrid, who is in charge of darkness, who is immersed in gloom, of whom those who are among the languid ones are afraid.

(Faulkner 1985: 48–49)

Demons were thought to behead, slit throats, draw out hearts, and initiate bloodbaths as forms of punishment. In the Litany of Re, blood-smeared demons with sharp knives threaten to destroy souls and corpses and to tear out the hearts of mortals, even pharaohs. Tearing out the heart signified another ultimate annihilation. Bodies were cut into pieces, they were slashed, tortured, maimed, beheaded, hacked into pieces, forced to swim in their own blood and cannibalized. Even the *ba* birds of the guilty could be burned or cut into pieces (see Figure 8.2), as was depicted for the enemies of Osiris.

Just as the burned body signified annihilation, so did cutting it into pieces or devouring it. These individuals were eternally consumed without hope of other possible trajectories. Demons fed on hearts, intestines and blood in an endless cycle of destruction and consumption. In the Book of Gates these demons have the names Rapacious, Squeezer, Brutal, Terror, Exacting, and Ripper (Hornung 1990: 153–155). Other examples suggest that these otherworldly torments mimicked those of real-world punishments: pulling the fingernails, breaking bones, twisting arms and so on. Punishment was also extended to the constituents of the self, alongside the material body.

These visions were inflected with a harsh reality, that practices of bodily torture were enacted in living contexts. Texts describe how victims were bound, tied, fettered, and ensnared. Human bodies began to emulate bound sacrificial animals, regularly offered in cultic practice—hapless creatures that lacked agency or identity. Impaling is described in various texts and shown in reliefs. Textual sources stemming back to the Coffin Texts attest to this as a punishment for one's enemies, along with other bodily spectacles such as hanging corpses from the prow of a royal boat. Specific bodily injunctions seem to have been desired.

Beyond ultimate death, mutilation lay at the core of these punishments. The heart was torn out, ripped from the living body while the chest bled, the blood was drunk, kidneys clawed out, the head too could be severed and so on. Preventative spells such as 154 in the Book of the Dead implore that *my brains are not destroyed, I am not mutilated* (Zandee 1960: 147). The tortured body stands in distinction to the intact, radiant body of the mummy, and represents the greatest fear of dismemberment, obviously for those still alive and those desiring life eternal. Wholeness and perfection were paramount. This was not an ideology of spirit alone, but one of flesh and bone.

Mutilated bodies formed a recurrent iconic motif of royal power over foreign bodies on civic monuments as well as portents for the damned in royal tomb iconography. In the tombs of Ramesses VI and IX we see rows of enemies, beheaded and painted red, indicating their bloodiness, or black for their eternal non-being. There is considerable iconographic overlap between the two contexts. In the temple of Ramesses III at Medinet Habu pharaoh is shown defeating his enemies and mutilating their dead bodies by removing their genitals (see below).

Bodily mutilation such as this easily destroyed earthly wholeness and perfection and similarly removed any chance of surviving into the hereafter, let alone achieving the physical perfection that Egyptian culture required. Heads and hands were cut off and various temple scenes depict the hands of enemies being presented to pharaoh. Bodily mutilation extended beyond representational spheres since we know that ordinary criminals had their feet beaten, their noses cut, ears removed and, for heinous crimes, they could be burned alive or impaled on sticks. Archaeologists have also uncovered the fetters that bound Nubian captives in particularly gruesome ways.

Bodily mutilation was not only horrific as a torture, but ensured long-term humiliation since the body constantly signified its crime. Punitive measures taken on earth in real time were paralleled in the Egyptian's hellish construction of the netherworld. Therefore, to some degree, these visionary images had a substrate of fact and in turn these nightmare visions contributed to the suite of bodily tortures enacted upon the bodies of enemies and others.

The most graphic of these images is of royal design, emblazoned on the temples and monuments of New Kingdom pharaohs. On the first court of the East Wall at Medinet Habu, Ramesses III reviews both his human and material booty as bound captives are brought before him. On an upper register a scribe records a pile of severed hands while below in the next register a parallel scene takes place. This time the hands are paralleled by a pile of severed uncircumcised penises and the scribe records them with acute specificity. The genitals of the victims have been removed and heaped up, as hands were, suggesting this was a way of metonymically rendering the fallen enemy.

Other scenes show severed penises with the testicles attached, an altogether different way of graphically representing the genitals (O'Connor 1990: 53). As a signifier the severed penis seems to have been a violent and potent reminder of Egyptian domination over the physical bodies of individuals as well as their territories. Whether such depictions actually record specific uncircumcised or circumcised penises is unknown. We are still uncertain as to how many ordinary Egyptians would have been circumcised (Meskell 2002: 87–88). Were these acts carried out after death or were they part of the punishment leading up to death?

The severing of the penis was a recurrent theme that marked even the earliest representations of Egyptian supremacy. On the Predynastic Narmer Palette we see the severed genitals of enemies juxtaposed against the victims'

149

heads, also separated from their bodies. Scenes of Ramesses II's troops at the battle of Qadesh display Egyptians cutting the hands from fallen captives while still alive. On the walls of his temple at Abydos a similar, now canonical, scene occurs where a scribe counts the number of severed hands of the enemy, lying haphazardly in various piles. Scribes pick up each hand by its thumb as the count progresses. This representation of bodily mastery was a way of proving fighting prowess, as measured by overseeing scribes. Scenes of performative fighting and wrestling between foreigners and Egyptians were similarly popular, featuring violent hand-to-hand combat, while pharaoh and his officials looked on.

Foreign bodies in tortured positions, decapitated heads and severed penises are potent motifs of the New Kingdom. Similar mutilations are denoted in the tomb sphere, such as those who are damned after judgment. In the twentieth Dynasty Book of the Night, the damned were displayed naked and bound in a posture of defenselessness. They are depicted without genitals so that they will not have descendants and presumably to deny them a sexual identity and after-life, paralleling the punishments doled out by pharaoh in the context of war.

The bodily gestures of the defeated on royal monuments signify their impending damnation. Images of defeated Hittites on the first pylon of the north tower at Medinet Habu show a mass of overturned bodies in contorted poses simulating the chaos of slaughter and battle. A similar range of postures is shown for the defeated Libyans, with arms tied behind them at the elbows and bound in the same positions as those of the damned in the underworld. They are trampled underfoot by the advancing Egyptians. Ramesses III is portrayed twice their size in his advancing war chariot. The neat order and symmetry of Egyptian iconography is itself overturned through this visual violence.

On the north wall Ramesses hold his bound captives by the hair, a common motif for domination, suppression and victory. The Libyans are bound around the elbows, but there are a variety of bodily contortions that follow on from this. Their hairstyles and clothing all render their corporeal difference. In the first pylon of the south tower Ramesses is shown smiting the chiefs of all foreign lands before various manifestations of Amun, a multiplicity of bodies lined up against each other in perfect symmetry, some forty-two of them held by one royal hand.

Torture was inflicted on the animal body as it was upon the human body, echoing back to the theme of the damned victim as a trapped animal. Iconic images of dangerous animals such as lions, snake, and crocodiles, depicted as hieroglyphic symbols on tomb walls, were often cut or mutilated by the artist. Other hieroglyphs were rendered incomplete by the artist so as to impede activation of their animal powers that might threaten the dead. Scribes found it meaningful to omit, dismember or mutilate these graphic signs, since they had the threatening potential of the real, attesting to the extraordinary power of these iconic signifiers.

This impels us to re-situate these traditionally considered art objects within an anthropological theory of art. The bodies of birds such as ducks or owls, which were common in the hieroglyph script, were also mutilated since they might easily fly away, leaving the inscription and the tomb bereft (Goldwasser 1995: 79). It was believed that the iconic image could also be re-animated and brought back to life through magical prowess.

The acts of *damnatio memoriae* that effaced and erased were also extended to individuals. Altering the historical record, attacking personal enemies, censoring a religious event, are all motives for the "mark of the second hand," erasure, which presupposes a certain level of knowledge by the perpetrator (Der Manuelian 1999: 286).

Just as statues were considered beings in their own right, images of people, animals and others could have real-time efficacy. An anthropological theory of art challenges once traditional taxa of objects as "exclusively" art objects, since this elides their cultural and contextual specificities. More productively we could explore the domain, the interstices, in which *objects* merge with *people* and *deities* by virtue of the existence of social relations between persons and things, and persons and persons *via* things (Gell 1998: 12). By depicting or creating images, whether of the transfigured self or of the defeated enemy, a certain agency was conferred on those represented in power or seen to be controlling the image. Images had agency and conferred agency. Agency is attributable to those persons and things that are seen as "initiating causal sequences of a particular type, that is, events caused by acts of mind or will or intention, rather than the mere concatenation of physical events. An agent is one who 'causes events to happen' in their vicinity" (Gell 1998: 16). Thus the erasure or mutilation of persons, animals or things alternatively diminished their agency, reducing them to ineffectual non-beings in all worlds.

Embodied evil

The Egyptians certainly had a fear of evil that inhabited the spirit realm, something unseen and ghostly that could manifest as a deceased relative or jealous demon. Yet the most vivid evocations of evil inhabit the somatic realm that was represented in the most potent sphere: the tomb. Here the threat of evil and annihilation was both symbolized by an inhuman embodiment and was actualized by inflicting bodily tortures upon the victim in perpetuity. In both domains, bodily distortion was requisite. Far from the world of perfect aesthetics and somatic integrity, this was a demonic world of torture and dismemberment. The great enemy to both living and dead was the demon Apep (or Apophis) who took the unmistakable form of a snake—perhaps the first incarnation of this embodied evil, seen so often in Christian theology. Yet the snake, as an animal, was not considered evil. The Egyptians had some thirty snake deities, including the important goddess Wadjet who symbolized the eye of the sun, and Renenutet, goddess of the harvest and of prosperity (Germond and Livet 2001: 178).

Apep was the eternal enemy of the gods. Known as the destroyed one, he did not belong with the existent, and had no beginning or end, like the snake who swallows its tail. He was *the one who was spat out*, the product of Neith's saliva in the primeval water who was already there at the creation of the world. Apep was endlessly regenerating, although he was physically imperfect since he could not see or hear. Unlike the countless ears and eyes that enhanced the power of the divine gods, Apep was deprived of his senses (Hornung 1982: 169). Although he was fearsome, he was physically compromised, reiterating the emphasis on bodily functions, impairments and mutilations in the domain of the underworld. Every day and every night, powerful magic was required to repel his advances. He constantly reappeared, as seen in the Book of Gates, with twelve human heads emerging from his coils. These were the heads of people he had devoured and then incorporated into his own bodily being.

Yet, as the sun god traveled past, a powerful reversal was set in motion. At this time the human heads devoured the body of the snake, consuming and destroying Apep through a form of self-cannibalization. As soon as the god passed, however, the heads entered their coils again. Thus the snake body defied destruction, alternating between death and resurrection (Hornung 1982: 158–159). Spell 39 of the Book of the Dead (Faulkner 1985: 61) states:

> *Get back! You shall be decapitated with a knife, your face shall be cut away all round, your head shall be removed by him who is in his land, your bones shall be broken, your limbs shall be cut off; the earth-god has condemned you, O Apep, you enemy of Ra.*

In the burial chamber of pharaoh Amenhotep II in the Valley of the Kings, this vital journey of the sun god through the twelve hours of the night is depicted. It details in gruesome specificity the decapitated bodies of enemies, while another register shows the body of Apep with knives stuck in him, as the snake tries to stop the journey of the sun each night. The wall painting mimics the color and style of an unrolled papyrus in cream color, with human figures in stick-like form painted red and black. It is further decorated with a funerary text known as the Amduat, or the Book of the Hidden Chamber. This was the chief religious text in the royal tombs after Tuthmosis I until the Amarna period (Hornung 1982: 155).

The Egyptians imagined the underworld as a dangerous place that was capable of operating in contrary ways to the known universe (Robins 1997a: 122). People were forced to walk on their heads, eat excrement and undergo other forms of bodily reversals. Apep represented the chaos of non-being, a demonic entity who signified the real threats of a lack of existence and bodily being after death. The underworld had dangers, specifically those directed toward the fragility of the human form. But at the same time it also offered countless possibilities for renewal—a cyclical renewal that operated on a daily basis. In this vein the royal tomb was mobilized as a microcosm of the under-world, embodying the sun passing from sunset to sunrise.

The fearful world of otherness

There is nothing in Classic Maya iconography or the as-yet deciphered textual record that corresponds to ancient Egyptian visions of an eternal domain of bodily torment following death. Spanish clerics in the sixteenth century iden-tified the Christian Hell with the Highland Maya concept of *Xibalba*, one of the major locales of the epic tales of hero twins recorded in the colonial period Quiche Maya manuscript known as *Popol Vuh* (Tedlock 1985). Certainly, the young hero twins underwent a series of unpleasant challenges in Xibalba, the elder pair of twins were permanently defeated, and even the ultimately victo-rious younger twins first had to suffer a painful death. Perhaps the games of chance which the hero twins lost can be thought of as a form of judgment, but if so, it was one entirely lacking the moral dimension of the Egyptian weighing of the heart. The means by which the younger hero twins triumphed are at best amoral (if not outright immoral), as they act the classic trickster role, enticing the lords of Xibalba into voluntarily being sacrificed.

But in many ways, the terrestrial underworld of the Classic Maya, the visual predecessor to the much later verbal depiction of Xibalba, does seem to have occupied a similar place in a Maya imaginary as the Egyptian under-world. The sources for understanding the Classic Maya underworld are rela-tively limited, if we do not follow the usual and historically questionable route of using post-colonial texts as if they were unchanged records of much earlier beliefs. Texts and images on monuments do not seem to represent the underworld and its terrors. Instead, it is from paintings on specific pottery vessels, of the kinds included in burials, that we can gain the sense that Classic Maya people's everyday existence was framed in distinction with a dangerous and possibly unpleasant inverse (Coe 1978; Reents-Budet 1994: 273–278; Schele and Miller 1986: 265–300). As burial furnishings, these pots were filled with the bitter red–brown drink, *cacao*, whose substance may have recalled blood and ground bones. Left with the deceased in tombs whose form suggested the sleeping rooms of palaces, these vessels perhaps suggest experiences newly open to the dead person's immaterial spirit, freed of the limitations of the solid flesh.

The pottery paintings that have been taken as representations of under-world scenes are commonly set against a black background, perhaps implying the lack of solar light that is a characteristic of the underworld domain in the beliefs of later peoples of Central America. The underworld was the place where the sun went when it set at night, a transition Classic Maya texts suggest was seen as a daily death. The underworld was understood in terms of Classic

Maya experience of caves, which riddle the land around major sites (Bassie-Sweet 1991, 1996). Within caves, extensive dripstone formations and still bodies of water surround sometimes vast spaces where the Maya marked their presence with painted images and texts (Stone 1995). Where caves were not naturally present, the Classic Maya excavated chambers below the pyramids they constructed and named as "mountains," creating analogues in the experiential world for locations of significant mythic events such as the birth of corn (Brady and Ashmore 1999). A domain of primordial power, it would appear that the Classic Maya underworld, while a place very different from that of everyday life, and potentially dangerous, was not a land of torment.

Against the black background of underworld vase paintings, a kind of parody of courtly life is depicted, in which are echoed actions shown in palace scenes depicting living mortals. Rather than a strict reversal of the world of everyday order, the underworld would seem to be a kind of mirror double for it. In underworld court scenes, many of the roles of subordinates are played by animal hybrids, notably the rabbit scribe and flying messengers with features of night birds and mosquitoes. Many of these vessels show dances, like those of the earthly world, whose participants are solely human/animal hybrids, notably including monkeys, whose physical resemblance to humans was clearly a subject of fascination in Maya society (Grube and Nahm 1994). Floral scrolls emanate from the anus of some animal hybrids, suggesting both that a pervasive stench characterized this domain (Schele and Miller 1986: 268), and a reversal of the desirable living experience of the emission of breath and speech from the mouth.

At the apex of underworld society reigned old gods, whose distinctive regalia can be traced through the succeeding Postclassic period, and who appear in a few unusual monuments from the Classic Maya site of Palenque (Coe 1978; Gillespie and Joyce 1998; Schele 1976; Schele and Miller 1986: 286–287). For the dead nobles who ideally lived to old age, these aged underworld lords would have been physical doubles, showing the lines of age that were banished from representation of living nobles. The most prominent of the old gods depicted in underworld scenes on polychromes, God L, wears a jaguar-skin cape and a wide-brimmed hat with feathers (Gillespie and Joyce 1998). He is often shown smoking tobacco, derived from *Nicotiana rustica*, whose spiral smoke links it to other immaterial bodily substances, from which it differs in smoke color, smell, and mildly intoxicating effects. Through his bodily extensions of jaguar skin and *mo'an* bird feathers, this old god is identified with warrior sacrifice (Grube and Schele 1994). Despite his attitude of ease and decorum, characteristic of living Maya lords, this underworld lord is linked substantially with the violence of warfare and sacrifice.

Scholars associate the Classic Maya underworld most closely with ball-game sacrifice, through the much later *Popol Vuh* text, in which hero twins journey to Xibalba to compete with underworld lords in ball games (Tedlock 1985). A first set of twins never succeed in playing the ball game, since they fail the first tests they are set. A second set of twins, born of an underworld daughter impregnated by the decapitated head of one of the older twins, manages to survive long enough to play ball against the underworld lords. Defeated, they are also sacrificed, their bones ground up and thrown into the water.

Ballcourt architecture and ball-game costume systematically marked living participants in ball games as standing at the threshold between worlds (Gillespie 1991). But Classic texts and images do not represent detailed narratives of underworld ball-game contests. Some images do represent decapitation of ball players and the transformation of blood spurting from the neck into flourishing plants (Freidel 1992; Miller and Houston 1987; Schele and Freidel 1991; Schele and Miller 1986: 241–264). Some texts describe decapitation as a consequence of ball games, and equate skulls linguistically with seeds (Schele and Freidel 1991).

Taken literally, these images and texts have been viewed as evidence that human sacrifice was a stage in ball-game ceremonial (Miller and Houston 1987). The recovery of a cache of human crania and cervical vertebrae near the ballcourt at Seibal (Smith 1982) and the depiction of crania displayed on pole racks carved into a platform near the Great Ballcourt at Chichen Itza have been offered as evidence that these practices really did take place, at least in some times and places. Given the equation drawn in Maya texts between the living visage and its doubles, the display of masks as belt ornaments also echoes the theme of decapitation. In this sense, Classic Maya representation and performance instantiated as lived experience on the earthly plane aspects of the underworld, particularly the experiences of violence and pain.

Violence and pain

Violence perpetrated on victims of battle raids lent itself to representation in terms of consumption of the defeated by the victors, given the prominence among the Classic Maya of human/animal and human/plant hybrids, especially human/maize hybrids. Violence was systematically conflated with the embodiment of other mundane experience. War captives destined for sacrifice are presented within the confines of noble residences on pottery vessels destined for use within such palaces (Reents-Budet 1994: 257–259). Other pottery vessels used in the same locales display captives destined for sacrifice on scaffolds—a scene tied to accession to rule (Taube 1988). Such paintings on vessels inserted violence into everyday life and court ceremonial, and metaphorized struggle between warriors with human domination of the animal and plant worlds. The metaphorical equation of such violence with everyday life was further promoted by ambiguities in the tools used in everyday activities.

The lance shown as a major prosthetic extension of warriors in battle is also depicted as the hunter's tool in scenes of ceremonial deer hunts on pottery and other small-scale objects, probably regalia and possibly parts of individual costume (Pohl 1981; Reents-Budet 1994: 263–264). The hearts held in the claws of jaguar and eagle hybrids at Chichen Itza (see Figure 5.12) are shown being removed from the chest with bifaces identical to lance points, shown as sharp teeth in the mouths of animal/stone hybrids (Schele 1983). The instrument of decapitation, a hafted ground stone celt, is indistinguishable from the domestic tool used to clear trees from land intended for cultivation as maize fields (see Figure 2.17). Ears of corn, identified with the head of the maize plant, were stripped of their outer covering of husks, exposing the kernels that were removed and eaten, leaving the dry cob behind. The decapitation and flaying of the facial skin of sacrificial victims (Schele and Freidel 1990: 243, 409) was thus metaphorically linked to harvesting and eating the flesh of another, whether such cannibalism was ever really practiced (compare Fitzsimmons 2002: 76–78).

The context in which Classic Maya patrons, on present evidence primarily noble men, caused images of decapitation and other forms of sacrifice to be produced was insistently one of alterity: these were the consequences of war experienced by others. But the relationship of captor and captive was fundamentally one of identification, so the display of such images would also have been a potent reminder of risk and danger for the young men who engaged in Classic Maya raids. Captors assimilated the names of their victims as part of their own ever-changing nominal identity (Stuart 1985). The homonymy between the words for captive and bone made the record of capture an explicit claim to sharing durable bodily materiality.

The war dances depicted in Classic Maya art presented both captives and captors as objects for the violence of the gaze of senior male nobles. Seated serenely, such elder males survey the exposed bodies of young men engaged in captive sacrifice, ball games, and personal bloodletting (Joyce 2000d). The visual relations evident in pottery painting reinforce the identification of young men as phallic extensions controlled by elder men. These images record the perpetration of social control over bodily materiality through the practice of piercing the body to produce blood to be converted through burning into sacrificial smoke directed at immaterial beings (Freidel et al. 1991; Stuart 1984; Schele and Miller 1986: 175–208).

Auto-sacrifice, the practice of personally cutting one's own body, has undoubtedly been over-emphasized in scholarship on Classic Maya society. It is reasonable to propose caution in assuming that rulers routinely carried out a painful practice on their own bodies, and to question whether they did so in public. Discursive texts recording personal bloodletting by rulers need not have referenced the physical body of the ruler, given the clear pattern of extending the personhood of nobles to other corporeal beings. The actions of young men, categorically described in terms that equate them with the penis, could easily be absorbed by the expansive personhood of older males.

Complementing the potentially ambiguous textual record, the Classic Maya site of Yaxchilan has produced a series of images unambiguously depicting the act of bloodletting carried out by noble women (Tate 1992;

Schele and Miller 1986: 186–190). The tongue of these women takes the place of the penis, and a meticulously detailed rope, sometimes studded with spines, is shown in the moment of being drawn through the tongue. Regardless of whether these images served to commemorate real embodied activity or were metaphoric of another physical or immaterial action, they would have been strong expressions of a form of potential, socially sanctioned violence. While the hands that draw the rope through the tongue are those of the women themselves, they are juxtaposed in these images to male figures, often shown towering over them as they kneel. The use of carefully depicted images of rope identical to those shown binding war captives links these images to those of conquest. They have been read as unambiguous expressions of sexualized domination of women (Stone 1988). This practice, if carried out, would have differentially affected these women's capacity for speech—a highly valued expression in Classic Maya society—just as the use of labrets affected women's expression in Northwest Coast society (Moss 1996).

Linking speech at least temporarily to pain is clearly a form of bodily discipline of verbal expression. To the extent that male subjects actually took part in the practice of piercing the penis, one of the products of this activity would have been a similar discipline of bodily expression: the creation of a linkage between sexuality and pain. A number of authors have argued that the effect of this practice would have been to achieve ecstatic trance and spiritual transcendence of bodily boundaries. Most notably, this argument has been supported by juxtaposing reliefs from Yaxchilan in narrative sequences that imply that women's bloodletting produces visions of hybrid serpents conducting ancestral spirits into the physical plane. The murals decorating three rooms at Bonampak have similarly been described as a sequence in which personal bloodletting by young men, emphasized by a whirling dance, is part of battle ceremonies that led the participants to a state of transcendance (Schele and Miller 1986: 177–178).

Without denying the human possibilities for using pain as a vehicle to achieve altered states, it is well to remember that the condition of such altered states is to first submit to bodily pain, at risk, without guarantees. In Classic Maya art, the subjects of such violence were all subordinated to select male nobles. Whether metaphoric or real, Classic Maya society thematized in visual discourse the embodiment of domination as the literal experience of pain, the literal threat of death and dismemberment, and the literal possibility of bodily partition. These aspects of bodily discipline were not deferred to a post-mortem level of experience; they were part of the everyday possibility. The underworld may have served as a supernatural, eternal, and primordial warrant for hierarchy (Susan Gillespie, personal communication). But it was in the real world of embodied experience that Classic Maya elders disciplined the bodies of children from the moment of birth, shaping a suitable social being. This was a process that was unrelenting, until the moment of death opened the possibility—at least for some people—of taking the place of the immaterial presence of an ancestor.

157

9

EPILOGUE

The personhood of Classic Maya and New Kingdom Egyptian subjects has not been irretrievably lost; it continues to persist today in the form of material extensions that are part of the basis for our examination of personhood in these ancient societies. Within these ancient societies, such durable objects clearly supported the commemoration of persons even after the dissolution of the flesh, and their survival of post-mortem dangers.

Commemoration of the person is epitomized by Classic Maya monuments with inscriptions using a calendar system that allows precise designation of dates of events in a single, continuous, framework. For as long as the objects survive, these inscriptions place persons regarding monuments in the present in relation to persons recalled from the past. The primary communicative effect of such texts, beyond the incidents of biography and history that they relate, is the performance of memory (Joyce 2003). Maya calendars and writing systems worked as technologies of memory, practices of inscription (after Connerton 1989), through which social memories were constructed.

Signs of memory more commonplace than monuments were more pervasive in Classic Maya settlements. The durable representations of bodily ideals of perfection found in monumental art are not the only material forms of memory of embodiment that circulated through history, preserving, against all threats, the personhood of Classic Maya subjects. Small, hand-held figurines made and used in residential compounds of non-ruling elites are notable for the representation of a wide range of subjects, including infants, adults, and the elderly, engaged in everyday activities like grinding corn and weaving (Joyce 1993). Such figurines are of course ambiguous; they may represent an attempt to inscribe traditional roles and activities as orthodoxy, and in some places they include representations of hierarchically privileged subjects. But they are also distinctly different from monumental images and painted pottery in their depiction of quotidian subjects, the diversity of forms of embodiment they commemorate and make subjects of possible discourse, and the openness to narrative that they allow, especially if they were used in multi-figure scenes. We may not know the other kinds of imaginings that human subjects outside

158

the central core of Maya political life engaged in, but we can suggest that there was scope for conceptions of existence distinct from the violently reinforced regimes of bodily perfection and hierarchy so amply underwritten by Classic Maya elites.

Through the repetition of some extremely conservative body practices, and the use of material objects reproduced to enable these practices, memories of persons were reproduced among restricted social groups, elite families constructing social relations over many generations. In some cases, such material cues of implicit memory were transformed so that they serve today as evidence of explicit commemoration equivalent in content, if not in scale or audience, to the more obvious medium of commemorative sculpture. The transformation of objects employed in practical action into explicit commemorative records, accomplished by inscribing body ornaments with texts, changed implicit memory into explicit recall, merging personal and historical memory (Joyce 2000b, 2003).

In New Kingdom Egypt, even after the trials of death and the complex negotiations of the underworld, it was possible to participate in an earthly existence by virtue of one's kin and their ongoing responsibilities to remember and commemorate the dead. Through a system of ritual observances, instantiated and mediated through material culture and visual representation, one could recall the deceased and call upon him or her to intervene in the world of the living. Through devotional practices directed toward effigies of the deceased it was possible to include them and petition them to help in daily practice. The effectiveness of these rites formed a corpus of techniques, a set of technologies for communicating between worlds and between individuals (Meskell forthcoming). Object worlds furnished the medium for mediation between realms, direct communication between specific persons, and desired outcomes for living and dead in specific situations. Ancestral images were thus congealed memory, yet they also operated as contextual knowledge—a pre-science that offered strategies to induce change.

Ancestor busts and stelae representing deceased kin materially invoked their presence and potent potential to intervene in contemporary affairs. These beings were known as *effective spirits of Re* and occupied a primary position in the afterlife. They could retain human form but could miraculously commune with deities such as Re and Osiris in the netherworld (Friedman 1994). The individuals depicted on stelae were deceased members of the community who were being implored or appeased; not the long dead who had fallen from memory, but the fathers, sons, brothers and husbands who were part of living memory. Dedicants would have been keen to propitiate the deceased since their perceived actions could impact the living positively or negatively, particularly since they mingled with such omnipotent deities. The position of the image, within the house or chapel, localized within the community itself, was crucial to the salience of the devotion and its desired results. Stelae or ancestor busts placed in the house were in the image of the deceased while representations of the deceased in statue form were traditionally situated at the tomb chapel. Both received offerings and were associated with a deceased individual and were thus concurrently part of domestic and funerary cult. We should also add to this corpus the inscribed stone libation basins, some of which are also dedicated to the blessed dead, that have been regularly found in houses like those at Deir el Medina (Demarée 1983).

Places of memory anchor the past in the present and, alternately, the present in the past. The long, interleaved history of Egyptian monuments and cultural landscapes would imply a fruitful context for the analysis of memory and the re-working of memory (Meskell 2003). Egyptian culture embodied a strong "sense" of the past; they were surrounded by its materiality, but it did not always evoke feelings of reverence. Individuals frequently incorporated older funerary monuments into new constructions and regularly robbed tombs in the process of burial preparations. In the vital area of the world of the dead, they inhabited and inspired to inhabit a doubly dead landscape in which the funerary monuments around them provided a model of achievement, even in their decayed form, as well as a physical environment into which they awkwardly inserted their current passage to a deceased status through destruction, usurpation, and re-use (Baines and Lacovara 2002). In Egyptian culture, death was not considered as the end of one's existence or of one's effectiveness on earth. The dead were powerful beings who could intervene in the world of the living in both benevolent and malevolent ways. Ancestor busts and stelae are testament to this interplay since they provided a focus for these spheres of interaction and attested to the dead's willingness to intercede in the terrestrial. It is often said that the dead kept the living in line.

We cannot assume a universal relationship between memory and the object. In many cultural settings the object does not follow a Western taxonomy of the object (Gell 1998). Archaeologists and anthropologists have both come to acknowledge that memory is performed. Practices of remembering and forgetting can only come about through discursive bodily actions and performance. Habitual bodily practice informs memory and serves to refashion and reiterate certain aspects of the past. Memory does not exist by itself; it must be given material form, narrated and re-narrated by people and to others in order to persist or return (Davis 1997: 189).

When an image was venerated a ritual memory exercise was accomplished and when this was coupled with larger festive offerings and performances, the effect must have been heightened. At their core, Egyptian festivals were fundamentally acts of commemoration and remembrance. Bodily memory was enhanced through ritual observances, funerals, ceremonies for the dead, festivals, and daily personal venerations. Embracing the dead through living practice was equally important for sustaining both collectivities. Festivals and funerals were transitional moments that served many functions: emotional outpouring and remembering, feasting, social interaction, religious observance and communing with the gods. Key to each was the reinstatement of

160

dead individuals, through commemorating their lives and their continued presence among the living. The entire notion of personhood, temporally and spatially situated, is a component of innumerable cultural institutions and practices. Egyptian conceptions of self traversed life and death, since both worlds were porous, such that the contexts of existence had a shared substrate. This set of practices fits nicely with Connerton's (1989: 7) view of recollection as operating in two distinct arenas of social activity: *commemorative ceremonies* and *bodily practices.*

Cult activities involving stelae and busts were enacted in houses, but also chapels, tomb environs, and temples. Their size and portability facilitated movement from and around a number of contexts. Processions of ancestral images were probably linked to the festival calendar. The Beautiful Festival of the Wadi was a key example of a festival of the dead, which took place between the harvest and the Nile flood. In it, the divine boat of Amun traveled from the Karnak temple to the necropolis of Western Thebes. A large procession followed and living and dead were thought to commune near the tombs, which became *houses of the joy of the heart* on that occasion. It is likely that the images of deceased individuals were taken along in the procession and then returned to the grave. On a smaller scale, family festivals also took place in which the deceased again took part (Bleeker 1967: 137).

All the practices of memory through which ancient Maya and Egyptian personhood survived involved groups that provided individuals with "frameworks within which their memories are localised by a kind of mapping. We situate what we recollect within the mental spaces provided by the group" (Connerton 1989: 37). Following Halbwachs (1980), these mental spaces always have material referents and refer back to the material spaces that particular social groups occupy. Durable objects change little, particularly at the pre-industrial village level, and offer a sense of permanence and stability within the particular spatiality. The illusion of reinstating the past in the present that the performance of memory provides, aided by enduring objects situated within spatial contexts, was implicit in the practices of embodiment and the commemorative ceremonies whose traces we can read today. Through the reconstruction of memory, in which we participate here, the personhood of these long-vanished people continues to have a material existence.

From a hermeneutic perspective, the specificities of memory can only endure within sustained contexts (Halbwachs 1980) and memory cannot be miraculously transmitted without continual revision and refashioning. Constructing memory then entails diverse moments of modification, re-use, ignoring and forgetting, and investing with new meanings. And certainly there was an active strategy of forgetting, evidenced in the textual and material record in communities like Deir el Medina, where individuals were purposely forgotten in a process of moving on and when the need arose. Forgetting was required when the needs of the living intervened, specifically in the case of assigning tombs and spaces for burial in the Ramesside Period. Appropriating tombs, against the cultural mores and better judgments of Egyptian society, undoubtedly necessitated a form of religious and moral amnesia or at least a suspension of memory.

One such forgettable individual was a man from Deir el Medina called Amenemope who lived in the early part of the reign of Ramesses II. Members of his family apparently disappeared from the village by the 20th Dynasty when the chief workmen of the village inspected his tomb in the Western Necropolis, before handing it over to the workman Menna (McDowell 1999: 71). With the sweep of a scribal hand the materiality of Amenemope's memory was thus erased, although not irretrievably, as our ability to see this episode of forgetting makes clear. Such events must have been regular occurrences. They demonstrate the importance of a person's family, those who could remember and propitiate, at the point of burial and continuing on into the realm of commemoration. This indeed made the name, and thus the individual, live.

Coming full circle, we see the interconnections between the individual and their networks of kin, the centrality of embodied life in all its sensual and sexual specificity, and the intricate strategies ancient peoples engaged in to overcome the materiality of death and the immateriality of the self and memory. Ancient Egyptian and Mayan materials are evocative fragments of past life to think through our own cultural contexts, to understand the importance of our different legacies and refigure our own taxonomies and experiences with the recognition of cultural difference firmly in mind. Archaeological accounts can in many ways parallel ethnographic or sociological inquiries, particularly given their rich material, iconographic and textual sources. It has been our aim here to reinstate the sensuous embodied aspects of ancient life through an anthropology of the past, and offer an additional avenue for pursuing a history of the body and of embodied lives.

BIBLIOGRAPHY

Allen, J. P. (1988) *Genesis in Egypt: The Philosophy of Ancient Egyptian Creation Accounts.* New Haven: Yale.

Althusser, L. (1971) Ideology and ideological state apparatuses (Notes towards an investigation). In *Lenin and Philosophy and Other Essays,* transl. B. Brewster, pp. 170–177. New York: Monthly Review Press.

Andrews, C. (1990) *Ancient Egyptian Jewelry.* London: British Museum Press.

—— (1994) *Amulets of Ancient Egypt.* London: British Museum Press.

Ashmore, W. (1989) Construction and cosmology: politics and ideology in lowland Maya settlement patterns. In *Word and Image in Maya Culture,* eds W. Hanks and D. S. Rice, pp. 272–286. Salt Lake City: University of Utah Press.

—— (1991) Site-planning principles and concepts of directionality among the ancient Maya. *Latin American Antiquity* 2(3): 199–226.

Assmann, J. (1982) Persönlichkeitsbegriff und -bewusstsein. In *Lexikon der Ägyptologie,* eds W. Helck and E. Otto, pp. 963–978, Band IV, Megiddo-Pyramiden. Wiesbaden: Otto Harrassowitz.

—— (1993) Literatur und Karneval im Alten Ägypten. In *Karnevaleske Phanomene in antiken und nachantiken Kulturen und Literaturen,* ed. S. Döpp, pp. 31–57. Trier: Verlag Trier.

—— (1996) Preservation and presentation of self in ancient Egyptian portraiture. In *Studies in Honor of William Kelly Simpson,* ed. P. Der Manuelian, pp. 55–81. Boston: Museum of Fine Arts.

—— (1999) A dialogue between self and soul: Papyrus Berlin 3024. In *Self, Soul and Body in Religious Experience,* eds A. I. Baumgarten, J. Assmann, and G. A. G. Stroumsa, pp. 384–403. Leiden: Brill.

—— (2001) *The Search for God in Ancient Egypt.* Ithaca: Cornell University Press.

Atran, S. (1993) Itza Maya tropical agro-forestry. *Current Anthropology* 34: 633–700.

Aveni, A. F. (1980) *Skywatchers of Ancient Mexico.* Austin: University of Texas Press.

Baines, J. (1985) *Fecundity Figures: Egyptian Personification and the Iconology of a Genre.* Warminster: Aris and Phillips.

—— (1991) Society, morality, and religious practice. In *Religion in Ancient Egypt,* ed. B. E. Shafer, pp. 123–200. London: Routledge.

—— (1999) Foreunners of narrative biographies. In *Studies in Honour of H. S. Smith,* eds J. Tait and A. Leahy, pp. 23–37. London: EES Occasional Publications, Egypt Exploration Society.

163

Baines, J. and P. Lacovara (2002) Burial and the dead in ancient Egyptian society: respect, formalism, neglect. *Journal of Social Archaeology* 2(1): 5–36.

Baines, J. and N. Yoffee (1998) Order, legitimacy and wealth in ancient Egypt and Mesopotamia. In *Archaic States: A Comparative Approach*, eds G. Feinman and J. Marcus, pp. 199–260. Santa Fe: School of American Research Press.

Bakhtin, M. (1984) *Rabelais and His World*, transl. H. Iswolsky. Bloomington, IN: Indiana University Press.

Ball, J. W. and J. M. Ladd (1992) Ceramics. In *Artifacts from the Cenote of Sacrifice, Chichen Itza, Yucatan: Textiles, Basketry, Stone, Bone, Shell, Ceramics, Wood, Copal, Rubber, Other Organic Materials, and Mammalian Remains*, ed. C. C. Coggins, pp. 191–233. Peabody Museum Memoirs 10(3). Cambridge, MA: Peabody Museum of Archaeology and Ethnology, Harvard University.

Barthes, R. (1974) *S/Z*. New York: Hill and Wang.

Bassie-Sweet, K. (1991) *From the Mouth of the Dark Cave: Commemorative Sculpture of the Late Classic Maya*. Norman: University of Oklahoma Press.

—— (1996) *At the Edge of the World: Caves and Late Classic Maya World View*. Norman: University of Oklahoma Press.

Bataille, G. (1986) *Eroticism, Death and Sexuality*. San Francisco: City Lights Books.

—— (1993) *The Accursed Share: Volumes II and III*. New York: Zone Books.

Battaglia, D. (1985) "We feed our father": Paternal nurture among the Sabarl of Papua New Guinea. *American Ethnologist* 12: 427–441.

Baudrillard, J. (1993) *Symbolic Exchange and Death*. London: Sage.

Becker, M. J. (1992) Burials as caches, caches as burials: A new interpretation of the meaning of ritual deposits among the Classic Period Lowland Maya. In *New Theories on the Ancient Maya*, eds E. C. Danien and R. J. Sharer, pp. 185–196. University Museum Symposium Series, vol. 3. Philadelphia: University of Pennsylvania.

Behrens, P. (1982) Phallus. In *Lexikon der Ägyptologie*, eds W. Helck and E. Otto, pp. 1018–1020, Vol. 4. Wiesbaden: Otto Harrassowitz.

Benson, E. P. (1974) Gestures and offerings. In "Primera Mesa Redonda de Palenque: A Conference on the Art, Iconography, and Dynastic History of Palenque, Palenque, Chiapas, Mexico, December 14–22, 1973", ed. M. G. Robertson, pp. 109–120. Pebble Beach, CA: Precolumbian Art Research, Robert Louis Stephenson School.

Bleeker, C. J. (1967) *Egyptian Festivals: Enactments of Religious Renewal*. Leiden: Brill.

Bochi, P. A. (1994) Images of time in ancient Egyptian art. *Journal of the American Research Centre in Egypt* 31: 55–62.

Brady, J. E. and W. Ashmore (1999) Mountains, caves, and water: ideational landscapes of the ancient Maya. In *Archaeologies of Landscape: Contemporary Perspectives*, eds W. Ashmore and A. B. Knapp, pp. 124–145. Oxford: Blackwell.

Brand, P. J. (2000) *The Monuments Seti I: Epigraphic, Historical and Art Historical Analysis*. Leiden: Brill.

Bricker, V. R. (1991) Faunal offerings in the Dresden Codex. In "Sixth Palenque Round Table, 1986", eds M. G. Robertson and V. M. Fields, pp. 285–292. Norman: University of Oklahoma Press.

—— (1992) A reading for the "Penis Manikin" glyph and its variants (Una interpretación del glifo "maniquí-pene" y sus variantes). Research Reports on

Ancient Maya Writing/Informes Sobre Investigaciones de la Antigua Escritura Maya 38, Washington DC and Mexico DF: Center for Maya Research and Instituto Nacional de Antropología e Historia.

Bricker, V. R. and C. Bill (1994) Mortuary practices in the Madrid Codex. In "Seventh Palenque Round Table, 1989", eds M. G. Robertson and V. M. Fields, pp. 195–200. San Francisco: Pre-Columbian Art Research Institute.

Bruhns, K. O. (1988) Yesterday the Queen wore … . An analysis of women and costume in public art of the Late Classic Maya. In *The Role of Gender in Precolumbian Art and Architecture*, ed. V. Miller, pp. 105–134. Lanham, MD: University Press of America.

Butler, J. (1990) *Gender Trouble: Feminism and the Subversion of Identity*. New York: Routledge.

—— (1993) *Bodies that Matter: On the Discursive Limits of "Sex"*. New York: Routledge.

Bynum, C. W. (2001) *Metamorphosis and Identity*. New York: Zone.

Campbell, L., T. Kaufman and T. C. Smith-Stark (1986) Meso-America as a linguistic area. *Language* 62(3): 530–570.

Chase, A. F. (1992) Elites and the changing organization of Classic Maya society. In *Mesoamerican Elites: An Archaeological Assessment*, eds D. Z. Chase and A. F. Chase, pp. 30–49. Norman: University of Oklahoma Press.

Chase, D. Z. and A. F. Chase (1996) Maya multiples: Individuals, entries, and tombs in Structure A34 of Caracol, Belize. *Latin American Antiquity* 7: 61–79.

—— (1998) The architectural context of caches, burials, and other ritual activities for the Classic period Maya. In *Function and Meaning in Classic Maya Architecture*, ed. S. D. Houston, pp. 299–332. Washington, DC: Dumbarton Oaks.

Clancy, F., C. C. Coggins and T. P. Culbert (1985) Catalogue. In *Maya: Treasures of an Ancient Civilization*, eds C. Gallenkamp and R. Johnson, pp. 97–231. New York: Harry N. Abrams and the Albuquerque Museum.

Closs, M. P. (1988) The penis-headed manikin glyph. *American Antiquity* 53: 804–811.

Coe, M. D. (1956) The funerary temple among the Classic Maya. *Southwestern Journal of Anthropology* 12: 387–394.

—— (1976) Early steps in the evolution of Maya writing. In *Origins of Religious Art and Iconography in Preclassic Mesoamerica*, ed. H. B. Nicholson, pp. 107–122. Los Angeles: University of California, Latin American Studies Center.

—— (1977) Supernatural patrons of Maya scribes and artists. In *Social Process in Maya Prehistory*, ed. N. Hammond, pp. 327–347. New York: Academic Press.

—— (1978) *Lords of the Underworld: Masterpieces of Classic Maya Ceramics*. Princeton: Princeton University Press.

—— (1988) Ideology of the Maya tomb. In *Maya Iconography*, eds E. P. Benson and G. G. Griffin, pp. 222–235. Princeton: Princeton University Press.

—— (1997) *The Art of the Maya Scribe*. London: Thames & Hudson.

Coggins, C. and J. M. Ladd (1992) Copal and rubber offerings. In *Artifacts from the Cenote of Sacrifice, Chichen Itza, Yucatan: Textiles, Basketry, Stone, Bone, Shell, Ceramics, Wood, Copal, Rubber, Other Organic Materials, and Mammalian Remains*, ed. C. C. Coggins, pp. 191–233. Peabody Museum Memoirs 10(3). Cambridge, MA: Peabody Museum of Archaeology and Ethnology, Harvard University.

Connerton, P. (1989) *How Societies Remember.* Cambridge: Cambridge University Press.

Csordas, T. J., ed. (1994) *Embodiment and Experience.* Cambridge: Cambridge University Press.

Culbert, T. P., ed. (1973) *The Classic Maya Collapse.* Albuquerque: University of New Mexico Press.

—— (1991) *Classic Maya Political History: Hieroglyphic and Archaeological Evidence.* Cambridge: Cambridge University Press.

Culbert, T. P. and D. Rice, eds. (1990) *Precolumbian Population History in the Maya Lowlands.* Albuquerque: University of New Mexico Press.

Davis, R. H. (1997) *Lives of Indian Images.* Princeton: Princeton University Press.

Demarée, R. J. (1983) *The 3h Ikr n R^c-Stelae: On Ancestor Worship in Ancient Egypt.* Leiden: Nederlands Instituut voor het Nabije Oosten te Leiden.

Depuydt, L. (1997) *Civil Calendar and Lunar Calendar in Ancient Egypt.* Leuven: Peeters, Departement Oosterse Studies.

Der Manuelian, P. (1999) Semi-literacy in Egypt: some erasures from the Amarna period. In *Gold of Praise: Studies on Ancient Egypt in Honor of Edward Wente*, eds E. Teeter and J. A. Larson, pp. 285–298. Chicago: Oriental Institute of the University of Chicago.

de Lauretis, T., ed. (1984) *Alice Doesn't: Feminism, Semiotics, Cinema.* Bloomington: Indiana University Press.

Derchain, P. (1975) La perruque et le cristal. *Studien zur Altägyptischen Kultur* 2: 55–74.

Derrida, J. (1987) *Cinders.* Lincoln: University of Nebraska Press.

Douglas, M. (1966) *Purity and Danger: An Analysis of the Concepts of Pollution and Taboo.* London: Routledge.

Edmonson, M. (1979) Some Postclassic questions about the Classic Maya. In "Tercera Mesa Redonda de Palenque, Vol. IV", eds M. G. Robertson and D. C. Jeffers, pp. 9–18. San Francisco: Pre-Columbian Art Research Institute.

Elliott, A. (1994) *Psychoanalytic Theory: An Introduction.* Cambridge: Blackwell Publishers.

—— (2001) *Concepts of the Self.* Cambridge: Polity.

Faulkner, R. O. (1985) *The Ancient Egyptian Book of the Dead.* London: British Museum Press.

Fitzsimmons, J. L. (2002) Death and the Maya: Language and Archaeology in Classic Maya Mortuary Ceremonialism. Unpublished doctoral dissertation. Cambridge, MA: Department of Anthropology, Harvard University.

Forman, W. and S. Quirke (1996) *Hieroglyphs and the Afterlife in Ancient Egypt.* London: British Museum Press.

Fox, M. V. (1985) *The Song of Songs and the Ancient Egyptian Love Songs.* Madison, WI: University of Wisconsin.

Frandsen, P. J. (1992) On the root *nfr* and a "clever" remark on embalming. In *The Heritage of Ancient Egypt: Studies in Honour of Erik Iversen*, eds J. Osing and E. K. Nielsen, pp. 49–62. Copenhagen: Cartsen Niebuhr Institute of Ancient Near Eastern Studies.

—— (1997) On categorization and metaphorical structuring: some remarks on Egyptian art and language. *Cambridge Archaeological Journal* 7(1): 71–104.

Freidel, D. A. (1992) Children of the First Father's skull: Terminal Classic warfare in the Northern Maya Lowlands and the transformation of kingship and elite hierarchies. In *Mesoamerican Elites: an Archaeological Assessment*, eds A. F. Chase and D. Z. Chase, pp. 99–117. Norman: University of Oklahoma Press.

Freidel, D. A., M. Masucci, S. Jaeger and R. A. Robertson (1991) The bearer, the burden, and the burnt: the stacking principle in the iconography of the Late Preclassic Maya lowlands. In "Sixth Palenque Round Table, 1986", eds M. G. Robertson and V. M. Fields, pp. 175–183. Norman: University of Oklahoma Press.

Friedman, F. (1994) Aspects of domestic life and religion. In *Pharaoh's Workers. The Villagers of Deir el Medina*, ed. L. H. Lesko, pp. 95–117. New York: Cornell University Press.

Gardiner, A. (1935) *Hieratic Papyri in the British Museum I*. London: British Museum Press.

Gatens, M. (1996) *Imaginary Bodies*. Routledge: London.

Gell, A. (1998) *Art and Agency: An Anthropological Theory*. Oxford: Oxford University Press.

Germond, P. and Livet, J. (2001) *An Egyptian Bestiary*. New York: Thames & Hudson.

Giddy, L. (1999) *The Survey of Memphis II. Kom Rabiʿa: The New Kingdom and Post-New Kingdom Objects*. London: Egypt Exploration Society.

Gillespie, S. D. (1991) Ballgames and boundaries. In *The Mesoamerican Ballgame*, eds V. L. Scarborough and D. R. Wilcox, pp. 317–345. Tucson: University of Arizona Press.

—— (2000) Maya "nested houses": the ritual construction of place. In *Beyond Kinship: Social and Material Reproduction in House Societies*, eds R. A. Joyce and S. D. Gillespie, pp. 135–160. Philadelphia: University of Pennsylvania Press.

—— (2001) Personhood, agency, and mortuary ritual: a case study from the ancient Maya. *Journal of Anthropological Archaeology* 20(1): 73–112.

—— (2002) Body and soul among the Maya: Keeping the spirits in place. In *The Space and Place of Death*, eds H. Silverman and D. B. Small, pp. 67–78. Archeological Papers Number 11. Arlington, VA: American Anthropological Association.

Gillespie, S. D. and R. A. Joyce (1997) Gendered goods: The symbolism of Maya hierarchical exchange relations. In *Women in Prehistory: North America and Mesoamerica*, eds C. Claassen and R. A. Joyce, pp. 189–207. Philadelphia: University of Pennsylvania Press.

—— (1998) Deity relationships in Mesoamerican cosmologies: The case of the Maya God L. *Ancient Mesoamerica* 9: 1–18.

Goldwasser, O. (1995) *From Icon to Metaphor: Studies in the Semiotics of the Hieroglyphs*. Fribourg: University of Fribourg.

Gossen, G. H. (1996) Animal souls, co-essences, and human destiny in Mesoamerica. In *Monsters, Tricksters, and Sacred Cows: Animal Tales and American Identities*, ed. A. J. Arnold, pp. 80–107. Charlottesville, VA: University Press of Virginia.

Graham, M. M. (1992) Art-tools and the language of power in the early art of the Atlantic watershed of Costa Rica. In *Wealth and Hierarchy in the Intermediate Area*, ed. F. Lange, pp. 165–206. Washington, DC: Dumbarton Oaks.

Grosz, E. (1994) *Volatile Bodies: Toward a Corporeal Feminism*. Bloomington: Indiana University Press.

—— (1995) *Space, Time and Perversion*. New York and London: Routledge.

167

Grube, N. (1992) Classic Maya dance: evidence from hieroglyphs and iconography. *Ancient Mesoamerica* 3(2): 201–218.

Grube, N. and W. Nahm (1994) A census of Xibalba: a complete inventory of way characters on Maya ceramics. In *The Maya Vase Book*, vol. 4, eds B. Kerr and J. Kerr, pp. 686–715. New York: Kerr Associates.

Grube, N. and L. Schele (1994) Kuy, the owl of omen and war. *Mexicon* 16(1): 10–17.

Halbwachs, M. (1980) *The Collective Memory*. New York: Harper & Row.

Hall, G. D. (1989) Realm of Death: Royal Mortuary Customs and Polity Interaction in the Classic Maya Lowlands. Unpublished doctoral dissertation. Cambridge, MA: Department of Anthropology, Harvard University.

Hall, G. D., S. M. Tarka, Jr., W. J. Hurst, D. Stuart and R. E. W. Adams (1990) Cacao residues in ancient Maya vessels from Rio Azul, Guatemala. *American Antiquity* 55(1): 138–143.

Hammond, N. (1991) Inside the black box: defining Maya polity. In *Classic Maya Political History: Hieroglyphic and Archaeological Evidence*, ed. T. P. Culbert, pp. 253–284. Cambridge: Cambridge University Press.

Hanks, W. F. (1989a) Elements of Maya style. In *Word and Image in Maya Culture: Explorations in Language, Writing, and Representation*, eds W. F. Hanks and D. S. Rice, pp. 92–111. Salt Lake City: University of Utah Press.

—— (1989b) Word and image in a semiotic perspective. In *Word and Image in Maya Culture: Explorations in Language, Writing, and Representation*, eds W. F. Hanks and D. S. Rice, pp. 8–21. Salt Lake City: University of Utah Press.

—— (1990) *Referential Practice: Language and Lived Space among the Maya*. Chicago: University of Chicago Press.

Hare, T. (1999) *ReMembering Osiris: Number, Gender, and the Word in Ancient Egyptian Representational Systems*. Stanford: Stanford University Press.

Harrison, P. D. and B. L. Turner II, eds. (1978) *Pre-Hispanic Maya Agriculture*. Albuquerque: University of New Mexico Press.

Hayles, N. K. (1999) *How We Became Posthuman: Virtual Bodies in Cybernetics, Literature, and Informatics*. Chicago: University of Chicago Press.

Hekman, S. J. (1990) *Gender and Knowledge: Elements of a Postmodern Feminism*. Cambridge: Polity Press.

Henderson, J. S. (1997) *The World of the Ancient Maya*, 2nd ed. Ithaca: Cornell University Press.

Henderson, J. S. and R. A. Joyce (2002) Brewing distinction: The development of cacao beverages in Formative Mesoamerica. A paper presented at the annual meeting of the American Anthropological Association, New Orleans.

Hendon, J. A. (1991) Status and power in Classic Maya society: An archeological study. *American Anthropologist* 93(4): 894–918.

—— (1992) Variation in Classic Maya sociopolitical organization. *American Anthropologist* 94(4): 940–941.

—— (1996) Archaeological approaches to the organization of domestic labor: Household practice and domestic relations. *Annual Review of Anthropology* 25: 45–61.

—— (1997) Women's work, women's space, and women's status among the Classic-Period Maya elite of the Copan Valley, Honduras. In *Women in Prehistory: North America and Mesoamerica*, eds C. Claassen and R. A. Joyce, pp. 33–46. Philadelphia: University of Pennsylvania Press.

—— (1999) Multiple sources of prestige and the social evaluation of women in

Prehispanic Mesoamerica. In *Material Symbols: Culture and Economy in Prehistory*, ed. J. Robb, pp. 257–276. Center for Archaeological Investigations, Occasional Paper No. 26. Carbondale: Southern Illinois University.

—— (2000) Having and holding: Storage, memory, knowledge, and social relations. *American Anthropologist* 102: 42–53.

—— (2002) Social relations and collective identities: Household and community in ancient Mesoamerica. In *The Dynamics of Power*, ed. M. O'Donovan, pp. 273–300. Center for Archaeological Investigations, Occasional Paper No. 30. Carbondale: Southern Illinois University.

Héritier-Augé, F. (1989) Semen and blood: Some ancient theories concerning their genesis and relationship. In *Fragments for a History of the Human Body, Part Three*, ed. M. Feher, pp. 158–175. New York: Zone.

Hodel-Hoenes, S. (2000) *Life and Death in Ancient Egypt: Scenes from Private Tombs in New Kingdom Thebes*. Ithaca and London: Cornell University Press.

Hornung, E. (1982) *Conceptions of God in Ancient Egypt: The One and the Many*, transl. J. Baines. Ithaca: Cornell.

—— (1990) *The Valley of the Kings: Horizon of Eternity*. New York: Timken.

—— (1992) *Idea into Image: Essays on Ancient Egyptian Thought*. New York: Timken.

—— (1999) *The Ancient Egyptian Books of the Afterlife*. Ithaca: Cornell University Press.

Houston, S. D. (1996) Symbolic sweatbaths of the Maya: architectural meaning in the Cross Group at Palenque, Mexico. *Latin American Antiquity* 7(2): 132–151.

—— (2000) Into the minds of ancients: Advances in Maya glyph studies. *Journal of World Prehistory* 14: 121–201.

—— (2001) Decorous bodies and disordered passions: representations of emotion among the Classic Maya. *World Archaeology* 33(2): 206–219.

Houston, S. D. and D. Stuart (1989) The *way* glyph: evidence for "co-essences" among the Classic Maya. Research Reports in Classic Maya Writing 30. Washington, DC: Center for Maya Research.

—— (1996) Of gods, glyphs and kings: divinity and rulership among the Classic Maya. *Antiquity* 70 (268): 289–312.

—— (1998) The ancient Maya self: personhood and portraiture in the Classic period. *Res* 33: 73–101.

Houston, S. D. and K. A. Taube (2000) An archaeology of the senses: Perceptual psychology in Classic Maya art, writing, and architecture. *Cambridge Archaeological Journal* 10(2): 261–294.

Houston, S. D., J. Robertson and D. Stuart (2000) The language of Classic Maya inscriptions. *Current Anthropology* 41(3): 321–356.

Hunt, E. (1977) *The Transformation of the Hummingbird: Cultural Roots of a Zinacantecan Mythical Poem*. Ithaca: Cornell University Press.

Ikram, S and A. Dodson (1998) *The Mummy in Ancient Egypt: Equipping the Dead for Eternity*. London: Thames & Hudson.

Ingold, T. (1994) *What is an Animal?* London: Routledge.

Inomata, T. (2001a) The Classic Maya palace as a political theater. In *Reconstruyendo la ciudad Maya: El urbanismo en las sociedades antiguas*, eds A. Ciudad Ruiz, M. J. Iglesias Ponce de León and M. del C. Marínez Martínez, pp. 341–362. Publicación S.E.E.M. No. 6. Madrid: Sociedad Española de Estudios Mayas.

169

—— (2001b) Power and ideology of artistic creation: elite craft specialists in Classic Maya society. *Current Anthropology* 42(3): 321–349.

Inomata, T. and S. D. Houston, eds. (2001) *Royal Courts of the Ancient Maya.* Boulder: Westview Press.

Jackson, M. (1989) *Paths Toward a Clearing: Radical Empiricism and Ethnographic Inquiry.* Bloomington and Indianapolis: Indiana University Press.

Joralemon, D. (1974) Ritual blood-sacrifice among the ancient Maya, Part 1. In "Primera Mesa Redonda de Palenque, Part 2", ed. M. G. Robertson. Pebble Beach, CA: Robert Louis Stevenson School.

Joyce, R. A. (1993) Women's work: images of production and reproduction in pre-Hispanic southern Central America. *Current Anthropology* 34(3): 255–274.

—— (1996) The construction of gender in Classic Maya monuments. In *Gender in Archaeology: Essays in Research and Practice*, ed. R. Wright, pp. 167–195. Philadelphia: University of Pennsylvania Press.

—— (1998) Performing the body in Prehispanic Central America. *Res* 33: 147–165.

—— (1999) Symbolic dimensions of costume in Classic Maya monuments: The construction of gender through dress. In *Mayan Clothing and Weaving Through The Ages*, eds B. Knoke de Arathoon, N. L. Gonzalez and J. M. Willemsen Devlin, pp. 29–38. Guatemala: Museo Ixchel del Traje Indígena.

—— (2000a) Girling the girl and boying the boy: The production of adulthood in ancient Mesoamerica. *World Archaeology* 31(3): 473–483.

—— (2000b) Heirlooms and Houses: Materiality and social memory. In *Beyond Kinship: Social and Material Reproduction in House Societies*, eds R. A. Joyce and S. D. Gillespie, pp. 189–212. Philadelphia: University of Pennsylvania Press.

—— (2000c) High culture, Mesoamerican civilization, and the Classic Maya tradition. In *Order, Legitimacy, and Wealth in Ancient States*, eds J. Richards and M. Van Buren, pp. 64–76. Cambridge: Cambridge University Press.

—— (2000d) A Precolumbian gaze: Male sexuality among the ancient Maya. In *Archaeologies of Sexuality*, eds B. Voss and R. Schmidt, pp. 263–283. London: Routledge Press.

—— (2001a) *Gender and Power in Prehispanic Mesoamerica.* Austin: University of Texas Press.

—— (2001b) Negotiating sex and gender in Classic Maya Society. In *Gender in Pre-Hispanic America*, ed. C. Klein, pp. 109–141. Washington, DC: Dumbarton Oaks.

—— (2002) Desiring women: Classic Maya sexualities. In *Ancient Maya Gender Identity and Relations*, eds L. Gustafson and A. Trevelyan, pp. 329–344. Westport, CT: Greenwood Publishing.

—— (2003) Concrete memories: Fragments of the past in the Classic Maya present (ad500–1000). In *Archaeologies of Memory*, eds S. Alcock and R. van Dyke. Oxford: Blackwell.

Joyce, R. A. and J. A. Hendon (2000) Heterarchy, history, and material reality: "Communities" in Late Classic Honduras. In *The Archaeology of Communities*, eds M.-A. Canuto and J. Yaeger, pp. 143–160. London: Routledge Press.

Justeson, J. S. (1986) Origin of writing systems: Preclassic Mesoamerica. *World Archaeology* 17(3): 437–458.

Justeson, J. S., W. M. Norman and N. Hammond (1988) The Pomona flare: A Preclassic Maya hieroglyphic text. In *Maya Iconography*, eds E. P. Benson and G. G. Griffin, pp. 94–151. Princeton: Princeton University Press.

Kadish, G. E. (1979) The scatophagus Egyptian. *Journal of the Society for the Study of Egyptian Antiquities* 9(4): 203–217.

Kolata, A. L. (1984) The tree, the king and the cosmos: Aspects of tree symbolism in ancient Mesoamerica. *Field Museum of Natural History Bulletin* 55(3): 10–19.

Kristeva, J. (1982) *Powers of Horror: an Essay on Abjection*, transl. L.S. Roudiez. New York: Columbia University Press.

Krochock, R. (1998) The Development of Political Rhetoric at Chichen Itza, Yucatan, Mexico. Unpublished doctoral dissertation. Department of Anthropology, Southern Methodist University.

Kurbjuhn, K. (1985) Busts in flowers: a singular theme in Jaina figurines. In "Fourth Palenque Round Table, 1980", ed. E. P. Benson, pp. 221–234. San Francisco: Pre-Columbian Art Research Institute.

Lacan, J. (1996) The meaning of the Phallus. In *Psychoanalysis and Gender*, ed. R. Minsky, pp. 269–280. London: Routledge.

—— (2001) *Écrits: A Selection*. London and New York: Routledge.

Lakoff, G. (1987) *Women, Fire, and Dangerous Things: What Categories Reveal about the Mind*. Chicago: University of Chicago Press.

Lakoff, G. and M. Johnson (1980) *Metaphors We Live By*. Chicago: University of Chicago Press.

Landa, D. de (1941) *Relacion de las cosas de Yucatan*, ed. and transl. A. M. Tozzer. Peabody Museum Papers vol. 18. Cambridge, MA: Peabody Museum of Archaeology and Ethnology, Harvard University.

Leahy, A. (1984) Death by fire in ancient Egypt. *Journal of the Economic and Social History of the Orient* 27(2): 199–206.

Lichtheim, M. (1976) *Ancient Egyptian Literature: Volume II. The New Kingdom*. Berkeley: University of California Press.

—— (1980) *Ancient Egyptian Literature: Volume III. The Late Period*. Berkeley: University of California Press.

Lingis, A. (1994) *Foreign Bodies*. New York: Routledge.

Lloyd, G. (1993) *The Man of Reason: "Male" and "Female" in Western Philosophy*. London: Routledge.

Lock, M. (1993) Cultivating the body: Anthropology and epistemologies of bodily practice and knowledge. *Annual Reviews in Anthropology* 22: 133–155.

Looper, M. G. (1995) *The Sculpture Programs of Butz-Tiliw, an eighth-century Maya king of Quirigua, Guatemala*. Doctoral thesis, Department of Art History, University of Texas at Austin. Ann Arbor: UMI.

Lounsbury, F. G. (1974) The inscription of the Sarcophagus lid at Palenque. In "Primera Mesa Redonda de Palenque: A Conference on the Art, Iconography, and Dynastic History of Palenque, Palenque, Chiapas, Mexico, December 14–22, 1973", ed. M. G. Robertson, pp. 5–19. Pebble Beach, CA: Precolumbian Art Research, Robert Louis Stephenson School.

—— (1985) Identities of the mythological figures in the Cross group inscriptions of Palenque. In "Fourth Palenque Round Table, 1980", ed. E. P. Benson, pp. 45–58. San Francisco: Pre-Columbian Art Research Institute.

—— (1991) Distinguished lecture: recent work in the decipherment of Palenque's hieroglyphic inscriptions. *American Anthropologist* 93: 809–825.

Lyon, M. L. and J. M. Barbalet (1994) Society's body: emotion and the "somatization" of social theory. In *Embodiment and Experience: The Existential*

Ground of Culture and Self, ed. T. Csordas, pp. 48–66. Cambridge: Cambridge University Press.

McAnany, P. A. (1995) *Living with the Ancestors: Kinship and Kingship in Ancient Maya Society*. Austin: University of Texas Press.

—— (1998) Ancestors and the Classic Maya built environment. In *Function and Meaning in Classic Maya architecture*, ed. S. D. Houston, pp. 271–298. Washington, DC: Dumbarton Oaks.

McDowell, A. G. (1999) *Village Life in Ancient Egypt: Laundry Lists and Love Songs*. Oxford: Oxford University Press.

Macri, M. J. (1997) Noun morphology and possessive constructions in old Palenque Ch'ol. In *The Language of Maya Hieroglyphs*, eds M. J. Macri and A. Ford, pp. 89–95. San Francisco: Pre-Columbian Art Research Institute.

—— (2001) *Another example of T757 as the day Muluk*. Maya Hieroglyphic Database Project Glyph Dwellers Report Number 13. Davis: University of California.

Mann, T. (1978) *Joseph and His Brothers*. Harmondsworth: Penguin.

Marcus, J. (1992) Royal families, royal texts: examples from the Zapotec and Maya. In *Mesoamerican Elites: An Archaeological Assessment*, eds D. Z. Chase and A. F. Chase, pp. 221–241. Norman: University of Oklahoma Press.

Mathews, P. (1979) The glyphs from the ear ornament from Tomb A 1/1. In *Excavations at Altun Ha, Belize, 1964–1970, Volume 1*, ed. D. Pendergast, pp. 79–80. Toronto: Royal Ontario Museum.

Mathews, P. and L. Schele (1974) Lords of Palenque—the glyphic evidence. In "Primera Mesa Redonda de Palenque: A Conference on the Art, Iconography, and Dynastic History of Palenque, Palenque, Chiapas, Mexico, December 14–22, 1973", ed. M. G. Robertson, pp. 63–75. Pebble Beach, CA: Precolumbian Art Research, Robert Louis Stephenson School.

Mauss, M. (1985 [1938]) A category of the human mind: The notion of person, the notion of self. In *The Category of the Person: Anthropology, Philosophy, History*, eds M. Carrithers, S. Collins and S. Lukes, pp. 1–25. Cambridge: Cambridge University Press.

—— (2001 [1950]) *A General Theory of Magic*. London: Routledge.

Meeks, D. and C. Favard-Meeks (1997) *Daily Life of the Egyptian Gods*. London: John Murray.

Merleau-Ponty, M. (1962) *The Phenomenology of Perception*, transl. C. Smith. London: Routledge and Kegan Paul.

Merwin, R. E. and G. C. Vaillant (1932) *The Ruins of Holmul, Guatemala*. Peabody Museum Memoirs, vol. 3, no. 2. Cambridge, MA: Peabody Museum of American Archaeology and Ethnology, Harvard University.

Meskell, L. M. (1994) Dying young: The experience of death at Deir el Medina. *Archaeological Review from Cambridge* 13(2): 35–45.

—— (1996) The somatisation of archaeology: institutions, discourses, corporeality. *Norwegian Archaeological Review* 29(1): 1–16.

—— (1998a) An archaeology of social relations in an Egyptian village. *Journal of Archaeological Method and Theory* 5(3): 209–243.

—— (1998b) Size matters: Sex, gender, and status in Egyptian iconography. In *Redefining Archaeology: Feminist Perspectives*, eds M. Casey, D. Donlon, J. Hope and S. Welfare, pp. 175–181. Canberra: The Australian National University.

—— (1999a) *Archaeologies of Social Life: Age, Sex, Class etc. in Ancient Egypt.* Oxford: Blackwell.

—— (1999b) Archaeologies of life and death. *American Journal of Archaeology* 103: 181–199.

—— (2000a) Cycles of life: narrative homology and archaeological realities. *World Archaeology: Lifecycles* 31(3): 423–441.

—— (2000b) Re-embedding sex: domesticity, sexuality and ritual in New Kingdom Egypt. In *Archaeologies of Sexuality*, eds B. Voss and R. Schmidt, pp. 253–262. London: Routledge.

—— (2002) *Private Life in New Kingdom Egypt.* Princeton, NJ: Princeton University Press.

—— (2003) Memory's materiality: ancestral presence, commemorative practice and disjunctive locales. In *Archaeologies of Memory*, eds S. Alcock and R. van Dyke. Oxford: Blackwell.

—— (forthcoming) *Material Biographies: Object Worlds from Ancient Egypt and Beyond.* London: Berg.

Milbrath, S. (1999) *Star Gods of the Maya: Astronomy in Art, Folklore, and Calendars.* Austin: University of Texas Press.

Milde, H. (1991) *The Vignettes in the Book of the Dead of Neferenpet.* Leiden: Nederlands Instituut voor het Nabije Oosten.

Miller, A. G. (1986) *Maya Rulers of Time: A Study of Architectural Sculpture at Tikal, Guatemala.* Philadelphia: University Museum, University of Pennsylvania.

Miller, M. E. (1986) *The Murals of Bonampak.* Princeton, NJ: Princeton University Press.

—— (1999) *Maya Art and Architecture.* New York: Thames & Hudson.

Miller, M. E. and S. D. Houston (1987) The Classic Maya ballgame and its architectural setting: A study of relations between text and image. *Res* 14: 46–65.

Minsky, R. (1995) *Psychoanalysis and Gender.* London: Routledge.

Moholy-Nagy, H., J. M. Ladd and F. Trembour (1992) Objects of stone, shell, and bone. In *Artifacts from the Cenote of Sacrifice, Chichen Itza, Yucatan: Textiles, Basketry, Stone, Bone, Shell, Ceramics, Wood, Copal, Rubber, Other Organic Materials, and Mammalian Remains*, ed. C. C. Coggins, pp. 191–233. Peabody Museum Memoirs 10(3). Cambridge, MA: Peabody Museum of Archaeology and Ethnology, Harvard University.

Monaghan, J. (1998) The person, destiny, and the construction of difference in Mesoamerica. *Res* 33: 137–146.

Montgomery, J. (2002) *Dictionary of Maya Hieroglyphics.* New York: Hippocrene Books.

Morris, B. (2000) *Animals and Ancestors.* London: Berg.

Morris, W. F. (1985a) Fall fashions: Lagartero figurine costumes at the end of the Classic period. In Palenque Round Table Series, Volume VII, eds M. G. Robertson and V. M. Fields, pp. 245–254. San Francisco: Pre-Columbian Art Research Institute.

—— (1985b) Warped glyphs: A reading of Maya textiles. In Palenque Round Table Series, Volume VII, eds M. G. Robertson and V. M. Fields, pp. 317–323. San Francisco: Pre-Columbian Art Research Institute.

Moss, M. L. (1996) Gender, social inequality, and cultural complexity: Northwest Coast women in prehistory. In *Debating Complexity*, eds D. A. Meyer, P. C. Dawson and D. T. Hanna, pp. 81–88. Calgary: University of Calgary Archaeological Association.

Munn, N. D. (1986) *The Fame of Gawa: A Symbolic Study of Value Transformation in a Massim (Papua New Guinea) Society.* Durham, NC: Duke University Press.

Newsome, E. A. (2001) *Trees of Paradise and Pillars of the World: The Serial Stela Cycle of "18-Rabbit-God K", King of Copán.* Austin: University of Texas Press.

Nunn, J. F. (1996) *Ancient Egyptian Medicine.* London: British Museum Press.

O'Connor, D. (1990) The nature of the Tjemhu (Libyan) society in the later New Kingdom. In *Libya and Egypt c. 1300–750*, ed. A. Leahy, pp. 29–113. London: SOAS Centre of Near and Middle Eastern Studies and The Society for Libyan Studies.

Omlin, J. A. (1973) *Der Papyrus 55001 und seine satirisch-erotischen Zeichnungen und Inschrifen.* Turin: Museo Egizio di Torino.

Parkinson, R. B. (1995) "Homosexual" desire in Middle Kingdom literature. *Journal of Egyptian Archaeology* 81: 57–76.

—— (1999) *Cracking Codes: The Rosetta Stone and Decipherment.* London: British Museum Press.

—— (2000) Imposing words: The entrapment of language in the Tale of the Eloquent Peasant. In *Reading the Eloquent Peasant*, ed. A.M. Gnirs, pp. 27–51. Göttingen: Seminar für Ägyptologie und Koptologie.

Paxton, M. (2001) *The Cosmos of the Yucatec Maya: Cycles and Steps from the Madrid Codex.* Albuquerque: University of New Mexico Press.

Philo, C. and C. Wilbert (2000) Animal spaces, beastly places. In *Animal Spaces, Beastly Places*, eds C. Philo and C. Wilbert, pp. 1–34. London: Routledge.

Piankoff, A. (1954) *The Tomb of Ramesses VI.* New York: Pantheon Books.

——(1964) *The Litany of Re.* New York: Pantheon Books.

Pinch, G. (1993) *Votive Offerings to Hathor.* Oxford: Griffith Institute.

—— (1994) *Magic in Ancient Egypt.* London: British Museum Press.

Pohl, M. D. (1981) Ritual continuity and transformation in Mesoamerica: Reconstructing the ancient Maya *cuch* ritual. *American Antiquity* 46(3): 513–529.

Pohl, M. D., ed. (1985) Prehistoric Lowland Maya Environment and Subsistence Economy. Peabody Museum Papers, vol. 77. Cambridge, MA: Peabody Museum of Archaeology and Ethnology, Harvard University.

Proskouriakoff, T. (1961) Portraits of women in Maya art. In *Essays in Pre-Columbian Art and Archaeology*, ed. Samuel K. Lothrop, pp. 81–99. Cambridge: Harvard University Press.

—— (1963) Historical data in the inscriptions of Yaxchilan. *Estudios de Cultura Maya* 3: 149–167.

—— (1973) The hand-grasping-fish and associated hieroglyphs on Classic Maya monuments. In *Mesoamerican Writing Systems*, ed. E. P. Benson, pp. 165–178. Washington, DC: Dumbarton Oaks.

——(1974) *Jades from the Cenote of Sacrifice, Chichen Itza, Yucatan.* Peabody Museum Memoirs 10(1). Cambridge, MA: Peabody Museum of Archaeology and Ethnology, Harvard University.

—— (1993) *Maya History.* Austin: University of Texas Press.

Quirke, S. (1992) *Ancient Egyptian Religion.* London: British Museum Press.

Rands, R. (1965) Jades of the Maya Lowlands. In *Handbook of Middle American*

Indians, Vol. 3, eds R. Wauchope and G. Willey, pp. 561–580. Austin: University of Texas.

Reents-Budet, D. (1991) "Holmul dancer" theme in Maya art. In "Sixth Palenque Round Table, 1986", eds M. G. Robertson and V. M. Fields, pp. 217–222. Norman: University of Oklahoma Press.

—— (1994) *Painting the Maya Universe: Royal Ceramics of the Classic Period.* Durham, NC: Duke University Press.

Reeves, N. (1990) *The Complete Tutankhamun.* London: Guild Publishing.

Rice, D. S. (1993) Eighth-century physical geography, environment, and natural resources in the Maya Lowlands. In *Lowland Maya Civilization in the Eighth Century AD,* eds J. A. Sabloff and J. S. Henderson, pp. 11–63. Washington DC: Dumbarton Oaks.

Ritner, R.K. (1993) *The Mechanics of Ancient Egyptian Magical Practice.* Chicago: Oriental Institute University of Chicago.

Robertson, M. G. (1974) The quadripartite badge—A badge of rulership. In "Primera Mesa Redonda de Palenque, Part 1", ed. M. G. Robertson, pp. 77–83. Pebble Beach, CA: The Robert Louis Stevenson School.

Robins, G. (1993) *Women in Ancient Egypt.* London: British Museum Press.

—— (1994) Some principles of compositional dominance and gender hierarchy in Egyptian art. *Journal of the American Research Center in Egypt* 31: 33–40.

—— (1997a) *The Art of Ancient Egypt.* London: British Museum.

—— (1997b) The "feminization" of the male figure in New Kingdom two-dimensional art. In *Chief of Seers: Egyptian Studies in Memory of Cyril Aldred,* eds E. Goring, N. Reeves and J. Ruffle, pp. 251–265. London: Kegan Paul International.

Romanosky, E. (2001) Min. In *The Oxford Encyclopedia of Ancient Egypt,* ed. D. Redford, pp. 413–415. Oxford: Oxford University Press.

Romero, J. (1970) Dental mutilation, trephination, and cranial deformation. In *Handbook of Middle American Indians, vol. 9,* eds R. Wauchope and T. D. Stewart, pp. 50–67. Austin: University of Texas.

Roth, A. M. (1993) Fingers, stars, and the "Opening of the Mouth": the nature and function of the *ntrwj*-blades. *Journal of Egyptian Archaeology* 79: 57–79.

Russmann, E. R. (2001) *Eternal Egypt: Masterworks of Ancient Art from the British Museum.* Berkeley and Los Angeles: University of California Press.

Ruz Lhuillier, A. (1965) Tombs and funerary practices in the Maya Lowlands. In *Handbook of Middle American Indians, vol. 2: The Archaeology of Southern Mesoamerica, Part 1,* eds R. Wauchope and G. R. Willey, pp. 441–461. Austin: University of Texas Press.

Sabloff, J. A. and J. S. Henderson, eds. (1993) *Lowland Maya Civilization in the Eighth Century AD.* Washington, DC: Dumbarton Oaks.

Sahagún, Bernardino de (1969) *Florentine Codex: General History of the Things of New Spain, Book 6, Rhetoric and Moral Philosophy,* transl. Arthur J. O. Anderson and Charles E. Dibble. Monographs of the School of American Research, number 14, Part VII. Santa Fe: School of American Research and the University of Utah Press.

Schafer, H. (1986) *Principles of Egyptian Art,* transl. J. Baines. Oxford: Griffith Institute.

Schaffer, A.-L. (1991) The Maya "posture of royal ease". In "Sixth Palenque Round Table, 1986", eds M. G. Robertson and V. M. Fields, pp. 203–216. Norman: University of Oklahoma Press.

Schele, L. (1976) Accession iconography of Chan-Bahlum in the Group of the Cross at Palenque. In "Art, Iconography and Dynastic History of Palenque, Part III: Proceedings of the Segunda Mesa Redonda de Palenque, Palenque, Chiapas, Mexico, December 14–21, 1974", ed. M. G. Robertson, pp. 9–34. Pebble Beach, CA: Robert Louis Stevenson School, Pre-Columbian Art Research.

—— (1979) Genealogical documentation on the tri-figure panels at Palenque. In "Tercera Mesa Redonda de Palenque, Vol. IV", eds M. G. Robertson and D. C. Jeffers, pp. 41–70. San Francisco: Pre-Columbian Art Research Institute.

—— (1983) Human sacrifice among the Classic Maya. In *Ritual Human Sacrifice in Mesoamerica*, ed. E. Boone, pp. 7–48. Washington, DC: Dumbarton Oaks.

—— (1988) The Xibalba shuffle: a dance after death. In *Maya Iconography*, eds E. P. Benson and G. G. Griffin, pp. 294–317. Princeton: Princeton University Press.

—— (1997) *Hidden Faces of the Maya*. Impetus [Mexico]: Comunicacíon S.A. de C.V.

Schele, L. and D. Freidel (1990) *A Forest of Kings: The Untold Story of the Ancient Maya*. New York: William Morrow.

—— (1991) The courts of creation: Ballcourts, ballgames and portals to the Maya Otherworld. In *The Mesoamerican Ballgame*, eds V. L. Scarborough and D. R. Wilcox, pp. 289–315. Tucson: University of Arizona Press.

Schele, L. and M. E. Miller (1986) *The Blood of Kings: Dynasty and Ritual in Maya Art*. Fort Worth: Kimball Art Museum.

Shafer, B. E. (1997) Temples, priests, and rituals: an overview. In *Temples in Ancient Egypt*, ed. B.E. Shafer, pp. 1–30. Ithaca, NY: Cornell University Press.

Singer, P. (2001) Heavy petting. *Prospect* 62(April): 12–13.

Smith, A. L. (1982) *Excavations at Seibal, Department of Peten, Guatemala: Major architecture and caches*. Peabody Museum Memoirs, v. 15, no. 1. Cambridge, MA: Peabody Museum of Archaeology and Ethnology, Harvard University.

Stone, A. J. (1985) Variety and transformation in the cosmic monster theme at Quirigua, Guatemala. In "Fifth Palenque Round Table, 1983", ed. V. M. Fields, pp. 39–48. San Francisco: Pre-Columbian Art Research Institute.

—— (1988) Sacrifice and sexuality: Some structural relationships in Classic Maya art. In *The Role of Gender in Precolumbian Art and Architecture*, ed. V. Miller, pp. 75–103. Lanham, MD: University Press of America.

—— (1995) *Images from the Underworld: Naj Tunich and the Tradition of Maya Cave Painting*. Austin: University of Texas Press.

—— (2002) Spirals, ropes, and feathers: The iconography of rubber balls in Mesoamerican art. *Ancient Mesoamerica* 13: 21–39.

Storey, R. (1992) Children of Copan: Issues in paleopathology and paleodemography. *Ancient Mesoamerica* 3(1):161–167.

Strathern, A. (1996) *Body Thoughts*. Ann Arbor: University of Michigan Press.

Strathern, M. (1988) *The Gender of the Gift: Problems with Women and Problems with Society in Melanesia*. Berkeley: University of California Press.

Stuart, D. (1984) Royal auto-sacrifice among the Maya: A study of image and meaning. *Res* 7/8: 6–20.

—— (1985) "Count-of-captives" epithet in Classic Maya writing. In "Fifth Palenque Round Table, 1983", ed. V. M. Fields, pp. 97–101. San Francisco: Pre-Columbian Art Research Institute.

—— (1988) Blood symbolism in Maya iconography. In *Maya Iconography*, eds E. P. Benson and G. G. Griffin, pp. 175–221. Princeton: Princeton University Press.

—— (1996) Kings of stone: A consideration of stelae in ancient Maya ritual and representation. *Res* 29/30: 148–171.

—— (1998) "The fire enters this house": Architecture and ritual in Classic Maya texts. In *Function and meaning in Classic Maya architecture*, ed. S. D. Houston, pp. 373–425. Washington, DC: Dumbarton Oaks.

Sweely, T. (1999) Gender, space, people and power at Ceren, El Salvador. In *Manifesting Power: Gender and the Interpretation of Power in Archaeology*, ed. T. Sweeley, pp. 155–171. London: Routledge.

Tate, C. (1992) *Yaxchilan: The Design of a Maya Ceremonial City*. Austin: University of Texas Press.

Taube, K. A. (1985) The Classic Maya Maize God: A reappraisal. In "Fifth Palenque Round Table, 1983", eds M. G. Robertson and V. Fields, pp. 171–181. San Francisco: Pre-Columbian Art Research Institute.

—— (1988) A study of Classic Maya scaffold sacrifice. In *Maya Iconography*, eds E. P. Benson and G. G. Griffin, pp. 331–351. Princeton: Princeton University Press.

—— (1989a) The maize tamale in Classic Maya diet, epigraphy, and art. *American Antiquity* 54: 31–51.

—— (1989b) Ritual humor in Classic Maya religion. In *Word and Image in Maya Culture: Explorations in Language, Writing, and Representation*, eds W. F. Hanks and D. S. Rice, pp. 351–382. Salt Lake City: University of Utah Press.

—— (1992) *The Major Gods of Ancient Yucatan. Studies in pre-Columbian Art and Archaeology, no. 32*. Washington, DC: Dumbarton Oaks.

—— (1998) The jade hearth: Centrality, rulership, and the Classic Maya temple. In *Function and Meaning in Classic Maya Architecture*, ed. S. D. Houston, pp. 427–478. Washington, DC: Dumbarton Oaks.

Taussig, M. (1993) *Mimesis and Alterity: A Particular History of the Senses*. New York: Routledge.

Taylor, J. H. (2001) *Death and the Afterlife in Ancient Egypt*. London: British Museum Press.

Tedlock, D., transl. (1985) *Popol Vuh*. New York: Simon and Schuster.

Teeter, E. (2000) Body in Egyptian texts and representations. *Bulletin of the American Society of Papyrologists* 37: 149–170.

te Velde, H. (1967) *Seth, God of Confusion: A Study of his Role in Egyptian Mythology and Religion*. Volume 6. Leiden: Brill.

—— (1990) Some remarks on the concept "Person" in the Ancient Egyptian culture. In *Concepts of Person in Religion and Thought*, eds H. G. Kippenberg, Y. B. Kuiper, and A. F. Sanders, pp. 83–101. Berlin: Mouton de Gruyter.

Thompson, J. E. S. (1946) *Tattooing and Scarification Among the Maya. Notes on Middle American Archaeology and Ethnology, No. 63*, pp. 18–25. Washington, DC: Carnegie Institution of Washington.

—— (1961) A blood-drawing ceremony painted on a Maya vase. *Estudios de Cultura Maya* 1: 13–20.

Tourtellot, G., III (1983) Assessment of Classic Maya household composition. In *Prehistoric Settlement Patterns: Essays in Honor of Gordon R. Willey*, eds E. Z. Vogt and R. Leventhal, pp.35–54. Albuquerque: University of New Mexico Press.

—— (1990) *Excavations at Seibal, Department of Peten, Guatemala: Burials*. Peabody Museum Memoirs, v. 17, no. 2. Cambridge, MA: Peabody Museum of Archaeology and Ethnology, Harvard University.

Tozzer, A. M. (1957) *Chichen Itza and Its Cenote of Sacrifice: A Comparative Study of Contemporaneous Maya and Toltec.* Cambridge, MA: Peabody Museum of American Archaeology and Ethnology, Harvard University.

Troy, L. (1986) *Patterns of Queenship in Ancient Egyptian Myth and History.* Uppsala: Acta Universitatis Upsalensis.

Turner, B. S. (1984) *The Body and Society.* Oxford: Basil Blackwell.

—— (1996) *The Body and Society.* London: Sage.

Ventura, C. (1996) Symbolism of Jakaltek Maya tree gourd vessels and corn drinks in Guatemala. *Journal of Ethnobiology* 16: 169–183.

Vogelsang-Eastwood, G. (1993) *Pharaonic Egyptian Clothing.* Leiden: Brill.

—— (1999) *Tutankhamun's Wardrobe: Garments from the Tomb of Tutankhamun.* Rotterdam: Barjesteh van Waalwijk van Doorn and Co.

Walker, J. H. (1996) *Studies in Ancient Egyptian Anatomical Terminology.* Warminster: Aris and Phillips.

Weismantel, M. J. (1995) Making kin: kinship theory and Zumbagua adoptions. *American Ethnologist* 22: 685–704.

Welsh, W. (1988) *An Analysis of Classic Lowland Maya Burials.* BAR International Series 409. Oxford: British Archaeological Reports.

Wilkinson, R. H. (1991/2) Ancient Near Eastern raised arm figures and the iconography of the Egyptian god Min. *Bulletin of the Egyptological Seminar* 11: 109–118.

Willey, Gordon R. (1972) *The Artifacts of Altar de Sacrificios.* Peabody Museum of Archaeology and Ethnology, Harvard University, Papers vol. 64(1). Cambridge, MA.

Williams, S. J. and G. Bendelow (1998) *The Lived Body: Sociological Themes, Embodied Issues.* London: Routledge.

Woodbury, R. (1965) Artifacts of the Guatemalan Highlands. In *Handbook of Middle American Indians* vol. 2, eds R. Wauchope and G. R. Willey, pp. 163–179. Austin: University of Texas.

Zandee, J. (1960) *Death as an Enemy According to Ancient Egyptian Conceptions.* Leiden: Brill.

Zizek, S. (1991) *Looking Awry: An Introduction to Jacques Lacan through Popular Culture.* Cambridge: The MIT Press.

—— (1996) "I hear you with my eyes"; or, the invisible master. In *Gaze and Voice as Love Objects,* eds R. Salecl and S. Zizek, pp. 90–126. Durham, NC: Duke University Press.

INDEX